GRAMMAR AND BEYOND 1B

Second Edition

with Academic Writing

Randi Reppen

CAMBRIDGE
UNIVERSITY PRESS

University Printing House, Cambridge CB2 8BS, United Kingdom

One Liberty Plaza, 20th Floor, New York, NY 10006, USA

477 Williamstown Road, Port Melbourne, VIC 3207, Australia

314–321, 3rd Floor, Plot 3, Splendor Forum, Jasola District Centre, New Delhi – 110025, India

79 Anson Road, #06–04/06, Singapore 079906

Cambridge University Press is part of the University of Cambridge.

It furthers the University's mission by disseminating knowledge in the pursuit of education, learning and research at the highest international levels of excellence.

cambridge.org
Information on this title: cambridge.org/9781108779784

© Cambridge University Press 2021

This publication is in copyright. Subject to statutory exception and to the provisions of relevant collective licensing agreements, no reproduction of any part may take place without the written permission of Cambridge University Press.

First published 2013
Second edition 2021

20 19 18 17 16 15 14 13 12 11 10 9 8 7 6 5 4 3 2 1

Printed in Dubai by Oriental Press

A catalogue record for this publication is available from the British Library

ISBN Student's Book 1B with Online Practice 978-1-108-77978-4

Additional resources for this publication at www.cambridge.org/grammarandbeyond

Cambridge University Press has no responsibility for the persistence or accuracy of URLs for external or third-party internet websites referred to in this publication, and does not guarantee that any content on such websites is, or will remain, accurate or appropriate. Information regarding prices, travel timetables, and other factual information given in this work is correct at the time of first printing but Cambridge University Press does not guarantee the accuracy of such information thereafter.

About the Author

Randi Reppen is Professor of Applied Linguistics and TESL at Northern Arizona University (NAU) in Flagstaff, Arizona. She has over 20 years' experience teaching ESL students and training ESL teachers, including 11 years as the Director of NAU's Program in Intensive English. Randi's research interests focus on the use of corpora for language teaching and materials development. In addition to numerous academic articles and books, she is the author of *Using Corpora in the Language Classroom* and a co-author of *Basic Vocabulary in Use*, 2nd edition, both published by Cambridge University Press.

Corpus Consultants

Michael McCarthy is Emeritus Professor of Applied Linguistics at the University of Nottingham, UK, and Adjunct Professor of Applied Linguistics at Pennsylvania State University. He is a co-author of the corpus-informed *Touchstone* series and the award-winning *Cambridge Grammar of English*, both published by Cambridge University Press, among many other titles, and is known throughout the world as an expert on grammar, vocabulary, and corpus linguistics.

Jeanne McCarten has over 30 years of experience in ELT/ESL as a teacher, publisher, and author. She has been closely involved in the development of the spoken English sections of the *Cambridge International Corpus*. Now a freelance writer, she is co-author of the corpus-informed *Touchstone* series and *Grammar for Business*, both published by Cambridge University Press.

Advisory Panel

The ESL advisory panel has helped to guide the development of this series and provided invaluable information about the needs of ESL students and teachers in high schools, colleges, universities, and private language schools throughout North America.

Neta Simpkins Cahill, Skagit Valley College, Mount Vernon, WA
Shelly Hedstrom, Palm Beach State College, Lake Worth, FL
Richard Morasci, Foothill College, Los Altos Hills, CA
Stacey Russo, East Hampton High School, East Hampton, NY
Alice Savage, Lone Star College-North Harris, Houston, TX

Scope and Sequence

Unit	Theme	Grammar	Topics
PART 1 The Verb *Be*			
UNIT 1 page 2	Tell Me About Yourself	Statements with Present of *Be*	Present of *Be*: Affirmative Statements (p. 4) Present of *Be*: Negative Statements (p. 8)
UNIT 2 page 14	Schedules and School	*Yes/No* Questions and Information Questions with *Be*	*Yes/No* Questions and Short Answers with *Be* (p.18) Information Questions with *Be* (p. 22)
PART 2 Nouns, Determiners, and Pronouns			
UNIT 3 page 28	Gadgets	Count Nouns; *A/An*; *Have* and *Be*	Nouns; *A/An* (p. 30) *Be* with *A/An* + Noun (p. 33) *Have* (p. 35)
UNIT 4 page 40	The Workplace	Demonstratives and Possessives	Demonstratives (*This*, *That*, *These*, *Those*) (p. 42) Possessives and *Whose* (p. 47)
PART 3 Prepositions and Adjectives			
UNIT 5 page 54	Skills and Qualities for Success	Descriptive Adjectives	Adjectives (p. 56) Questions with *What . . . like?* and *How* + Adjective (p. 59)
UNIT 6 page 68	Around the House	Prepositions	Prepositions of Place: Things at Home and in the Neighborhood (p. 70) Prepositions of Place: Locations and Other Uses (p. 74) Prepositions of Time (p. 77)
UNIT 7 page 84	Local Attractions	*There Is* and *There Are*	*There Is* / *There Are* (p. 86) *Yes/No* Questions with *There Is* / *There Are* (p. 81)

Avoid Common Mistakes	Academic Writing
Avoiding *be + no*; avoiding sentences beginning with *be*	**Thinking about Speaking and Writing** • Compare the skills • Add information in a chart
Remembering capital letters and punctuation; avoiding contractions with short answers to *yes/no* questions	**Writing about a Person** Writing prompt: *Write about someone in your family.* • Use pronouns to avoid repetition • Brainstorm
Remembering *a/an*; remembering subject/verb agreement	• Write simple sentences
Using *this/that* and *these/those*; using possessives	• Use *and* to add details • Revise and edit
Remembering where to put adjectives; avoiding plural adjectives	**Writing about a Place** Writing prompt: *Write about your country.* • Identify main ideas • Classify key words
Remembering *in*, *on*, and *at*	• Paragraph structure and topic sentences • Use prepositional phrases to write about places • Use an outline to organize ideas
Using *there is / there are*; avoiding contractions in academic writing	• Use *there is* and *there are* to introduce details • Write, revise, and edit paragraphs

Unit	Theme	Grammar	Topics
PART 4 Simple Present			
UNIT 8 page 98	Lifestyles	Simple Present	Simple Present: Affirmative and Negative Statements (p. 100) Statements with Adverbs of Frequency (p. 106)
UNIT 9 page 114	Daily Habits	Simple Present *Yes/No* Questions and Short Answers	Simple Present *Yes / No* Questions and Short Answers (p. 116)
UNIT 10 page 122	Cultural Holidays	Simple Present Information Questions	Simple Present Information Questions (p. 124) Questions with *How Often* (p. 130)
PART 5 Conjunctions			
UNIT 11 page 134	Time Management	Conjunctions: *And, But, Or; Because*	*And, But, Or* (p. 136) *Because* (p. 139)
PART 6 Simple Past			
UNIT 12 page 146	Success Stories	Simple Past Statements	Simple Past Statements: Regular Verbs (p. 148) Simple Past Statements: Irregular Verbs (p. 153)
UNIT 13 page 162	Business Ideas	Simple Past Questions	Simple Past *Yes / No* Questions (p. 164) Simple Past Information Questions (p. 167)
UNIT 14 page 172	Life Stories	Simple Past of *Be*	Simple Past of *Be*: Affirmative and Negative Statements (p. 174) Simple Past of *Be*: Questions and Answers (p. 176)
UNIT 15 page 184	Luck and Loss	Past Time Clauses with *When, Before,* and *After*	Past Time Clauses with *When, Before,* and *After* (p. 186)

Avoid Common Mistakes	Academic Writing
Avoiding *do/does* in negative statements with *be*; avoiding *be* with simple present verbs	**Writing about Daily Life** Writing prompt: *Write about the life of a classmate.* • Brainstorm
Remembering *Do/Does* in simple present questions with *have*; Avoiding *Do/Does* in questions with *be*	• Identify main ideas and details • Use a chart to organize details
Remembering *do/does*; avoiding *-s* with *he/she/it*	• Write a paragraph • Add details about time and place • Revise and edit
Remembering a comma with conjunctions; using conjunctions	**Writing Formal Emails** Writing prompt: *Write an email to a professor.* • Write a formal email
Remembering simple past verbs to talk about the past; remembering the base form of the verb after *did not / didn't*	**Narrative Paragraph** Writing prompt: *Write a paragraph about the history of a business.* • Use a timeline to put past events in order • Brainstorm and research
Remembering *did* + subject + base form of the verb; avoiding the past form in information questions	• Add details to main events • Use a paragraph planner to organize ideas
Using *was/were*; Remembering the correct form with *born*	• Use time-order transition signals • Write a narrative paragraph
Remembering the correct spelling of *when*, *before*, and *after*; Remembering the subject in the main clause and the time clause	• Use past time clauses • Revise and edit

Unit	Theme	Grammar	Topics
PART 7 More About Nouns, Determiners, and Pronouns			
UNIT 16 page 194	Eating Habits	Count and Noncount Nouns	Count and Noncount Nouns (p. 196) Units of Measure; *How Many . . . ?* and *How Much . . . ?* (p. 201)
UNIT 17 page 212	Languages	Quantifiers: *Some, Any, A Lot Of, A Little, A Few, Much, Many*	Quantifiers: *Some* and *Any* (p. 214) Quantifiers: *A Lot Of, A Little, A Few, Much, Many* (p. 219)
UNIT 18 page 228	Changes and Risks	Articles: *A / An* and *The*	Articles: *A / An* and *The* (p. 230) Article or No Article? (p. 235)
UNIT 19 page 242	Meals Around the World	Possessive Pronouns and Indefinite Pronouns	Possessive Pronouns (p. 244) Indefinite Pronouns (p. 249)
PART 8 Imperatives and Modals			
UNIT 20 page 256	Social Customs	Imperatives	Imperatives (p. 258)
UNIT 21 page 270	Making Connections	Ability and Possibility	*Can* and *Could* for Ability and Possibility (p. 272) *Be Able To* and *Know How To* for Ability (p. 277)
UNIT 22 page 284	College Life	Requests and Permission	*Can, Could,* and *Would* for Requests (p. 286) *Can, Could,* and *May* for Permission (p. 290)
PART 9 Present and Past Progressive			
UNIT 23 page 298	Body Language	Present Progressive	Present Progressive Statements (p. 300) Present Progressive Questions (p. 305) Present Progressive and Simple Present (p. 307)
UNIT 24 page 316	Inventions and Discoveries	Past Progressive and Simple Past	Past Progressive (p. 318) Time Clauses with Past Progressive and Simple Past (p. 323)

Avoid Common Mistakes	Academic Writing
Avoiding *a / an* with noncount nouns; avoiding the plural with noncount nouns	**Descriptive Paragraphs** Writing prompt: *Write about popular food in your country.*<ul><li>Use an idea map to brainstorm</li></ul>
Remembering *many* with plural nouns; remembering *any* with negative statements and *some* with affirmative statements	<ul><li>Use an idea map to organize</li><li>Complete an outline</li><li>Use quantifiers to describe food</li></ul>
Avoiding *a/an* with noncount nouns; Avoiding *the* to talk about things or people in general	<ul><li>Use articles in a paragraph</li><li>Write descriptive paragraphs</li></ul>
Avoiding the plural with possessive pronouns; remembering *any* + in negative statements	<ul><li>Use collocations</li><li>Revise and edit</li></ul>
Avoiding *no* in negative imperatives; remembering an apostrophe in *don't*	**Expository Paragraph** Writing prompt: *Write a paragraph about someone who is a good role model to you. Explain why that person is a good role model.*<ul><li>Balance facts and qualities</li><li>Brainstorm</li></ul>
Avoiding *-s* with *can* and *could*; remembering the base form with *can* and *could*	<ul><li>Write concluding sentences</li><li>Use statements of ability</li><li>Organize ideas</li></ul>
Remembering the correct word order for making requests; remembering the base form of the verb after *can*, *could*, *may*, or *would*	<ul><li>Use adjectives and adverbs to describe challenges</li><li>Write an expository paragraph</li><li>Revise and edit</li></ul>
Remembering *be* and verb + *-ing* for the present progressive	**Process Paragraph** Writing prompt: *Describe the Sydney Triathlon.*<ul><li>Use a line diagram to think about steps in a process</li><li>Brainstorm</li></ul>
Remembering *was / were* + verb + *-ing* for the past progressive	<ul><li>Use transition words to order events in a process</li><li>Describe a process diagram</li><li>Organize events</li></ul>

Unit	Theme	Grammar	Topics
PART 10 Subjects, Objects, and Complements			
UNIT 25 page 330	Fast Food or Slow Food	Subject and Object Pronouns; Questions About Subjects and Objects	Subject and Object Pronouns (p. 332) Questions About the Subject and the Object (p. 335)
UNIT 26 page 342	Do What You Enjoy Doing	Infinitives and Gerunds	Infinitives (p. 344) Gerunds (p. 347)
PART 11 The Future			
UNIT 27 page 356	The Years Ahead	Future with *Be Going To*, Present Progressive, and *Will*	Future with *Be Going To* or Present Progressive (p. 358) Future with *Will* (p. 363)
UNIT 28 page 372	Will We Need Teachers?	*Will*, *May*, and *Might* for Future Possibility; *Will* for Offers and Promises	*May* and *Might*; Adverbs with *Will* (p. 374) Offers and Promises (p. 379)
PART 12 More Modals			
UNIT 29 page 384	Study Habits	Suggestions and Advice	Suggestions and Advice (p. 386) Asking for and Responding to Suggestions and Advice (p. 389)
UNIT 30 page 396	Getting What You Want	Necessity and Conclusions	Necessity and Conclusions with *Have To*, *Need To*, *Must* (p. 398)
PART 13 Adjective and Adverbs			
UNIT 31 page 408	Making a Good Impression	Adjectives and Adverbs	Adjectives and Adverbs of Manner (p. 410) Adjectives with Linking Verbs; Adjectives and Adverbs with *Very* and *Too* (p. 414)
UNIT 32 page 424	Progress	Comparative Adjectives and Adverbs	Comparative Adjectives (p. 426) Comparative Adverbs (p. 431)
UNIT 33 page 440	Facts and Opinions	Superlative Adjectives and Adverbs	Superlative Adjectives (p. 442) Superlative Adverbs (p. 447)

Avoid Common Mistakes	Academic Writing
Using subject and object pronouns; avoiding putting the pronoun before the noun	• Remove unrelated information from a paragraph • Write a process paragraph
Using infinitives and gerunds; Avoiding *wanna* in writing	• Use gerunds to add information • Revise and edit
Remembering the verb *be* in *be going to*; remembering *will* for predictions	**Opinion Paragraph** Writing prompt: *"The Internet wastes our time. It does not help us do more work."* Do you agree or disagree? • Recognize advantages and disadvantages. • Brainstorm advantages and disadvantages • What to do after brainstorming
Avoiding using *can* for predictions; avoiding using *can* for certainty	• Analyze a writing prompt/ question • Use a table to organize details • Write a topic sentence for an opinion paragraph
Using *should* and *ought*; avoiding putting *probably* after the *ought to*	• Use phrases to introduce opinions • Write an opinion paragraph
Avoiding *to* after *must*; avoiding *need to* for conclusions	• Connect ideas with *and*, *also*, and *too* • Revise and edit
Avoiding *-ly* in irregular adverbs; avoiding confusion with *good* and *well*; avoiding putting the adverb between a verb and its object	**Description and Opinion** Writing prompt: *Describe the place where you live now or where you are from. Write about its positive and negatives. Include your opinions.* • Use a T-chart to brainstorm positives and negatives
Avoiding *more* with *better* and *worse*; avoiding *that* and *then* after a comparative	• Use comparative adjectives to describe a place • Use a T-chart to take notes and organize ideas
Avoiding the comparative for more than two things; avoiding using *most* and *-est* together	• Use contrast words to signal a shift • Write a descriptive paragraph with opinion • Use superlative adjectives • Revise and edit

Appendices   A1
Index & Credits   I1

Introduction to *Grammar and Beyond*, 2nd edition

Grammar and Beyond is a research-based and content-rich grammar and academic writing series for beginning to advanced-level students. The series focuses on the most commonly used English grammar structures and practices all four skills in a variety of authentic and communicative contexts.

Grammar and Beyond is Research-Based

The grammar presented in this series is informed by years of research on the grammar of written and spoken English as it is used in college lectures, textbooks, academic essays, high school classrooms, and conversations between instructors and students. This research, and the analysis of over one billion words of authentic written and spoken language data known as the *Cambridge International Corpus*, has enabled the authors to:

- Present grammar rules that accurately represent how English is actually spoken and written
- Identify and teach differences between the grammar of written and spoken English
- Focus more attention on the structures that are commonly used, and less on those that are rarely used, in writing and speaking
- Help students avoid the most common mistakes that English language learners make
- Choose reading topics that will naturally elicit examples of the target grammar structure
- Introduce important vocabulary from the Academic Word List

Special Features of *Grammar and Beyond*

Realistic Grammar Presentations

Grammar is presented in clear and simple charts. The grammar points presented in these charts have been tested against real-world data from the *Cambridge International Corpus* to ensure that they are authentic representations of actual use of English.

Data from the Real World

Many of the grammar presentations and application sections include a feature called Data from the Real World. Concrete and useful points discovered through analysis of corpus data are presented and practiced in exercises that follow.

Avoid Common Mistakes

Every unit features an Avoid Common Mistakes section that develops students' awareness of the most common mistakes made by English language learners and gives them an opportunity to practice detecting and correcting these errors. This section helps students avoid these mistakes in their own work. The mistakes highlighted in this section are drawn from a body of authentic data on learner English known as the *Cambridge Learner Corpus*, a database of over 35 million words from student essays written by non-native speakers of English and information from experienced classroom teachers.

Academic Vocabulary

Every unit in *Grammar and Beyond* includes words from the Academic Word List (AWL), a research-based list of words and word families that appear with high frequency in English-language academic texts. These words are introduced in the opening text of the unit, recycled in the charts and exercises, and used to support the theme throughout the unit. By the time students finish each level, they will have been exposed several times to a carefully selected set of level-appropriate AWL words, as well as content words from a variety of academic disciplines.

Academic Writing

Every unit ends with an Academic Writing section. In Levels 1 through 3, this edition of *Grammar and Beyond* teaches students to write academically using writing cycles that span several units. Each writing cycle is organized around a writing prompt and focuses on a specific type of academic writing, such as descriptive, narrative, and process. Students move through the steps of the writing process - Brainstorm, Organize, Write, Edit - while learning and practicing new writing skills and ways to incorporate the unit grammar into their writing. In Level 4, the entire scope and sequence is organized around the types of essays students write in college, and focuses on the grammar rules, conventions, and structures needed to master them.

Series Levels

The following table provides a general idea of the difficulty of the material at each level of *Grammar and Beyond*. These are not meant to be interpreted as precise correlations.

	Description	TOEFL IBT	CEFR Levels
Level 1	Beginning	20 – 34	A1 – A2
Level 2	Low Intermediate to Intermediate	35 – 54	A2 – B1
Level 3	High Intermediate	55 – 74	B1 – B2
Level 4	Advanced	75 – 95	B2 – C1

Student Components

Student's Book with Online Practice

Each unit, based on a high-interest topic, teaches grammar points appropriate for each level in short, manageable cycles of presentation and practice. Academic Writing focuses on the structure of the academic essay in addition to the grammar rules, conventions, and structures that students need to master in order to be successful college writers. Students can access both the Digital Workbook and Writing Skills Interactive using their smartphones, tablets, or computers with a single log-in. See pages xviii–xxiii for a Tour of a Unit.

Digital Workbook

The Digital Workbook provides additional online exercises to help master each grammar point. Automatically-graded exercises give immediate feedback for activities such as correcting errors highlighted in the Avoid Common Mistakes section in the Student's Book. Self-Assessment sections at the end of each unit allow students to test their mastery of what they learned. Look for   in the Student's Book to see when to use the Digital Workbook.

Writing Skills Interactive

Writing Skills Interactive is a self-grading course to practice discrete writing skills, reinforce vocabulary, and give students an opportunity with additional writing practice. Each unit has:

- Vocabulary review
- Short text to check understanding of the context
- Animated presentation of target unit writing skill
- Practice activities
- Unit Quiz to assess progress

Teacher Resources

A variety of downloadable resources are available on Cambridge One (cambridgeone.org) to assist instructors, including the following:

Teacher's Manual

- Suggestions for applying the target grammar to all four major skill areas, helping instructors facilitate dynamic and comprehensive grammar classes
- An answer key and audio script for the Student's Book
- Teaching tips, to help instructors plan their lessons
- Communicative activity worksheets to add more in-class speaking practice

Assessment

- Placement Test
- Ready-made, easy-to-score Unit Tests, Midterm, and Final in .pdf and .doc formats
- Answer Key

Presentation Plus

Presentation Plus allows teachers to digitally project the contents of the Student's Book in front of the class for a livelier, interactive classroom. It is a complete solution for teachers because it includes easy-to-access answer keys and audio at point of use.

Acknowledgements

The publisher and author would like to thank these reviewers and consultants for their insights and participation:

Marty Attiyeh, The College of DuPage, Glen Ellyn, IL

Shannon Bailey, Austin Community College, Austin, TX

Jamila Barton, North Seattle Community College, Seattle, WA

Kim Bayer, Hunter College IELI, New York, NY

Linda Berendsen, Oakton Community College, Skokie, IL

Anita Biber, Tarrant County College Northwest, Fort Worth, TX

Jane Breaux, Community College of Aurora, Aurora, CO

Anna Budzinski, San Antonio College, San Antonio, TX

Britta Burton, Mission College, Santa Clara, CA

Jean Carroll, Fresno City College, Fresno, CA

Chris Cashman, Oak Park High School and Elmwood Park High School, Chicago, IL

Annette M. Charron, Bakersfield College, Bakersfield, CA

Patrick Colabucci, ALI at San Diego State University, San Diego, CA

Lin Cui, Harper College, Palatine, IL

Jennifer Duclos, Boston University CELOP, Boston, MA

Joy Durighello, San Francisco City College, San Francisco, CA

Kathleen Flynn, Glendale Community College, Glendale, CA

Raquel Fundora, Miami Dade College, Miami, FL

Patricia Gillie, New Trier Township High School District, Winnetka, IL

Laurie Gluck, LaGuardia Community College, Long Island City, NY

Kathleen Golata, Galileo Academy of Science & Technology, San Francisco, CA

Ellen Goldman, Mission College, Santa Clara, CA

Ekaterina Goussakova, Seminole Community College, Sanford, FL

Marianne Grayston, Prince George's Community College, Largo, MD

Mary Greiss Shipley, Georgia Gwinnett College, Lawrenceville, GA

Sudeepa Gulati, Long Beach City College, Long Beach, CA

Nicole Hammond Carrasquel, University of Central Florida, Orlando, FL

Vicki Hendricks, Broward College, Fort Lauderdale, FL

Kelly Hernandez, Miami Dade College, Miami, FL

Ann Johnston, Tidewater Community College, Virginia Beach, VA

Julia Karet, Chaffey College, Claremont, CA

Jeanne Lachowski, English Language Institute, University of Utah, Salt Lake City, UT

Noga Laor, Rennert, New York, NY

Min Lu, Central Florida Community College, Ocala, FL

Michael Luchuk, Kaplan International Centers, New York, NY

Craig Machado, Norwalk Community College, Norwalk, CT

Denise Maduli-Williams, City College of San Francisco, San Francisco, CA

Diane Mahin, University of Miami, Coral Gables, FL

Melanie Majeski, Naugatuck Valley Community College, Waterbury, CT

Jeanne Malcolm, University of North Carolina at Charlotte, Charlotte, NC

Lourdes Marx, Palm Beach State College, Boca Raton, FL

Susan G. McFalls, Maryville College, Maryville, TN

Nancy McKay, Cuyahoga Community College, Cleveland, OH

Dominika McPartland, Long Island Business Institute, Flushing, NY

Amy Metcalf, UNR/Intensive English Language Center, University of Nevada, Reno, NV

Robert Miller, EF International Language School San Francisco – Mills, San Francisco, CA

Marcie Pachino, Jordan High School, Durham, NC

Myshie Pagel, El Paso Community College, El Paso, TX

Bernadette Pedagno, University of San Francisco, San Francisco, CA

Tam Q Pham, Dallas Theological Seminary, Fort Smith, AR

Mary Beth Pickett, GlobalLT, Rochester, MI

Maria Reamore, Baltimore City Public Schools, Baltimore, MD

Alison M. Rice, Hunter College IELI, New York, NY

Sydney Rice, Imperial Valley College, Imperial, CA

Kathleen Romstedt, Ohio State University, Columbus, OH

Alexandra Rowe, University of South Carolina, Columbia, SC

Irma Sanders, Baldwin Park Adult and Community Education, Baldwin Park, CA

Caren Shoup, Lone Star College – CyFair, Cypress, TX

Karen Sid, Mission College, Foothill College, De Anza College, Santa Clara, CA

Michelle Thomas, Miami Dade College, Miami, FL

Sharon Van Houte, Lorain County Community College, Elyria, OH

Margi Wald, UC Berkeley, Berkeley, CA

Walli Weitz, Riverside County Office of Ed., Indio, CA

Bart Weyand, University of Southern Maine, Portland, ME

Donna Weyrich, Columbus State Community College, Columbus, OH

Marilyn Whitehorse, Santa Barbara City College, Ojai, CA

Jessica Wilson, Rutgers University – Newark, Newark, NJ

Sue Wilson, San Jose City College, San Jose, CA

Margaret Wilster, Mid-Florida Tech, Orlando, FL

Anne York-Herjeczki, Santa Monica College, Santa Monica, CA

Hoda Zaki, Camden County College, Camden, NJ

We would also like to thank these teachers and programs for allowing us to visit:

Richard Appelbaum, Broward College, Fort Lauderdale, FL

Carmela Arnoldt, Glendale Community College, Glendale, AZ

JaNae Barrow, Desert Vista High School, Phoenix, AZ

Ted Christensen, Mesa Community College, Mesa, AZ

Richard Ciriello, Lower East Side Preparatory High School, New York, NY

Virginia Edwards, Chandler-Gilbert Community College, Chandler, AZ

Nusia Frankel, Miami Dade College, Miami, FL

Raquel Fundora, Miami Dade College, Miami, FL

Vicki Hendricks, Broward College, Fort Lauderdale, FL

Kelly Hernandez, Miami Dade College, Miami, FL

Stephen Johnson, Miami Dade College, Miami, FL

Barbara Jordan, Mesa Community College, Mesa, AZ

Nancy Kersten, GateWay Community College, Phoenix, AZ

Lewis Levine, Hostos Community College, Bronx, NY

John Liffiton, Scottsdale Community College, Scottsdale, AZ

Cheryl Lira-Layne, Gilbert Public School District, Gilbert, AZ

Mary Livingston, Arizona State University, Tempe, AZ

Elizabeth Macdonald, Thunderbird School of Global Management, Glendale, AZ

Terri Martinez, Mesa Community College, Mesa, AZ

Lourdes Marx, Palm Beach State College, Boca Raton, FL

Paul Kei Matsuda, Arizona State University, Tempe, AZ

David Miller, Glendale Community College, Glendale, AZ

Martha Polin, Lower East Side Preparatory High School, New York, NY

Patricia Pullenza, Mesa Community College, Mesa, AZ

Victoria Rasinskaya, Lower East Side Preparatory High School, New York, NY

Vanda Salls, Tempe Union High School District, Tempe, AZ

Kim Sanabria, Hostos Community College, Bronx, NY

Cynthia Schuemann, Miami Dade College, Miami, FL

Michelle Thomas, Miami Dade College, Miami, FL

Dongmei Zeng, Borough of Manhattan Community College, New York, NY

Tour of a Unit

ACADEMIC WRITING FOCUS appears at the beginning of the unit.

GRAMMAR IN THE REAL WORLD presents the unit's grammar in a realistic context using contemporary texts.

UNIT 16: Count and Noncount Nouns
Eating Habits

1 Grammar in the Real World

ACADEMIC WRITING
Descriptive paragraphs

A Do you think your diet is healthy? Read the article from a health magazine. What kinds of food are part of a healthy diet?

B Comprehension Check Answer the questions. Use the article to help you.
1. How do colorful fruit and vegetables help your health?
2. Why is a little dark chocolate good for you?
3. What type of oil is good for you?
4. How much water is good to drink each day?

C Notice Find the sentences in the article, and complete them with a or an or Ø for no article.
1. When you turn on _____ television or read _____ newspaper, you often find _____ information about healthy eating.
2. _____ food and _____ health get a lot of attention in the news these days.
3. Maybe you think _____ fat is bad for you, but people need a little fat in their diet.
4. It is _____ challenge to change your diet, but even small changes can help you stay healthy and happy.

Look at the noun after each space. Which of the nouns are things you can count? Which are things you cannot count?

Food for Health

When you turn on a television or read a newspaper, you often find **information** about healthy eating. **Food** and **health** get a lot of **attention** in the **news** these **days**. Researchers seem to find new **things** about how our **diet** affects us every day.

Everyone knows it is important to eat **fruit** and **vegetables**. Did you know that eating **fruit** and **vegetables** with different colors is especially good for your **health**? Green, red, blue, and orange **fruit** and **vegetables** all have different **vitamins**[1] to help hydrate you, and they help prevent different **diseases**.

Did you know that dark **chocolate** is good for you, too? Research shows that a little **chocolate** helps your **heart** and your **mood**.[2]

How about **fat**?[3] Maybe you think **fat** is bad for you, but people need a little **fat** in their diet. One type of healthy **fat** is omega-3 **oil**.[4] It comes from **fish** and helps your **heart**, **skin**, and **brain** stay healthy. For **vegetarians** or non-fish eaters, many **seeds**[5] and **nuts** also contain omega-3 oil. Omega-3 **oil** comes in **pills**, too.

Finally, **water** is an important part of a healthy **diet**. Try to drink at least six **glasses** of **water** a day, and you don't need to buy it. In most places, tap **water** from the kitchen **faucet** is just fine and tastes great!

It is a **challenge** to change your **diet**, but even small **changes** can help you stay healthy and happy.

[1]**vitamin**: a natural substance in food that is important for good health
[2]**mood**: the way someone feels at a particular time
[3]**fat**: a substance in plants and animals, often used for cooking
[4]**omega-3 oil**: a kind of healthy fat
[5]**seed**: a small hard part of a plant from which new plants can grow

NOTICE ACTIVITIES draw students' attention to the structure, guiding their own analysis of form, meaning, and use.

GRAMMAR PRESENTATION

begins with an overview that describes the grammar in an easy-to-understand summary.

GRAMMAR APPLICATION

keeps students engaged with a wide variety of exercises that introduce new and stimulating content.

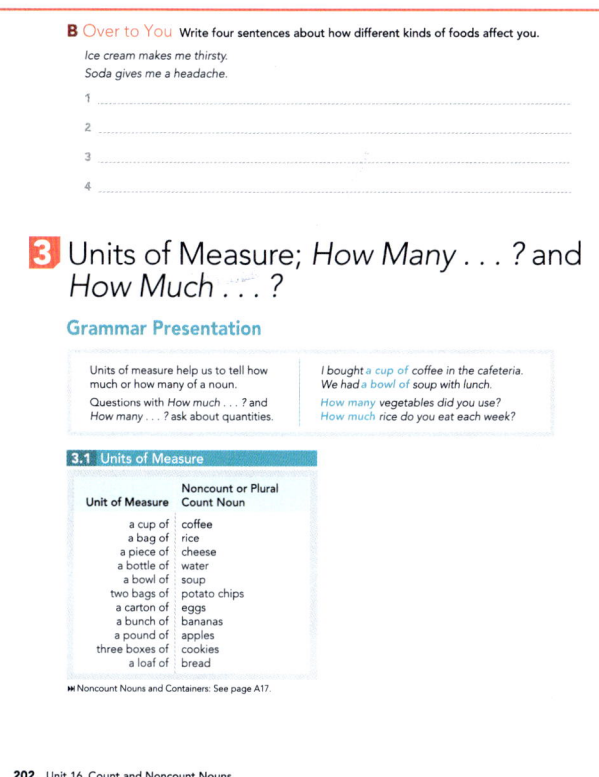

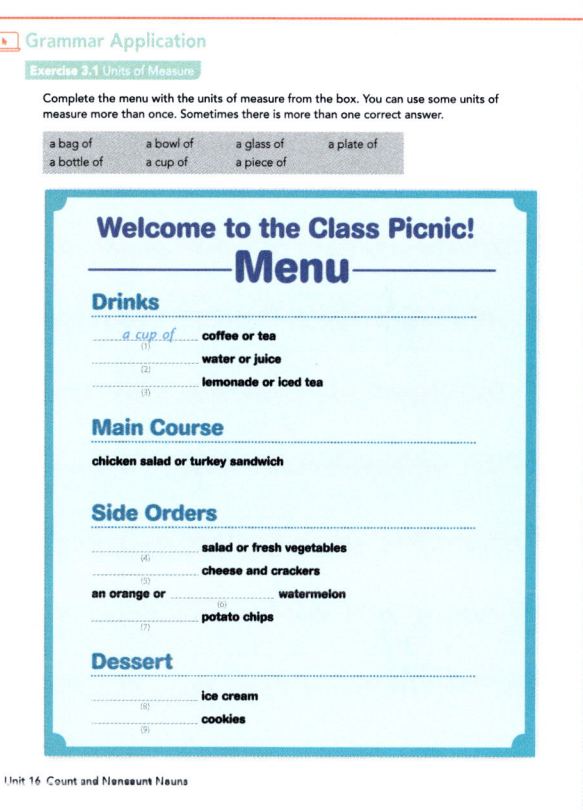

CHARTS

provide clear guidance on the form, meaning, and use of the target grammar for ease of instruction and reference.

THEME-RELATED EXERCISES

boost fluency by providing grammar practice in a variety of different contexts.

Tour of a Unit   xix

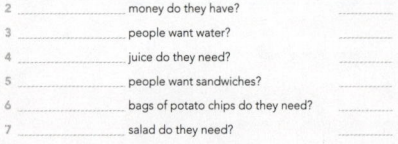

QR CODES

give easy access to audio at point of use.

CONTEXTUALIZED PRACTICE

moves from controlled to open-ended, teaching meaningful language for real communicative purposes.

DATA FROM THE REAL WORLD

takes students beyond traditional information and teaches them how the unit's grammar is used in authentic situations, including differences between spoken and written use.

HOW TO USE A QR CODE

1. Open the camera on your smartphone.
2. Point it at the QR code.
3. The camera will automatically scan the code. If not, press the button to take a picture.

* Not all cameras automatically scan QR codes. You may need to download a QR code reader. Search "QR free" and download an app.

Tour of a Unit

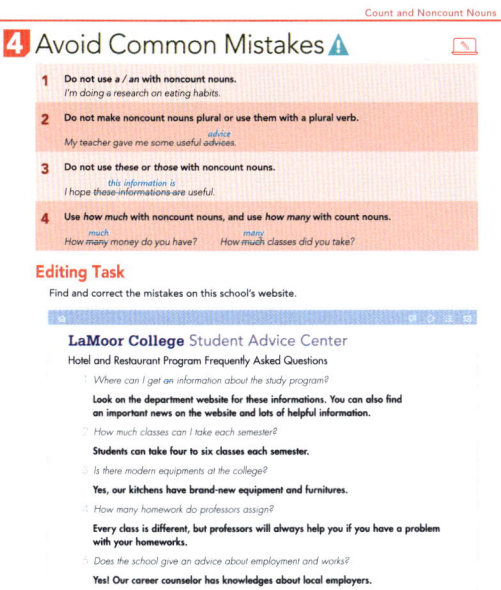

AVOID COMMON MISTAKES is based on a database of over 135,000 essays. Students learn to avoid the most common mistakes English language learners make and develop self-editing skills to improve their speaking and writing.

EDITING TASK gives learners an opportunity to identify and correct commonly made errors and develop self-editing skills needed in their university studies.

ACADEMIC WRITING concentrates on specific stages of the writing process: Brainstorm, Organize, Write, Edit.

REAL WORLD MODEL incorporates the unit grammar into common types of writing for students to understand and analyze.

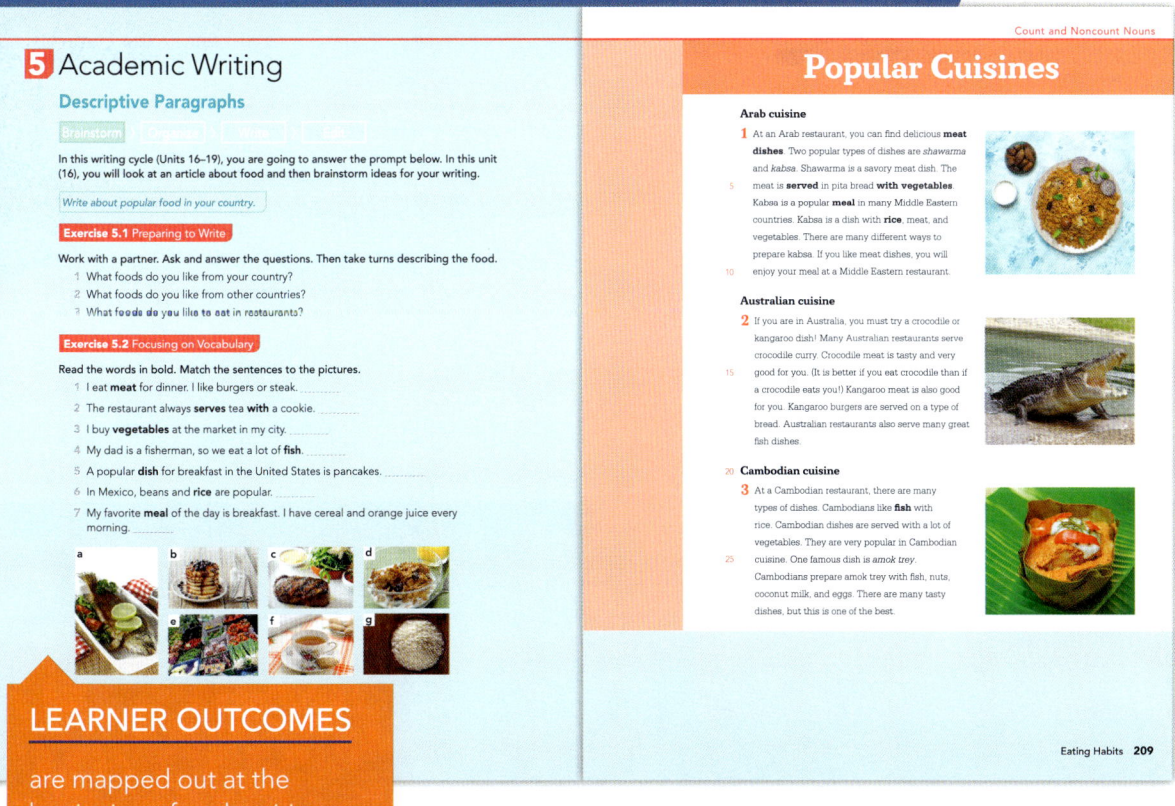

LEARNER OUTCOMES are mapped out at the beginning of each writing cycle and section.

SKILL BOXES

provide clear explanations of carefully selected writing skills.

MY WRITING

helps students develop their academic writing at various stages of the writing process.

Exercise 5.3 Comprehension Check

Read the text on page 209. Answer the questions.

1. Where is *kabsa* a very popular dish? _____
2. Which dishes are served in or on bread? _____
3. Which kinds of meat are good for you? _____
4. How many cuisines have rice dishes? Name them. _____
5. How many cuisines have fish dishes? Name them. _____

Exercise 5.4 Noticing the Grammar and Structure

Work with a partner. Complete the tasks.

1. Circle four examples of the article *a* in paragraph 1. Is the noun after each example count or non-count?
2. Underline the non-count nouns in paragraph 3.
3. What tense are the verbs in the text? Why does the writer use this tense?
4. Who is the writer's audience: college students, tourists, or chefs?

Using an Idea Map

An **idea map**, or **mind map**, is a diagram for brainstorming and organizing information. A good way to use an idea map is to write down all the words and ideas about a topic that you can think of. Then look for connections between those words and ideas.

Exercise 5.5 Applying the Skill

Work with a partner. Follow the steps to complete the idea map on page 211.

1. Look at paragraph 1 on page 209. Write the words that describe shawarma in the box. Add any other words and ideas that you know about the dish or Middle Eastern food.

    [   ]

2. Think of connections between these words and ideas. Use the questions to help you.
    - What is it made of?
    - What does it taste like?
    - What is it served with?

Count and Noncount Nouns

3. Write the connected words and ideas in one of the circles in the idea map below.

(idea map with "shawarma" in center circle)

My Writing

Exercise 5.6 Brainstorming

Work in groups of 2 or 3 students. If possible, work with classmates from different countries.

1. Brainstorm at least three popular dishes from your country.

    _____ _____ _____

2. Describe each dish. Use the questions to help you.
    - What is it made of?
    - What does it taste like?
    - What is it served with?
    - When do people eat it?
    - Do you like it? Why or why not?
3. Write three sentences about food from your country. Use count and non-count nouns correctly.

APPLICATION EXERCISES

give students scaffolded practice of the writing skills.

Kahoot!

for Grammar and Beyond
cambridge.org/kahoot/grammarandbeyond

What is Kahoot!?
Kahoot! is a game-based learning platform that makes it easy to create, share and play fun learning games and trivia quizzes in minutes. You can play Kahoot! on any mobile device or laptop with an internet connection.

What can you use kahoots for?
Kahoots can be used for review, formative assessment or homework.

When should you play Kahoot?
You can play kahoot quizzes before starting the unit as a diagnostic, during the unit as formative assessment, or at the end of a unit to test student knowledge.

To launch a live game in the classroom, find the kahoot for the level and unit and simply click on "play".

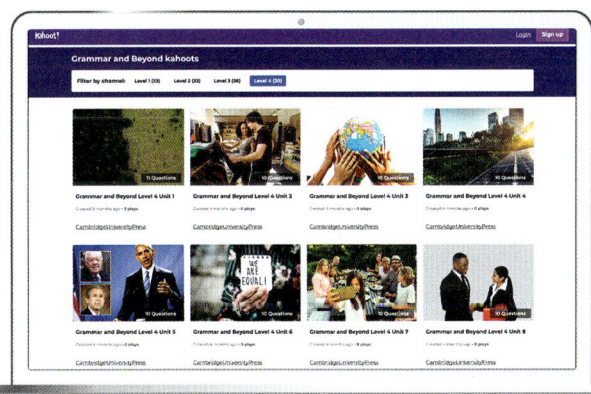

Quiz Your English app

Quiz Your English is a fun new way to practice, improve, and test your English by competing against learners from all around the world. Learn English grammar with friends, discover new English words, and test yourself in a truly global environment.

- Learn to avoid common mistakes with a special section just for *Grammar and Beyond* users
- Challenge your friends and players wherever they are
- Watch where you are on the leaderboards

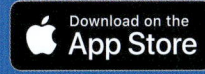

Tour of a Unit   xxiii

UNIT 16: Count and Noncount Nouns

Eating Habits

1 Grammar in the Real World

ACADEMIC WRITING

Descriptive paragraphs

A Do you think your diet is healthy? Read the article from a health magazine. What kinds of food are part of a healthy diet?

B Comprehension Check Answer the questions. Use the article to help you.
1. How do colorful fruit and vegetables help your health?
2. Why is a little dark chocolate good for you?
3. What type of oil is good for you?
4. How much water is good to drink each day?

C Notice Find the sentences in the article, and complete them with *a* or *an* or Ø for no article.

1. When you turn on _____ television or read _____ newspaper, you often find _____ information about healthy eating.

2. _____ food and _____ health get a lot of attention in the news these days.

3. Maybe you think _____ fat is bad for you, but people need a little fat in their diet.

4. It is _____ challenge to change your diet, but even small changes can help you stay healthy and happy.

Look at the noun after each space. Which of the nouns are things you can count? Which are things you cannot count?

Count and Noncount Nouns

Food for Health

When you turn on a television or read a **newspaper**, you often find **information** about healthy eating. **Food** and **health** get a lot of **attention** in the **news** these **days**. Researchers seem to find new **things** about how our **diet** affects us every day.

Everyone knows it is important to eat **fruit** and **vegetables**. Did you know that eating **fruit** and **vegetables** with different colors is especially good for your **health**? Green, red, blue, and orange **fruit** and **vegetables** all have different **vitamins**[1] to help hydrate you, and they help prevent different **diseases**.

Did you know that dark **chocolate** is good for you, too? Research shows that a little **chocolate** helps your **heart** and your **mood**.[2]

How about **fat**?[3] Maybe you think **fat** is bad for you, but people need a little **fat** in their diet. One type of healthy **fat** is omega-3 **oil**.[4] It comes from **fish** and helps your **heart**, **skin**, and **brain** stay healthy. For **vegetarians** or non-fish eaters, many **seeds**[5] and **nuts** also contain omega-3 **oil**. Omega-3 **oil** comes in **pills**, too.

Finally, **water** is an important part of a healthy **diet**. Try to drink at least six **glasses** of **water** a day, and you don't need to buy it. In most places, tap **water** from the kitchen **faucet** is just fine and tastes great!

It is a **challenge** to change your **diet**, but even small **changes** can help you stay healthy and happy.

---

[1]**vitamin:** a natural substance in food that is important for good health
[2]**mood:** the way someone feels at a particular time
[3]**fat:** a substance in plants and animals, often used for cooking
[4]**omega-3 oil:** a kind of healthy fat
[5]**seed:** a small hard part of a plant from which new plants can grow

Eating Habits

2 Count and Noncount Nouns

Grammar Presentation

Nouns are words for people, places, and things.

There are two types of nouns: count nouns and noncount nouns.

Count nouns name things you can count.
peas, vegetables, eggs, cookies

Noncount nouns name things you cannot count.
spinach, water, cheese, sugar

2.1 Count Nouns

A/An	Singular Count Noun	Singular Verb	
A	**vegetarian**	has	a meatless diet.
An	**apple**	is	a healthy snack.

Plural Count Noun	Plural Verb	
Vegetables	have	different vitamins.
Nuts	contain	healthy substances.

2.2 Noncount Nouns

Noncount Noun	Singular Verb	
Health	gets	a lot of attention in the news.
Water	is	an important part of a healthy diet.

➤➤ Noncount Nouns and Containers: See page A17.

2.3 Using Count Nouns

A Count nouns are things that you can count. You can use numbers with count nouns.	**one** egg, **six** eggs **one** banana, **two** bananas
B You can use *a/an* with singular count nouns.	Did you have **a** banana or **a** cookie?
Remember: Use *an* with words that start with a vowel sound.	I eat **an** apple and **an** orange every day.

2.3 Using Count Nouns (continued)

C	Count nouns can be plural. They can end in -s.	*Vegetables* are good for you. *Vitamins* keep you healthy.
	Remember: Some plural nouns are irregular.	*People* need good food. Some *children* don't like vegetables.
D	A singular count noun takes a singular verb.	A banana *is* good on cereal. My diet *isn't* very healthy.
E	A plural count noun takes a plural verb.	Nuts *contain* oil. Vegetarians *don't eat* meat.

2.4 Using Noncount Nouns

A	Noncount nouns are things you cannot count. Don't use numbers with count nouns.	milk, rice, sugar, cheese, spinach, tea, coffee NOT ~~one milk, one rice~~
	You can use numbers with drinks in a restaurant when you mean a cup of the drink.	Can we have *three coffees*, please?
B	Don't use *a/an* with noncount nouns.	Eat *spinach*. Drink *water*. Cook *shrimp*. NOT ~~a spinach, a water, a shrimp~~
C	Noncount nouns don't have a plural form. Don't add -s.	*Spinach* is good for you. NOT ~~Spinaches are~~ good for you.
D	A noncount noun takes a singular verb.	Fish *is* good for you. Fish oil *improves* your memory.

Grammar Application

Exercise 2.1 Count and Noncount Nouns

> **DATA FROM THE REAL WORLD**
>
> Research shows that noncount nouns are often the names of food and drink. The charts below show some of the most common food words in English.

A Which words are count nouns? Which are noncount nouns? Check (✓) the correct column.

	COUNT	NONCOUNT
apples	✓	
beans		
beef		
bread		
butter		
cheese		
cookies		
fish		
garlic		
ice cream		
meat		

	COUNT	NONCOUNT
milk		
potatoes		
rice		
sandwiches		
salt		
seafood		
shrimp		
sugar		
tomatoes		
vegetables		
water		

B Over to You Complete the lists with words from the chart. Write *count* after count nouns and *noncount* after noncount nouns.

I never eat / drink . . .	I often eat / drink . . .
apples – count	

198   Unit 16 Count and Noncount Nouns

Count and Noncount Nouns

Exercise 2.2 *A* and *An*

A Complete the survey questions. Write *a* or *an* before the count nouns. Write Ø before noncount nouns.

1. Do you usually have __*a*__ sandwich for lunch?

2. Do you often have _____ snack at bedtime?

3. Do you put _____ salt on your food?

4. Do you eat _____ garlic before a class?

5. How do you drink your tea or coffee? With _____ milk and _____ sugar?

6. Do you usually have _____ cookie with your tea or coffee?

7. Do you like _____ butter on your potatoes?

8. How often do you eat _____ pasta?

9. Which do you prefer: _____ apple or _____ banana?

10. Do you prefer _____ cereal or _____ bread for breakfast?

B **Pair Work** Ask a partner the survey questions in A.

A *Do you usually have a sandwich for lunch?*
B *No, I usually have an omelet or a Caesar salad.*

Eating Habits   199

Exercise 2.3 Count and Noncount Nouns

Read about the eating habits of these people. Change the singular count nouns in bold to plural nouns. Write Ø next to the noncount nouns.

Sean

I'm a vegetarian.

1. I don't eat **meat** __Ø__ .
2. I eat **egg**__s__ , but not every day.
3. I also eat **nut**__s__ , and I love fresh **vegetable**__s__ .
4. I also like **apple**__s__ and **cheese**__Ø__ a lot.

I don't like dairy food.

Isabel

5. I don't eat **cheese**__Ø__ or **butter**__Ø__ .
6. I don't drink **milk**__Ø__ .
7. I love **seafood**__Ø__ , but I'm allergic to **shrimp**__Ø__ .
8. My favorite food is **bean**__s__ .
9. I eat a lot of **pasta**__Ø__ .

I love fast food.

Lin

10. I love potato **chip**__s__ and **cookie**__s__ .
11. I don't eat **vegetable**__s__ very often.
12. I love desserts with **ice cream**__Ø__ .
13. I'm allergic to **chocolate**__Ø__ !

200 Unit 16 Count and Noncount Nouns

Exercise 2.4 Singular and Plural Verbs with Nouns

A Complete the sentences from a magazine article about food. Use the correct form of the verbs in parentheses.

FOOD FACTS

Food satisfies hunger, but it does other things, too. Food can have good and bad effects on your body and sometimes your mind. Did you know these facts about these common foods?

- Carrots __are__ (be) good for your eyes. (1)
- Pasta _____ (make) some people sleepy. (2)
- Bananas _____ (give) you energy. (3)
- Garlic _____ (be) good for your heart. (4)
- Ice _____ (give) some people a headache. (5)
- Ice cream _____ (make) some people thirsty. (6)
- Spinach _____ (contain) vitamin C. (7)
- Fish _____ (be) good for your brain. (8)
- Some people say green tea _____ (keep) you thin. (9)
- Some people say cheese _____ (give) them nightmares. (10)
- Some people say milk _____ (help) them sleep. (11)

B Over to You Write four sentences about how different kinds of foods affect you.

Ice cream makes me thirsty.
Soda gives me a headache.

1. _____
2. _____
3. _____
4. _____

3 Units of Measure; How Many . . . ? and How Much . . . ?

Grammar Presentation

Units of measure help us to tell how much or how many of a noun.

Questions with *How much . . . ?* and *How many . . . ?* ask about quantities.

I bought **a cup of** coffee in the cafeteria.
We had **a bowl of** soup with lunch.

How many vegetables did you use?
How much rice do you eat each week?

3.1 Units of Measure

Unit of Measure	Noncount or Plural Count Noun
a cup of	coffee
a bag of	rice
a piece of	cheese
a bottle of	water
a bowl of	soup
two bags of	potato chips
a carton of	eggs
a bunch of	bananas
a pound of	apples
three boxes of	cookies
a loaf of	bread

▸▸ Noncount Nouns and Containers: See page A17.

Count and Noncount Nouns

3.2 Using Units of Measure with Count and Noncount Nouns

A	You can use units of measure to count some noncount nouns.	My mother gave me **a bottle of** water. She drinks **a cup of** coffee every day. Did you eat **a piece of** cheese?
	You can make these expressions plural.	She took **two bottles of** water. I drank **three cups of** coffee today. We served **some pieces of** cheese.
B	You can use units of measure with count nouns.	I bought **a bag of** apples. David ate **a box of** cookies!
	You can make these expressions plural.	We collected **some bags of** apples. Lisa sold **six boxes of** cookies.

3.3 How Many . . . ? and How Much . . . ?

How Many	Count Noun	
	apples	did you eat?
How many	people	want food?
	bags	do you have?

How Much	Noncount Noun	
	coffee	do you drink every day?
How much	sugar	do you put in your coffee?
	money	do we need?

3.4 Using How Many . . . ? and How Much . . . ?

A	Use *How many . . . ?* to ask about count nouns.	*How many eggs* do you eat every week? *How many apples* do you bring to school every day?
B	Use *How much . . . ?* to ask about noncount nouns.	*How much milk* do you drink a day? *How much meat* do you eat in a week?

Grammar Application

Exercise 3.1 Units of Measure

Complete the menu with the units of measure from the box. You can use some units of measure more than once. Sometimes there is more than one correct answer.

| a bag of | a bowl of | a glass of | a plate of |
| a bottle of | a cup of | a piece of | |

Welcome to the Class Picnic!
Menu

Drinks

a cup of (1) coffee or tea

_____ (2) water or juice

_____ (3) lemonade or iced tea

Main Course

chicken salad or turkey sandwich

Side Orders

_____ (4) salad or fresh vegetables

_____ (5) cheese and crackers

an orange or _____ (6) watermelon

_____ (7) potato chips

Dessert

_____ (8) ice cream

_____ (9) cookies

Count and Noncount Nouns

Exercise 3.2 *How Much . . . ?* and *How Many . . . ?*

A Complete each question about the class picnic with *How much* or *How many*. Then listen to the conversation about the picnic and answer the questions.

1. _How many_ students are there in the class?   _18_
2. _____ money do they have?   _____
3. _____ people want water?   _____
4. _____ juice do they need?   _____
5. _____ people want sandwiches?   _____
6. _____ bags of potato chips do they need?   _____
7. _____ salad do they need?   _____
8. _____ cheese do people want?   _____
9. _____ people want an orange?   _____
10. _____ watermelon do they need?   _____

B **Pair Work** Plan a class picnic. Use the menu in Exercise 3.1 and the questions in A to help you.

A *How many students are there in our group?*
B *There are eight. How many people want water?*

🌐 DATA FROM THE REAL WORLD

Research shows that these are some of the most common noncount nouns:

equipment	homework	love	music	traffic
fun	information	mail	peace	weather
furniture	insurance	money	software	work

Noncount nouns are the names of:

materials: *oil, plastic, wood*
groups of things: *money, cash, furniture, jewelry*
subjects: *chemistry, geography, psychology*
weather: *snow, ice, fog*

Oil *costs a lot these days.*
The **jewelry** *in this store is expensive.*
Chemistry *doesn't interest me at all.*
There's always **snow** *in the winter here.*

Some noncount nouns end in -s, but they take a singular verb:

subjects: *economics, physics, politics*
activities: *aerobics, gymnastics*
other: *news*

Economics *was my best subject in high school.*
Gymnastics *is my favorite sport.*
The **news** *is really good.*

Students often make mistakes with noncount nouns, especially these:

information	equipment	advice	research	knowledge	furniture
behavior	work	homework	software	damage	training

Eating Habits

Exercise 3.3 Categories and Items

A Complete the chart. Use the words in the box.

a check	furniture	a keyboard	music	~~a ring~~
a couch	homework	knowledge	pop	traffic
equipment	information	money	rain	weather
an exercise	~~jewelry~~	motorcycles		

Category: _jewelry_ (1)

earrings
a necklace
a ring (2)

Category: _____ (3)

a table
a chair
_____ (4)

Category: _____ (5)

a computer
a printer
_____ (6)

Category: _____ (7)

names
dates
_____ (8)

Category: _____ (9)

cars
trucks
_____ (10)

Category: _____ (11)

an essay
a reading
_____ (12)

Category: _____ (13)

classical
hip-hop
jazz
_____ (14)

Category: _____ (15)

bills
coins
_____ (16)

Category: _____ (17)

snow
ice
_____ (18)

B Group Work Complete the chart with the words in the box. Then add as many words in each category as you can.

4 Avoid Common Mistakes ⚠️

1 **Do not use *a / an* with noncount nouns.**
I'm doing ~~a~~ research on eating habits.

2 **Do not make noncount nouns plural or use them with a plural verb.**
My teacher gave me some useful ~~advices~~ advice.

3 **Do not use *these* or *those* with noncount nouns.**
I hope ~~these informations are~~ this information is useful.

4 **Use *how much* with noncount nouns, and use *how many* with count nouns.**
How ~~many~~ much money do you have?   How ~~much~~ many classes did you take?

Editing Task

Find and correct the mistakes on this school's website.

LaMoor College Student Advice Center

Hotel and Restaurant Program Frequently Asked Questions

1. Where can I get ~~an~~ information about the study program?

   Look on the department website for these informations. You can also find an important news on the website and lots of helpful information.

2. How much classes can I take each semester?

   Students can take four to six classes each semester.

3. Is there modern equipments at the college?

   Yes, our kitchens have brand-new equipment and furnitures.

4. How many homework do professors assign?

   Every class is different, but professors will always help you if you have a problem with your homeworks.

5. Does the school give an advice about employment and works?

   Yes! Our career counselor has knowledges about local employers.

5 Academic Writing

Descriptive Paragraphs

Brainstorm > Organize > Write > Edit

In this writing cycle (Units 16–19), you are going to answer the prompt below. In this unit (16), you will look at an article about food and then brainstorm ideas for your writing.

> Write about popular food in your country.

Exercise 5.1 Preparing to Write

Work with a partner. Ask and answer the questions. Then take turns describing the food.

1. What foods do you like from your country?
2. What foods do you like from other countries?
3. What foods do you like to eat in restaurants?

Exercise 5.2 Focusing on Vocabulary

Read the words in bold. Match the sentences to the pictures.

1. I eat **meat** for dinner. I like burgers or steak. _____
2. The restaurant always **serves** tea **with** a cookie. _____
3. I buy **vegetables** at the market in my city. _____
4. My dad is a fisherman, so we eat a lot of **fish**. _____
5. A popular **dish** for breakfast in the United States is pancakes. _____
6. In Mexico, beans and **rice** are popular. _____
7. My favorite **meal** of the day is breakfast. I have cereal and orange juice every morning. _____

a

b

c

d

e

f

g

Popular Cuisines

Arab cuisine

1 At an Arab restaurant, you can find delicious **meat dishes**. Two popular types of dishes are *shawarma* and *kabsa*. Shawarma is a savory meat dish. The meat is **served** in pita bread **with vegetables**. Kabsa is a popular **meal** in many Middle Eastern countries. Kabsa is a dish with **rice**, meat, and vegetables. There are many different ways to prepare kabsa. If you like meat dishes, you will enjoy your meal at a Middle Eastern restaurant.

Australian cuisine

2 If you are in Australia, you must try a crocodile or kangaroo dish! Many Australian restaurants serve crocodile curry. Crocodile meat is tasty and very good for you. (It is better if you eat crocodile than if a crocodile eats you!) Kangaroo meat is also good for you. Kangaroo burgers are served on a type of bread. Australian restaurants also serve many great fish dishes.

Cambodian cuisine

3 At a Cambodian restaurant, there are many types of dishes. Cambodians like **fish** with rice. Cambodian dishes are served with a lot of vegetables. They are very popular in Cambodian cuisine. One famous dish is *amok trey*. Cambodians prepare amok trey with fish, nuts, coconut milk, and eggs. There are many tasty dishes, but this is one of the best.

Exercise 5.3 Comprehension Check

Read the text on page 209. Answer the questions.

1 Where is *kabsa* a very popular dish? _____

2 Which dishes are served in or on bread? _____

3 Which kinds of meat are good for you? _____

4 How many cuisines have rice dishes? Name them. _____

5 How many cuisines have fish dishes? Name them. _____

Exercise 5.4 Noticing the Grammar and Structure

Work with a partner. Complete the tasks.

1 Circle four examples of the article *a* in paragraph 1. Is the noun after each example count or non-count?
2 Underline the non-count nouns in paragraph 3.
3 What tense are the verbs in the text? Why does the writer use this tense?
4 Who is the writer's audience: college students, tourists, or chefs?

Using an Idea Map

An **idea map**, or **mind map**, is a diagram for brainstorming and organizing information. A good way to use an idea map is to write down all the words and ideas about a topic that you can think of. Then look for connections between those words and ideas.

Exercise 5.5 Applying the Skill

Work with a partner. Follow the steps to complete the idea map on page 211.

1 Look at paragraph 1 on page 209. Write the words that describe shawarma in the box. Add any other words and ideas that you know about the dish or Middle Eastern food.

[   ]

2 Think of connections between these words and ideas. Use the questions to help you.
 • What is it made of?
 • What does it taste like?
 • What is it served with?

3 Write the connected words and ideas in one of the circles in the idea map below.

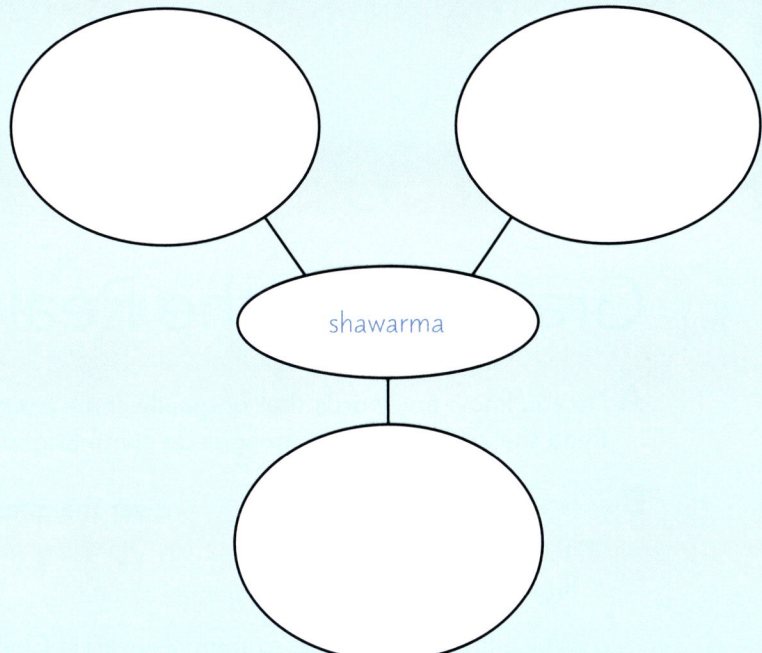

My Writing

Exercise 5.6 Brainstorming

Work in groups of 2 or 3 students. If possible, work with classmates from different countries.

1 Brainstorm at least three popular dishes from your country.

_____ _____ _____

2 Describe each dish. Use the questions to help you.
- What is it made of?
- What does it taste like?
- What is it served with?
- When do people eat it?
- Do you like it? Why or why not?

3 Write three sentences about food from your country. Use count and non-count nouns correctly.

_____
_____
_____
_____
_____

UNIT 17

Quantifiers: *Some, Any, A Lot Of, A Little, A Few, Much, Many*

Languages

1 Grammar in the Real World

ACADEMIC WRITING

Descriptive paragraphs

A Do you know any words that originally come from another language? Read the article. What languages do some English words come from?

B Comprehension Check Answer the questions. Use the article to help you.

1 From which language did *pajamas* come? _____
2 Which English words are commonly used in China? _____
3 Is *football* an original English word? _____
4 Which language did *ferry* come from? _____

C Notice Find the sentences in the article and complete them with *some* or *any*.

1 Let's go have _____ nachos.
2 Let's get _____ sushi.
3 The server asks, "Do you want _____ drinks?"

Compare the sentences with *some* and *any*. How are they different?

Quantifiers: Some, Any, A Lot Of, A Little, A Few, Much, Many

Sushi in the Café

[1] **import:** bring something into a country from another country

[2] **export:** send items to another country for sale or use

A woman says to a friend, "Let's go have **some** nachos." Her friend says, "I don't want nachos. Let's get **some** sushi." After they order their food, the server asks, "Do you want **any** drinks?" "Coffee, please," says the woman. "Cola for me," says her friend. What language did the women speak at the café? English, of course. However, **many** of the words they used are not originally English words. *Nachos, sushi, coffee,* and *cola* all come from other languages. They are called loanwords, words that started as foreign words and then became common.

Loanwords are not just names of food. We wear *cotton pajamas*, wash our hair with *shampoo*, and read *magazines*. *Pajamas* and *shampoo* come from Hindi, and *cotton* and *magazines* come from Arabic.

English words are loanwords in other languages, too. For example, the English words *model*, *baby*, and *computer* are now common in Chinese. In fact, **a lot of** English words are now international. People from **many** different countries understand them. **Some** examples include *football*, *ferry*, *flash*, and *Internet*.

Languages import[1] words and export[2] words because people are always in contact. The next time you learn a new word in English, use a dictionary to check where it comes from. You will be surprised that **a lot of** "English" words are really from **many** other languages.

Languages 213

2 Quantifiers: *Some* and *Any*

Grammar Presentation

> We use *some* and *any* to talk about an unknown quantity of something.
>
> Let's go have **some** sushi.
> Do you want **any** drinks?

2.1 Affirmative Statements with *Some*

	Some	Noncount Noun
I need		information.
Ricardo had	some	sushi.
We ordered		food.

	Some	Plural Noun
Let's have		nachos.
I know	some	Italian words.
Let's read		examples.

2.2 Negative Statements with *Any*

	Do / Does / Did + Not	Base Form of Verb	Any	Noncount Noun
I	don't	want		sushi.
The book	doesn't	have	any	information.
We	didn't	bring		food.

	Do / Does / Did + Not	Base Form of Verb	Any	Noncount Noun
I	don't	remember		Italian words.
Yuri	doesn't	want	any	nachos.
We	didn't	see		examples.

2.3 Yes/No Questions with *Some* and *Any*

	Some / Any	Noncount Noun	
Can I have	some	sushi?	
Do you have	any	information	about the English program?
Did you do	any	research	on loanwords?

Quantifiers: *Some, Any, A Lot Of, A Little, A Few, Much, Many*

2.3 Yes/No Questions with *Some* and *Any* (continued)

	Some / Any	Plural Noun	
Can you teach me	some	words	in Italian?
Do you have	any	books	on loanwords?
Are there	any	examples	in the book?

2.4 Using *Some* and *Any* in Statements

A Use *some* with noncount nouns and plural nouns in affirmative statements.

I found some information about loanwords in this book.

In affirmative statements *some* refers to small quantities or unknown quantities.

There are some words in English that come from Arabic, but I don't know how many.

B Use *some* for small amounts and numbers, not large amounts and numbers.

There are Latin and Greek words in English.
NOT *There are some Latin and Greek words in English.*
(There are thousands!)

C Use *any* with noncount nouns and plural nouns in negative statements.

There isn't any food in the refrigerator.

In negative statements, *any* refers to a zero quantity.

I don't remember any words in Italian.

2.5 Using Yes/No Questions with *Some* and *Any*

A Use *some* with noncount nouns and plural nouns to ask for something or to offer something that is there.

Can I get some information from you about Portuguese, please?

(The person asking knows the other person has information about Portuguese.)

Do you want to use some words from Russian for your paper about English loanwords?

(The person asking has words to give to the writer.)

B Use *any* with noncount nouns and plural nouns to ask for unknown quantities.

Did you make any progress with your paper?

(The questioner doesn't expect progress.)

Are there any English words that come from Swahili?

(There may be no English words that come from Swahili. The questioner doesn't know.)

Languages

Grammar Application

Exercise 2.1 Statements with *Some* and *Any*

A Julia and her classmates have some questions about loanwords. Complete their conversation with *some* or *any*.

Julia We use __some__ (1) Japanese words in English, for example, *karaoke* and *sushi*.

Simon Yeah, that's true. Do we use _____ (2) Indonesian words in English? Do you know, Taufik?

Taufik Yes, there are _____ (3) food words, for example, *satay*.

Nick Pilar told me _____ (4) Spanish words, for example, *papaya* and *Florida*. *Florida* means "a place with flowers."

Julia What about Arabic?

Taufik There aren't _____ (5) Arabic students in the class, so let's check online.

Nick Miriam, you lived in Ghana. Tell us _____ (6) words from African languages that we use in English.

Miriam Hmm. Yeah, sure. Well, *cola*, *jazz*, and *safari* are from African languages. There are probably _____ (7) more words, but I don't know _____ (8) others.

Julia Thanks, everyone. Now we know _____ (9) words in English that come from other languages. Let's organize them.

B Over to You Do you know any other English words that come from other languages? Tell the class.

A *I know some Italian words in English.*

B *Really? I don't know any Italian words. What words do you know?*

A *I know pesto and pizza. I don't know any others.*

Quantifiers: Some, Any, A Lot Of, A Little, A Few, Much, Many

Exercise 2.2 Yes/No Questions with Some and Any

A Complete the conversations. Write the questions. Use *some* or *any* and the words in parentheses.

Conversation 1

Samantha: So, Rafa, I know you're from Spain. You're from Barcelona, right?

Do you have any friends from Madrid
(1)
(have/friends/from Madrid)?

Rafa: Yes, I do. I have some friends who still live there. And you were born in Canada, right?

_____
(2)
(have/friends/from there)?

Samantha: Yes, I have some friends from Toronto and Montreal.

Conversation 2

Rafa: How's your English class, Tomoko?

_____
(3)
(have/classmates/from Latin America)?

Tomoko: Yes, I do. I have some classmates from Peru, Mexico, and Argentina.

Rafa: _____
(4)
(are there/students/from South Asia)?

Tomoko: I'm not sure, but I hope so! I want to meet people from all over the world.

Conversation 3

Tara: Hey, guys! I made chocolate chip cookies this morning.

_____
(5)
(want/cookies)?

Rafa: Oh, yes! Thanks!

_____
(6)
(have/milk)?

Tara: Yes, I do. It's in the refrigerator. Help yourself.

Languages 217

Conversation 4

Samantha Rafa, I like your CD collection.

_____ (7)
(can / I / listen to / music)?

Rafa Sure! Go ahead. I have a lot of salsa. It's fun to dance to!

Samantha Oh, I don't know how to dance salsa.

_____ (8)
(are there / salsa clubs / around here)?

Rafa Yes, there are some clubs downtown. They give dance lessons. Samantha,

_____ (9)
(want / to take / lessons)?

Samantha Sure!

Rafa Great! Let's go sometime!

B Pair Work Practice the conversations with a partner.

Exercise 2.3 Statements and Questions

A Write affirmative and negative statements using the verbs in parentheses. Make them true for you. Use *some* for affirmative statements and *any* for negative statements.

1. I ____*have some / don't have any*____ books in English at home. (have)
2. I _____ recording equipment. (own)
3. I _____ friends at work. (have)
4. I _____ words in Italian. (know)
5. I _____ people from El Salvador. (know)
6. I _____ TV shows in English. (watch)
7. I _____ podcasts from news websites. (download)
8. I _____ knowledge of French. (have)
9. I _____ e-mails in Portuguese. (write)
10. I _____ online music stores. (use)

B Pair Work Ask and answer questions with a partner based on your sentences in A. Use *any* in your questions.

A *Do you have any books in English at home?*

B *Yes, I have some books in English at home.*

Quantifiers: Some, Any, A Lot Of, A Little, A Few, Much, Many

3 Quantifiers: *A Lot Of, A Little, A Few, Much, Many*

Grammar Presentation

Quantifiers can refer to large or small amounts.

I know **a lot of** English words.
I need **a little** extra information for my paper on loanwords.

3.1 Affirmative Statements

	A Lot Of / A Little	Noncount Noun
I found	a lot of / a little	information.

	A Lot Of / A Few / Many	Plural Noun
She has	a lot of / a few / many	friends in Indonesia.

3.2 Yes/No Questions

	A Lot Of / A Little / Much	Noncount Noun
Did you learn	a lot of	English?
Did you need	a little	help?
Do you have	much	homework?

	A Lot Of / A Few / Many	Plural Noun
Did you meet	a lot of	people?
Do you have	a few	minutes?
Can you speak	many	languages?

Is There	A Lot Of / A Little / Much	Noncount Noun	
Is there	a lot of / a little / much	information	in the article?

Are There	A Lot Of / A Few / Many	Plural Noun	
Are there	a lot of / a few / many	people	in your class?

Languages 219

3.3 Using Quantifiers

A	In affirmative statements: Use *a lot of* for large quantities of plural nouns and noncount nouns.	I met **a lot of** Russian speakers in North Carolina. There is **a lot of** help available for students.
	Use *a little* for small quantities of noncount nouns.	I understand **a little** Swedish.
	Use *a few* for small quantities of plural nouns.	Dane has **a few** friends in Asia.
	Use *many* for large quantities of plural nouns.	There are **many** people that speak Swahili in the neighborhood.
B	In negative statements: Use *not a lot of* for small amounts of plural and noncount nouns.	There is**n't a lot of** information about some words. There are**n't a lot of** students from Denmark at the school.
	Use *not much* for small amounts of noncount nouns.	Two months is**n't much** time to learn a new language.
	Use *not many* for small amounts of plural nouns.	There are**n't many** people from Austria in my class.
C	In questions: Use *a lot of* with plural and noncount nouns.	Do you have **a lot of** relatives in Ireland? Is there **a lot of** bad weather in Maine?
	Use *much* in questions with noncount nouns.	Do you have **much** homework in Spanish class?
	Use *many* with plural nouns.	Are there **many** Chinese restaurants in Boston?
D	Don't use *much* in affirmative statements.	The website had **a lot of** information about Latin. NOT ~~The website had much information about Latin.~~
E	Use short answers with *a lot, a few,* and *not many* to refer to plural nouns.	"How **many** students did a presentation on loanwords?" "**A lot. / A few. / Not many.**"
	Use short answers with *a lot, a little,* and *not much* to refer to noncount nouns.	"How **much** work did you do on your paper?" "**A lot. / A little. / Not much.**"

Quantifiers: *Some, Any, A Lot Of, A Little, A Few, Much, Many*

Grammar Application

Exercise 3.1 Count and Noncount Nouns

Write *C* for the count nouns and *NC* for the noncount nouns.

dictionary __C__   homework ____   student ____   song ____   furniture ____

time ____   music ____   knowledge ____   word ____   Korean (language) ____

Exercise 3.2 *A Lot Of, A Little, A Few,* or *Many*

Listen and complete the paragraph about an English class with *a lot of, a little, a few,* or *many*.

Karina's English class at Dixon College is very international. Her class has __a few__ (1) Russians: Karina and two others. There are _____ (2) students from Brazil, perhaps 80 percent. There are _____ (3) students from Japan, but not many. The rest are from other Asian countries like Malaysia, Thailand, and Vietnam.

They come from all over the world and bring interesting stories with them. Rosa is from São Paulo, Brazil, and listens to _____ (4) Brazilian music. She loves it. She also has _____ (5) songs from Puerto Rico on her computer, but not many. Seri, from Penang, has _____ (6) beautiful furniture from Malaysia in her house. Keiko, from Japan, taught Karina and Rosa _____ (7) Japanese, but the words are difficult to remember. Noom, from Bangkok, loves his country's food. Sometimes he makes _____ (8) Thai food for his classmates, but not much because it's very hot for them. Linh, who moved from Vietnam, eats _____ (9) spicy food. She loves it! Sometimes, Karina brings in _____ (10) borscht, a Russian soup. Only Keiko and Noom like it, so she doesn't make a lot of it. The best part of Karina's diverse class is that she can hear _____ (11) languages besides English every day!

Languages

Exercise 3.3 *A Lot Of, A Little, A Few, Much,* or *Many*

A Circle the correct words.

Dustin Hi, Dr. Lanza. Thank you for doing this interview for *Student Voices*. First, are there **much / (many)** countries in Asia where English is the official language?
(1)

Dr. Lanza Well, there aren't **many / much**, but there are **a little / a few** – for example, Pakistan, Singapore, and the Philippines.
(2) (3)

Dustin How **many / much** words are there in English?
(4)

Dr. Lanza It's hard to say. Anywhere from 250,000 to 750,000, perhaps! Dictionaries have **much / a lot of** words, but they don't contain all of them. A big English dictionary has hundreds of thousands of words.
(5)

Dustin Really? That's **many / a lot**! How many words do native English speakers know? Do they know **a lot of / many** vocabulary?
(6) (7)

Dr. Lanza Yes, every native speaker knows **much / a lot of** words. Adults probably know 20,000 to 30,000 words.
(8)

Dustin Very interesting! Thanks for this interview, Dr. Lanza!

B Pair Work Tell a partner what you know about other cultures and languages. Use the conversation in A as a model. Remember to use *a lot of, a few, a little,* and *many*.

Exercise 3.4 Short Answers

Answer the questions that students in an English class are asking each other before class. Use *a lot, a few, a little, not many,* and *not much*.

1 How much time did you work on your paper?
   _A lot_____. I worked all day on it.

2 I wasn't in class yesterday. How much homework did we have for today?
   _____. The teacher only assigned two online exercises.

3 How many classes do you have today?
   _____. I only have two today. Tomorrow I have four!

4 How much time did you spend on homework last night?
   _____. I was very busy, so I didn't have a lot of time.

5 How many minutes do we have before class starts?
   _____. It's going to start in two minutes!

Quantifiers: Some, Any, A Lot Of, A Little, A Few, Much, Many

Exercise 3.5 *A Lot Of, Much, and Many*

DATA FROM THE REAL WORLD

People often use *a lot of* in speaking. In writing, they often use *much* and *many*.	**Say**: "There are a lot of different languages and cultures in South America." **Write**: There are many different languages and cultures in South America. **Say**: "Schools in poorer countries often don't have a lot of modern equipment." **Write**: Schools in poorer countries often do not have much modern equipment.	*a lot of* — bar chart showing small bar for writing and large bar for speaking
Use *a lot of* in speaking and writing in affirmative statements with noncount nouns.	The website has a lot of information about English as a global language.	

A Change *a lot of* to *much* or *many* in the essay.

Communication Shortage

                    many

In the twentieth century, ~~a lot of~~ young people had pen pals[1] from other countries. They wrote letters to them and learned about other countries, cultures, and languages. Traveling was expensive, so they did not have **a lot of** opportunities to meet their pen pals. There was not **a lot of** direct contact between people from different countries, so letters were
5 a good way to communicate.

      Now there are not **a lot of** traditional pen pals. Instead, there are **a lot of** social media sites on the Internet. People post photos, videos, and comments. People are busy and they don't have **a lot of** time, so now they use apps to send short messages around the world. Today apps such as Twitter® are popular. People typically send **a lot of** "tweets" every day. However, can
10 people exchange **a lot of** information in these very short messages? Can people learn **a lot of** interesting things about the other person's culture? These are good questions for discussion.

[1]**pen pal:** someone you exchange letters with as a hobby, especially someone from another country

B Pair Work Discuss the essay in A with a partner. Ask each other these questions.

1 What social media do you use to communicate with your friends? Why?
2 Do you think social media sites and apps are a good way to learn about other people and cultures?
3 What kinds of information do people exchange online?

4 Avoid Common Mistakes ⚠

1 **Use *many* with plural nouns.**

   Do you write ~~much~~ *many* essays?

2 **Use *much* with noncount nouns in negative statements and questions. In affirmative statements with noncount nouns, use *a lot of*, not *much*.**

   The students don't have ~~many~~ *much* work in the lab today.

   There is ~~much~~ *a lot of* information on loanwords online.

3 **For quantities, use *some* with noncount nouns. Do not use *a / an* with noncount nouns.**

   I need ~~an~~ *some* information about Korea.

4 **Use *any* with negative statements, and use *some* with affirmative statements.**

   I don't have ~~some~~ *any* dictionaries to use.   I learned ~~any~~ *some* Japanese words from a Japanese friend.

224 Unit 17 Quantifiers: *Some, Any, A Lot Of, A Little, A Few, Much, Many*

Quantifiers: *Some, Any, A Lot Of, A Little, A Few, Much, Many*

Editing Task

Find and correct 11 more mistakes in this interview with Dr. Matthew Sutton, Director of the Language Center at Marsland College.

Roberto Hello, Dr. Sutton. My name is Roberto Ferrer and I'm a student here at the college. I'd like to ask you ~~any~~ *some* questions about the Language Center for our college paper. How does the Language Center help language students?

Dr. Sutton Thanks for asking, Roberto. The center is very important. We give students much information about foreign languages and cultures, and we have much learning material for 30 different languages.

Roberto Wow, that sounds like much information on different languages that students can find here.

Dr. Sutton It is, Roberto. Much students find the center really helpful. You see, much students work and do not have many time to study. They can come to the center before or after class. They can spend a few minutes or one or two hours here. They can use our computers and equipment for projects, or just meet friends.

Roberto That sounds great. Do much students use the center?

Dr. Sutton Right now, about 100 students use the center every day.

Roberto Does the center have modern equipment?

Dr. Sutton Yes, it does. Every year, we buy a new equipment, for example, computers and 3D printers. We also spend much money to make the center a comfortable place. For example, we recently bought a new furniture. Please come and visit! We are open every day.

Roberto All right. Thanks for your time, Dr. Sutton!

5 Academic Writing

Descriptive Paragraphs

Brainstorm > Organize > Write > Edit

In Unit 16, you read about different foods and used an idea map to brainstorm for the prompt below. In this unit (17), you will continue brainstorming and begin organizing ideas for your paragraphs.

> Write about popular food in your country.

My Writing

Exercise 5.1 Using an Idea Map

Review your brainstorming and sentences on page 211. Complete an idea map like the one below for two of the dishes from your country. Write the name of the dish in the middle of each idea map. Brainstorm words to explain what each dish is made of, tastes like, and is served with.

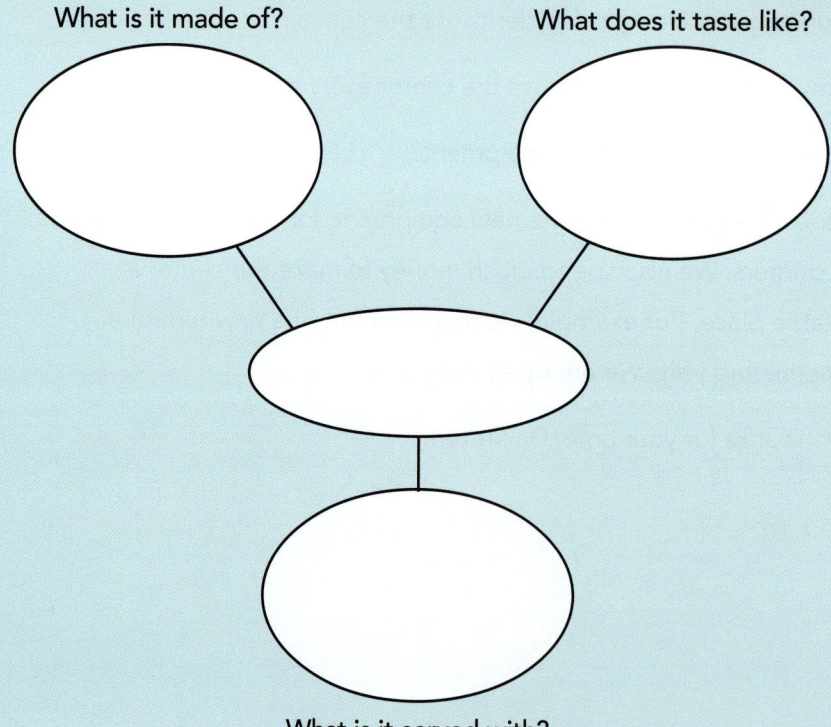

226 Unit 17 Quantifiers: *Some, Any, A Lot Of, A Little, A Few, Much, Many*

Quantifiers: *Some, Any, A Lot Of, A Little, A Few, Much, Many*

Exercise 5.2 Completing an Outline

Use your idea maps to complete the topic sentences and outline below.

Paragraph 1
A popular dish in _____ (my country) is _____ (name of first dish).
What it's made of:
1 _____
2 _____
What it tastes like:
1 _____
2 _____
What it's served with:
1 _____
2 _____

Paragraph 2
Another popular dish from _____ (my country) is _____ (name of second dish).
What it's made of:
1 _____
2 _____
What it tastes like:
1 _____
2 _____
What it's served with:
1 _____
2 _____

Exercise 5.3 Using Quantifiers to Describe Food

Complete the chart with ingredients that each of your dishes has or food that your dish is served with.

some...	*a lot of...*	*a few...*	*a little...*
some meat	a lot of vegetables	a few pieces of bread	a little salt

Languages 227

UNIT 18

Articles: *A / An* and *The*

Changes and Risks

1 Grammar in the Real World

ACADEMIC WRITING

Descriptive paragraphs

A Do you like to take risks?[1] Read the magazine article about how people respond to risk. When you make a decision, what steps do you take?

B Comprehension Check Circle the correct answers from the magazine article.

1 Making decisions during difficult times is
   a different for everyone.
   b always hard.
   c easy for everyone.

2 If you are an *ostrich*, you
   a like to take risks.
   b do not like to take risks.
   c look at your choices before you make a decision.

3 If you are a *rock climber*, you
   a like to take risks.
   b do not like to take risks.
   c look at your choices before you make a decision.

4 If you are an *analyst*, you
   a like to take risks.
   b do not like to take risks.
   c look at your choices before you make a decision.

C Notice Which article (*a* or *an*) comes before these words the first time they appear?

	a	an
1 ostrich		
2 car		
3 new job		
4 important decision		
5 business		

Compare the words that come after *a* with the words that come after *an*. Look at the beginning sounds of the words. How are they different?

[1] **take a risk:** do something where there is a possibility of being hurt or of a loss or defeat

DECISIONS IN RISKY TIMES

In uncertain or difficult times, it's sometimes hard for people to make decisions. For example, when **the** economy is bad, people worry about money and their jobs. Some take risks to try to make things better. Others don't take any risks and hope to stay safe. Guy Burgess,
5 of **the** University of Colorado, says people deal with difficult times differently.

Some people become *ostriches*.[1] **An** ostrich does not like risks. For example, Connor is nervous about **the** economy. He doesn't buy anything expensive, like **a** car, since **the** car he has still works. He doesn't look for **a** new job even though he hates **the** job he has. He knows **the**
10 job he has now is stable.[2]

Others become *rock climbers*. They love taking risks. For example, Kala found a new job and makes a lot more money. But **the** job does not have good health insurance, and it's short-term.[3] She isn't worried because she enjoys taking risks.

15 Finally, some become *analysts*.[4] For example, Lorena looks carefully at her choices before she makes **an** important decision. She decides to sell her house and put **the** money into a business. She knows she can make a lot of money with **the** business.

Some risks are worth taking and others are dangerous. It's important
20 to know which type of risk taker you are before you make big decisions.

---

[1]**ostrich:** here, a person who ignores reality or does not accept the truth
[2]**stable:** safe, not likely to change
[3]**short-term:** not for a long time
[4]**analyst:** someone who studies or examines something in detail, such as finances, computer systems, or the economy

2 Articles: *A / An* and *The*

Grammar Presentation

Articles are used with nouns. *A / An* is the indefinite article. *The* is the definite article.	Claire is **an** analyst. She thinks carefully before she makes **a** decision, especially when **the** decision is **an** important one.

2.1 Indefinite Article: *A / An*

A Use *a / an* with singular count nouns.	She made **a decision** about her job. **An analyst** examines something in detail.
B Use *a* when the noun begins with a consonant sound.	She made **a decision** about her job.
C Use *an* when the noun begins with a vowel sound.	**An analyst** examines something in detail.
D Use *a* before words such as adjectives or adverbs that begin with a consonant sound.	Tony found **a great** apartment in Chicago.
E Use *a* before words that begin with *u* when the *u* makes a "you" sound.	James went to **a university** in Boston. The economy is **a universal** concern.

2.2 Definite Article: *The*

You can use *the* before singular or plural count nouns and before noncount nouns.	**The job** is a good one. **The choices** were interesting. **The information** is very useful.

▸▸ Indefinite and Definite Articles: See page A19.

2.3 Using *A / An* and *The*

A Use *a / an* to introduce a person or thing for the first time to a listener. When you mention the person or thing again, use *the*.	Tom bought **a car**. (The listener does not know about this car.) **The car** was not very expensive. (Now the listener knows about this car.)

Articles: *A / An* and *The*

2.3 Using *A / An* and *The* (continued)

B Use *the* to talk about specific people or things that both the listener and speaker know about.

The president discussed **the plan**.
(Everyone knows the president and the plan.)
The moon and **the stars** were beautiful last night.
(Everyone knows the moon and the stars.)
"**The game** was interesting." "I agree."
(The speaker and listener are thinking of the same game.)

Grammar Application

Exercise 2.1 Sentences with *A / An*

A Complete the sentences with *a* or *an*.

1. A rock climber takes __a__ risk easily.
2. _____ analyst thinks about choices before he/she decides.
3. _____ ostrich doesn't like to take risks and wants to be safe.
4. Connor doesn't look for _____ job because he already has one.
5. Kala was glad she got _____ interview.
6. Lorena owns _____ business.
7. She made _____ decision about the business.
8. She decided to sell her house and rent _____ apartment.
9. I hope to go to _____ university in Europe.
10. I want to go to _____ information session and talk to _____ academic adviser.

B Over to You Which kind of risk taker are you? Discuss with a partner and explain your choice.

A I'm a rock climber because I love to take risks. I left a good job to go back to college.
B Oh, I'm an ostrich. I don't like to take risks at all.

Changes and Risks **231**

Exercise 2.2 Pronunciation Focus: Pronouncing *A* and *An*

We pronounce *a* and *an* with a weak sound, /ə/ or /ən/, because we don't stress the articles.	a decision	an analyst
	a business	an ostrich
	a risk	an opinion

A Listen and repeat the phrases in the chart above.

B Read the interview and complete the sentences with *a* or *an*.

Reporter Hi, my name is Steve. I'm a reporter with the *New Times*, and I have some questions for you about taking risks. Can you describe __a__ (1) decision that was really difficult for you?

Student Yes, I made _____ (2) decision to leave my job.

Reporter Do you think there was _____ (3) risk in that decision?

Student Yes, there was _____ (4) risk because I left _____ (5) good job, and I don't know about the new one yet.

Reporter Of the three types of risk takers – _____ (6) "ostrich," _____ (7) "rock climber," and _____ (8) "analyst" – which type are you?

Student Oh, I'm _____ (9) analyst!

Reporter Do you think analysts always make good decisions?

Student Yes, because _____ (10) analyst looks at all of the choices carefully.

Reporter How do you think _____ (11) ostrich manages stress?

Student Well, _____ (12) ostrich makes sure everything in his or her life is stable.

Reporter Do you know someone who is _____ (13) rock climber?

Student I do! My sister is _____ (14) rock climber. She always takes risks!

C Pair Work Practice the interview with a partner.

232 Unit 18 Articles: *A / An* and *The*

Articles: A / An and The

Exercise 2.3 A / An or The?

A Complete the conversation with *a*, *an*, or *the*.

Emma Guess what, Isabella? I want to start __a__ (1) catering business![1]

Isabella That's great! I know you love to cook!

Emma I went to ____(2) exciting class for new female entrepreneurs. ____(3) teacher for the class taught us a lot of things. For example, now I know how to get ____(4) loan[2] from a bank. When I get it, ____(5) loan can help me buy the equipment I need to start ____(6) business.

Isabella Are you nervous? Isn't it risky to start your own business?

Emma Of course! There is definitely ____(7) risk in starting your own business. When you know ____(8) risks, you can plan well. ____(9) class also taught me to write ____(10) marketing plan. ____(11) plan can guide my sales[3] of my catering services. I need to design ____(12) menu and make ____(13) website for my business. When ____(14) menu is ready and ____(15) website is up, I'll be ready to go!

Isabella Wow, that all sounds great! Do you need my help? I'm in ____(16) web design course right now. I can design something really great for your new business!

Emma Thanks! I'd like that.

---

[1]**catering business:** a business that provides and serves food and drinks for a particular event, such as a wedding or party
[2]**loan:** money that you can borrow but you have to pay back with interest (extra money)
[3]**sales:** the number of items sold

B Complete the story with *a*, *an*, or *the*.

Martin moved to New York City from Bogotá, Colombia, a year ago. He lives in __a__(1) neighborhood on the Upper West Side. He was worried because ____(2) neighborhood is expensive. He found ____(3) entry-level¹ job at ____(4) bank, but he did not make enough money. This made him uncomfortable because he does not like to take risks. His friends told him he could always get ____(5) second job. He took their advice and got ____(6) interesting job as a server at ____(7) coffee shop. ____(8) job is great! ____(9) coffee shop is near his apartment, so he can walk to work. ____(10) job is much more relaxing than ____(11) bank job. Martin gets to chat with ____(12) customers who come in as he fills their orders. He makes a lot of new friends there, too. Also, ____(13) second job allows him to save money. Now he feels much better and enjoys life in New York City!

¹**entry-level:** starting level

C **Pair Work** Talk to a partner about Emma in A and Martin in B. Is one of them an ostrich? An analyst? A rock climber? Why?

3 Article or No Article?

Grammar Presentation

We sometimes do not use an article before plural count and noncount nouns.	*Rock climbers love taking **risks**.* *I have **homework** to do.*

3.1 No Article

Use no article before plural count and noncount nouns when the nouns have a general meaning.	***Analysts** do not make quick decisions.* *I need **money** to buy that car!* ***Insurance** is very expensive.*

3.2 *The* and No Article with Geographical Places and Languages

A Use *the* before the names of:

• mountain ranges	*the Andes, the Himalayas, the Rocky Mountains*
• regions	*the Midwest, the Arctic, the Great Lakes*
• famous places and buildings	*the Grand Canyon, the Eiffel Tower, the White House*
• rivers	*the Amazon, the Nile, the Mississippi River*
• seas and oceans	*the Mediterranean, the Atlantic, the South China Sea*
• deserts	*the Sahara, the Mojave Desert*

B Use no article before the names of:

• most countries	*Canada, Colombia, Japan*
• continents	*Europe, Asia, Africa*
• individual mountains	*Mount Everest, Mount Kilimanjaro, Mount Fuji*
• individual lakes	*Lake Michigan, Lake Tahoe, Lake Victoria*

C Some countries have *the* in their names.

the United States, the United Kingdom, the United Arab Emirates, the Netherlands, the Philippines

D Use no article before the name of a language.

Can you speak Japanese?
 Chinese is a difficult language for English speakers.

Grammar Application

Exercise 3.1 *The* or No Article?

A Complete the conversation with **the** or Ø for no article.

Mi-Young You know, life as an international student is very stressful. We took a big risk to come to this new country!

Adriana You think so? I like taking risks. I think it's exciting. I don't worry about things. What do you worry about?

Mi-Young Oh, everything! I worry about __the__ (1) future. I worry about _____ (2) money. I worry about _____ (3) life in general.

Adriana Yeah, I guess it is a little stressful. We work and we study long hours. We also have to use _____ (4) English all the time!

Mi-Young True. We're at work or in class all day, and we never see _____ (5) sun. _____ (6) teachers are good, and our classmates are fun, but _____ (7) courses are really difficult. All I think about is _____ (8) home – there was no risk there!

Adriana I think _____ (9) risks are important, though. They sometimes help you succeed. Right now, _____ (10) education is important. That's what I worry about.

Mi-Young Aha! So you worry about something! You're just the same as everyone else!

Adriana I guess so. Well, everybody worries – _____ (11) life is like that!

B Pair Work Practice the conversation with a partner.

Exercise 3.2 More Practice with *The* and No Article

A Complete the professor's welcome speech with *the* or Ø for no article.

Welcome, __Ø__(1) international students! We're so excited to have you here. Get ready for a fun and busy year! We at __the__(2) university understand many of you are far away from __Ø__(3) home. We know that can be scary. You all took __Ø__(4) risks in coming here, and you're all very brave.

In your packets, there's __Ø__(5) information on housing. There are __Ø__(6) maps of __the__(7) entire campus and this part of __the__(8) city. You're all invited to __Ø__(9) weekly socials¹ where you can share __Ø__(10) information about what you learn. It's also a time to meet __Ø__(11) friends, both old and new!

We also assigned __Ø__(12) "language buddies." __The__(13) buddies are other students who help with __Ø__(14) English practice every day. When you need __Ø__(15) help with anything, please contact me! We want you to feel like this is your home away from __Ø__(16) home. Once again, welcome!

¹**socials:** get-togethers, or parties

B Over to You Talk to a partner about a time when you took a risk like the one in A. Did other people help you? What was helpful for you?

A *I enrolled in night classes. The college helped me find a part-time job during the day.*

B *How did the college help you do that?*

A *They gave me some information about local businesses. These companies needed part-time workers.*

Exercise 3.3 *The* and No Article with Languages and Geographic Places

Complete the blog with *the* or ∅ for no article.

Jenna's Travels

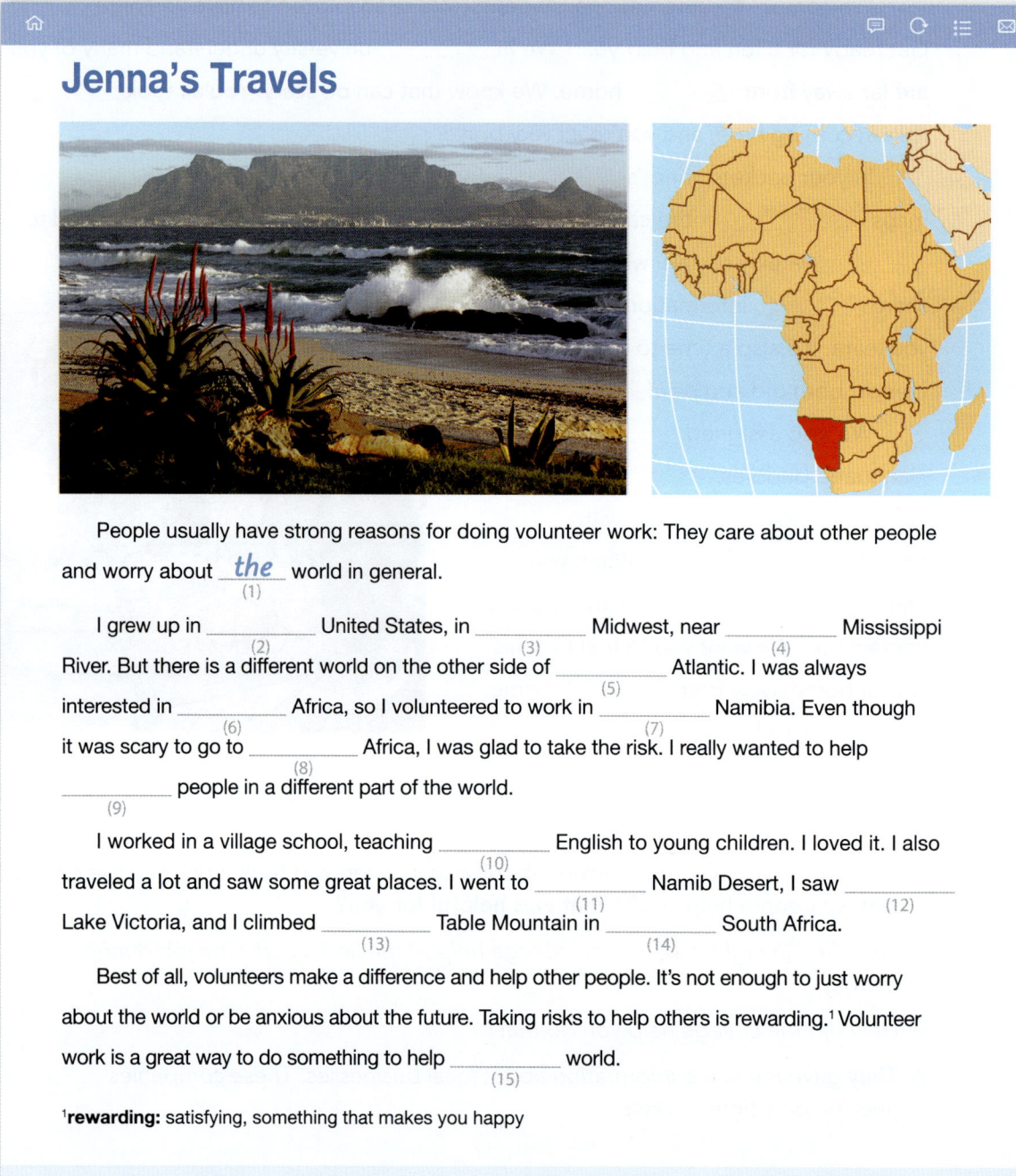

People usually have strong reasons for doing volunteer work: They care about other people and worry about __the__ (1) world in general.

I grew up in _____ (2) United States, in _____ (3) Midwest, near _____ (4) Mississippi River. But there is a different world on the other side of _____ (5) Atlantic. I was always interested in _____ (6) Africa, so I volunteered to work in _____ (7) Namibia. Even though it was scary to go to _____ (8) Africa, I was glad to take the risk. I really wanted to help _____ (9) people in a different part of the world.

I worked in a village school, teaching _____ (10) English to young children. I loved it. I also traveled a lot and saw some great places. I went to _____ (11) Namib Desert, I saw _____ (12) Lake Victoria, and I climbed _____ (13) Table Mountain in _____ (14) South Africa.

Best of all, volunteers make a difference and help other people. It's not enough to just worry about the world or be anxious about the future. Taking risks to help others is rewarding.[1] Volunteer work is a great way to do something to help _____ (15) world.

[1] **rewarding:** satisfying, something that makes you happy

4 Avoid Common Mistakes

1 Do not use *a / an* with a noncount noun.

I'm making ~~a~~ progress with my English.
I have ~~a~~ homework tonight.

2 Do not use *the* to talk about things or people in general.

Life
~~The life~~ is often difficult for ~~the~~ students.
Students get ~~the~~ homework every night.

3 Do not use *the* with the names of languages, most countries, or continents.

~~The~~ Japanese is a beautiful language.
I want to go to ~~the~~ Australia.

4 Use *a* before consonant sounds. Use *an* before vowel sounds.

a
I have to make ~~an~~ decision quickly!

an
There is ~~a~~ online university in Caracas.

Editing Task

Find and correct 10 more mistakes in these sentences about risk taking.

1 I read an interesting article about how ~~the~~ people manage risk.
2 The professor gave us an lecture on economics.
3 A ostrich worries about getting a good job when he or she finishes college.
4 Analysts hope they have an insurance at work, but will find an new job if they need to.
5 Some people feel a fear when they have to move to a new country.
6 I hope to become an volunteer in the South America after the college.
7 I don't speak the Spanish, so that's an risk. But maybe it can be fun!

5 Academic Writing

Descriptive Paragraphs

Brainstorm > Organize > **Write** > Edit

In Unit 17, you brainstormed and outlined ideas for the prompt below. In this unit (18), you will write the first draft of your paragraphs.

Write about popular food in your country.

Using Articles in a Paragraph

Writers often use *a* or *an* to introduce a person or thing in a paragraph. They use *the* to write about the person or thing again in the paragraph.

Exercise 5.1 Understanding the Skill

Read the paragraph. Fill in the blanks with the correct articles.

I live in (1)_____ small apartment in Miami. (2)_____ apartment is near the beach. It has (3)_____ bedroom and (4)_____ bathroom. (5)_____ bedroom is very small, but (6)_____ bathroom is very big. I have (7)_____ old dog too. She does not sleep in (8)_____ bedroom with me. She sleeps in (9)_____ bathroom because she is also big. My apartment is not very big, but it is comfortable, and I like it.

Exercise 5.2 Applying the Skill

For each sentence, write a second sentence with more information about the topic. Use *the* in the second sentence.

1 My neighbor has **an** interesting new job.

   _____

2 There is **a** rock-climbing gym near my apartment.

   _____

3 There is also **a** very good Argentinian restaurant on my street.

   _____

4 This morning I ate **an** omelet there for breakfast.

   _____

Articles: *A / An* and *The*

My Writing

Exercise 5.3 Planning Your Paragraphs

Look back at your outline on page 227.

1 Review the information. Make changes if necessary.

2 Think of information to add for each dish. Use the questions below to help you.

- When do people usually eat the dish?
- What kind of dish is it - a main meal, a side dish, a dessert?
- How long does it take to make the dish?
- Are there different types of the dish?

Exercise 5.4 Writing Your Paragraphs

Write two paragraphs, one about each dish. Follow the steps below to help you write each paragraph.

1 Write a topic sentence. Include the name of the dish and where it is from.

2 Write 1-2 sentences about the ingredients. (What is the dish made of?)

3 Write 1-2 sentences about the taste. (What does it taste like?)

4 Write 1-2 sentences about other food. (What is it served with?)

5 Write 1-2 more sentences about the information you added in Exercise 5.3.

6 Write a concluding sentence.

UNIT 19
Possessive Pronouns and Indefinite Pronouns
Meals Around the World

1 Grammar in the Real World

ACADEMIC WRITING

Descriptive paragraphs

A What is your favorite breakfast food? Read the conversation between three college roommates as they discuss typical breakfasts in their countries. What do people in your country usually eat for breakfast?

B Comprehension Check Complete the chart. Check (✓) the box next to the food people eat for breakfast in each place. Use the conversation in A to help you.

United States	Hong Kong	Mexico
☐ cereal	☐ cereal	☐ cereal
☐ coffee	☐ coffee	☐ coffee
☐ dumplings	☐ dumplings	☐ dumplings
☐ tea	☐ tea	☐ tea
☐ French bread	☐ French bread	☐ French bread

C Notice Circle the correct answer. Use the conversation to help you.

1 We always drink coffee or hot chocolate. My father loves strong coffee, and **his** is very sweet!

What noun does the pronoun   a my father   b my father's coffee
his replace?

2 They put cheese in their eggs, but I don't put it in **mine**.

What noun does the pronoun   a cheese   b eggs
mine replace?

3 Your grandparents ate a large breakfast! I'd like to try **theirs**.

What noun does the pronoun   a breakfast   b grandparents
theirs replace?

Possessive Pronouns and Indefinite Pronouns

WHAT'S FOR BREAKFAST?

Kyla - Is that all you eat for breakfast? It's so little!

Sara - Well, it's typical in Mexico to have coffee and a nice *bolillo*, or crusty French bread. It's all I want most days, but on weekends, I have a big breakfast with my family.

5   Meil-li - We do that in our family, too. In Hong Kong, we used to have *dim sum* every Saturday.

Sara - What's that?

Meil-li - It's a lot of small, light dishes: dumplings – steamed or fried dough filled with meat, seafood, or vegetables –
10   rice noodle rolls, *congee* – a sort of rice soup, thick like oatmeal – and tea, of course. What do you have at your family brunches?[1]

Sara - We have *huevos rancheros* – fried eggs with a spicy sauce and a *tortilla* – beans, a lot of fresh fruit,
15   sometimes fish that my father catches on his boat. We always drink coffee or hot chocolate. My father loves strong coffee, and **his** is very sweet!

Meil-li - Our breakfast is pretty good, Sara, but I want to try **yours**! How about breakfast in the United States, Kyla?

20   Kyla - Well, some people here say breakfast is the most important meal of their day. I have cereal, milk, fruit, yogurt, sometimes eggs – and always coffee. It's a lot of food, but it's not a heavy meal. It's not like the meals people had in the past. For example, my grandparents always had coffee, juice, potatoes, a big plate of
25   eggs with ham and cheese, and pancakes or donuts! They put cheese in their eggs, but I don't put it in **mine**.

Sara - Your grandparents ate a large breakfast! I'd like to try **theirs**. Did **everybody** eat like that?

30   Kyla - Many did, I think. People did hard physical work and needed a big meal in the morning. Today, some people still eat like that, and some don't have time to eat **anything** at all!

[1]**brunch:** a meal you sometimes eat in the late morning that combines breakfast and lunch

Meals Around the World   243

2 Possessive Pronouns

Grammar Presentation

| Possessive pronouns tell us who something belongs to. | That coffee is **mine**.
I think this one is **yours**.
Hers is still in the kitchen. |

2.1 Possessive Pronouns

Personal Pronouns	Possessive Determiners	Possessive Pronouns
I	**my** + noun **My** apples are sweet.	**mine** **Mine** are sweet.
you	**your** + noun **Your** apples are sweet.	**yours** **Yours** are sweet.
he	**his** + noun **His** apples are sweet.	**his** **His** are sweet.
she	**her** + noun **Her** apples are sweet.	**hers** **Hers** are sweet.
it	**its** + noun **Its** apples are sweet.	**Its** cannot be a pronoun. ~~Its are sweet.~~
we	**our** + noun **Our** apples are sweet.	**ours** **Ours** are sweet.
they	**their** + noun **Their** apples are sweet.	**theirs** **Theirs** are sweet.

▶▶ Subject and Object Pronouns: See page A18.

2.2 Using Possessive Pronouns

| **A** Possessive pronouns show who or what a noun belongs to. | This is my sister's cereal. The cereal is **hers**. |
| **B** When you use a possessive pronoun, don't repeat the noun or noun phrase. | Those apples are **mine**.
NOT Those are ~~mine~~ apples. |

Unit 19 Possessive Pronouns and Indefinite Pronouns

Possessive Pronouns and Indefinite Pronouns

2.2 Using Possessive Pronouns (continued)

C Possessive pronouns have one form. They do not change when the noun is plural.

This apple isn't **mine**. **Mine** is on the table.
These apples aren't **mine**. **Mine** are on the table.
NOT These apples aren't ~~mines~~. ~~Mines~~ are on the table.

The verb changes when the replaced noun is plural.

My apples are on the table.   **Mine are** on the table.
Mine is replacing *my apples*, so we need to use a plural verb.

D There is no possessive pronoun for *it*.

That tree's apples are juicy.   **Its** apples are juicy.
NOT ~~Its~~ are juicy.

DATA FROM THE REAL WORLD

Research shows that possessive determiners are much more common in writing.

I eat breakfast every day. **My** *breakfast is always delicious!*

Possessive pronouns are much more common in conversation.

"My breakfast is good. How is **yours***?"*
*"***Mine** *is delicious!"*

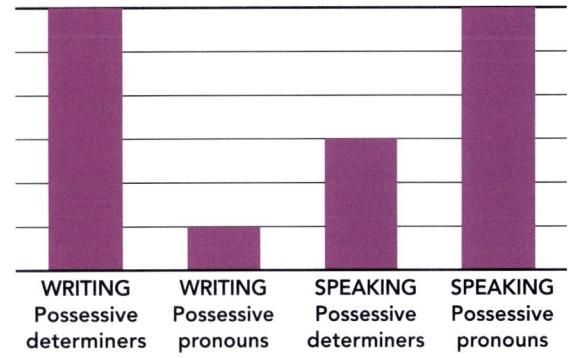

Use possessive pronouns to answer questions with **whose**.

"**Whose** peaches are these?"
"They're **mine**."

"**Whose** apple is this?"
"It's **hers**."

Grammar Application

Exercise 2.1 Possessive Pronouns

Rewrite each sentence. Replace the possessive determiner and noun in bold with a possessive pronoun.

1. That is **my coffee**.   *That is mine.*
2. Did you finish **your breakfast**?
3. **Their breakfast** tasted delicious.
4. John didn't take **my donut**; he took **her donut**!
5. Oh, you can have **our pancakes**.
6. **His hot chocolate** is probably the best.
7. I like fruit with **my breakfast**.

Meals Around the World   245

Exercise 2.2 More Possessive Pronouns

A Complete the sentences with *theirs*, *yours*, *his*, or *hers*.

Meal Times Around the World

People from all around the world eat their main meal at different times. Mexicans eat __theirs__ (1) in the afternoon. They eat between 2:00 and 4:00 p.m.

People in Spain have their main meal in the afternoon, too. Dinner in Spain is late. They usually eat _____ (2) at 10:00 p.m.! Some visitors don't like that custom. While in Spain, you can eat _____ (3) early because restaurants are open for travelers like you!

In Thailand, dinner is the main meal. Thais usually eat _____ (4) early in the evening.

In the United States, dinner is also the main meal. You might notice that families don't eat together all the time. For example, sometimes the father works late and misses dinner. In cases like this, he has _____ (5) when he gets home. Sometimes the daughter has soccer practice in the evening. These evenings, her parents make her an early dinner. She often eats _____ (6) at 5:00 p.m., before the rest of the family.

B Over to You Tell a partner about the eating habits in your country. What time do people eat their main meal? What do they eat?

Possessive Pronouns and Indefinite Pronouns

Exercise 2.3 Possessive Pronouns, Possessive Determiners, and Verbs

A Complete the sentences with the correct words. Then listen and check your answers.

Sara Kyla, let's cook dinner!

Kyla Wow, your kitchen is complicated. Look at all the shelves!

Sara Well, that's Franny's shelf. She eats a lot of junk food. Those bags of chips **is /(are)** (1) **her / hers** (2). As you can see, **her / hers** (3) shelf is full of chips and candy.

Kyla It looks like Su's shelf is full of healthy things.

Sara Yes. Those vitamins **is / are** (4) **her / hers** (5). **Her / Hers** (6) shelf is always very neat, too. Su and Mari share one shelf. That top shelf is **their / theirs** (7). It always has baskets of fruit on it.

Kyla Which shelf is **your / yours** (8)?

Sara This one **is / are** (9) **my / mine** (10).

Kyla Oh, so are those your bowls?

Sara Yes, those are **yours / mine** (11). They're from Japan.

Kyla They're very pretty. **Who's / Whose** (12) things are on this shelf?

Sara Oh, those are **ours / our** (13). We all share that shelf. OK. Well, let's start cooking.

Kyla Right. So, **who's / whose** (14) coming for dinner tonight?

Sara Our families. We have a lot of cooking to do.

B Pair Work Practice the conversation in A with a partner.

Exercise 2.4 Vocabulary Focus: *Theirs* and *There's*

Theirs and *there's* (*there is*) sound the same but mean different things. Be careful with the spelling of these two words.

I ate my lunch in the office, but they ate **theirs** in the park.
NOT I ate my lunch in the office, but they ate ~~there's~~ in the park.

Near the café **there's** a park.
NOT Near the café ~~theirs~~ a park.

Read the blog. Choose the correct words.

>> MY BLOG
Olof's Year Abroad
Friday, September 17

Hi! I'm Olof. I'm Swedish, and I study English in the United States. My new college friends had a party to welcome me. It was a party like we have in Sweden. In Sweden this party is a smorgasbord. Americans call ~~there's~~ / **theirs** (1) a potluck. Both parties have a variety of food, but ___there's / theirs___ (2) a small difference. With ___there's / theirs___ (3), all the guests bring a different dish to share. Sometimes a potluck host asks people to say what specific dish they want to bring. This way, people don't bring the same things. In Sweden, however, the host usually provides most of the food. The food at a smorgasbord is all Swedish, but the food at a potluck often is all different. In fact, ___there's / theirs___ (4) often food from different countries, like at my friends' potluck. ___There's / Theirs___ (5) included Mexican tamales, Thai spring rolls, and even Swedish meatballs! I had a lot of fun at the party. I especially liked the Swedish meatballs that my friends made. ___There's / Theirs___ (6) were just like the meatballs in Sweden!

Possessive Pronouns and Indefinite Pronouns

3 Indefinite Pronouns

Grammar Presentation

Indefinite pronouns refer to people or things that are not specific, not known, or not the focus of the sentence.

Everyone loved the food at the party.
Somebody made dinner.
Does *anyone* want breakfast?

3.1 Indefinite Pronouns

	-one	-body	-thing
some +	someone	somebody	something
any +	anyone	anybody	anything
every +	everyone	everybody	everything
no +	no one	nobody	nothing

3.2 Using Indefinite Pronouns

A Use an indefinite pronoun with *-one* or *-body* to refer to a person or a group of people.

Everyone knows fruit is good for you.
Somebody brought this delicious salad.

B Use an indefinite pronoun with *-thing* to refer to things (not people).

I know *something* about healthy food choices.
Everything I eat is from my garden.

C Use a third-person singular verb when the subject is an indefinite pronoun.

SUBJECT VERB
Something smells good!

SUBJECT VERB
Everyone eats food.

D Use indefinite pronouns with *some +*, *every +*, and *no +* in affirmative statements.

Someone ate all the apples.
Everyone eats vegetables.
No one eats junk food in my family.

E Use indefinite pronouns with *any +* in negative statements.

She *doesn't* eat lunch with *anybody*.
I *don't* see *anything* healthy about junk food.
He *doesn't* think *anyone* should eat fast food.

Don't use indefinite pronouns with *no +* in negative sentences.

NOT She ~~doesn't eat lunch with nobody~~.
NOT ~~I don't~~ want ~~nothing for dessert~~.

Meals Around the World 249

3.2 Using Indefinite Pronouns (continued)

F In *Yes/No* questions, use indefinite pronouns with *some +*, *any +*, or *every +*.

Is **someone** home?
Does **anyone** eat apples?
Is **everyone** here?

You can use indefinite pronouns with *no +* in *Yes/No* questions, but it's very formal.

Is **nobody** home?

3.3 Types of Statements That Use Indefinite Pronouns

	Affirmative Statements	Negative Statements	Yes/No Questions
anyone, anybody, anything	no	yes	yes
someone, somebody, something	yes	no	yes
everyone, everybody, everything	yes	no	yes
no one, nobody, nothing	yes	no	no

Grammar Application

Exercise 3.1 Indefinite Pronouns with *-one*, *-body*, or *-thing*

A Complete the words with *-one*, *-body*, or *-thing*. Sometimes there is more than one correct answer.

1. We sent every *one* in our class an invitation to our international dinner party last night.
2. Gladi wanted to bring dessert. She brought **some**_____ from Laos.
3. I didn't know **any**_____ about Laotian food before the party.
4. **Some**_____ brought some delicious Mexican *enchiladas*.
5. **No**_____ brought any Chinese food.
6. Maybe that's because our class doesn't have **any**_____ from China in it.
7. **Every**_____ was delicious, so people ate a lot.
8. By 10:00, there was **no**_____ left to eat, so we played games and danced instead!

B Pair Work Compare your answers with a partner. Which sentences can have more than one answer?

Possessive Pronouns and Indefinite Pronouns

Exercise 3.2 Yes/No Questions with Indefinite Pronouns

A Complete the questions with an indefinite pronoun. Sometimes there is more than one correct answer.

1 Do you know _anyone/anybody_ who eats rice for breakfast?
2 Does _____ eat dinner after 9:00 p.m.?
3 Do you know _____ in your neighborhood?
4 Do you know _____ about cooking?
5 Does _____ cook for you?
6 Can you tell me _____ about food in your country?

B Pair Work Ask and answer the questions in A with a partner.

A *Do you know anyone who eats rice for breakfast?*
B *Yes! I usually eat rice in the mornings.*

Exercise 3.3 Indefinite Pronouns

A Complete the sentences. Choose the correct indefinite pronoun.

Yuki Hello?

Lisa Yuki? Hi, it's Lisa. Did you get my message about coming over to my house for dinner?

Yuki Hi, Lisa. No, I didn't get your message. **Anybody /(Nobody)** told me you called! Sure, I can come for dinner. What time?
(1)

Lisa Come at 7:00. What do you want to eat?

Yuki I don't know **anybody / anything** about cooking, and I like **everyone / everything**, so you decide.
(2) (3)

Lisa Well, OK. I don't really cook either. How about sushi from Matsuri Restaurant? I know the owner. I can have **something / someone** there make us a special dinner.
(4)

Yuki That sounds great. So you don't mind calling? I don't know **no one / anyone** at that restaurant.
(5)

Lisa Sure. Do you want me to call Roberto? **Something / Someone** told me he loves sushi.
(6)

Yuki Oh, yes, I know. I can call him. Do you want to invite **anybody / anything** else?
(7)

Lisa I'm not sure if **no one / anyone** else is around tonight, but that's OK. See you tonight!
(8)

B Pair Work Practice the conversation in A with a partner.

Meals Around the World

Exercise 3.4 Indefinite Pronouns with -one and -body

🌐 DATA FROM THE REAL WORLD

In conversation, people usually use **'s not** and **'re not** after pronouns.

He**'s not** 21.
She**'s not** in class.
They**'re not** here.

They usually use **isn't** and **aren't** after names and nouns.

Carlos **isn't** 21.
Louise **isn't** in class.
The boys **aren't** here.

SPEAKING
someone
anyone
everyone
no one

WRITING
someone
anyone
everyone
no one

SPEAKING
somebody
anybody
everybody
nobody

WRITING
somebody
anybody
everybody
nobody

Check (✓) the box if the indefinite pronoun is more common in speaking or writing.

	Speaking	Writing
someone	☐	✓
everybody	☐	☐
anybody	☐	☐
anyone	☐	☐
no one	☐	☐
everyone	☐	☐
somebody	☐	☐
nobody	☐	☐

4 Avoid Common Mistakes

1 **Don't repeat the noun after the possessive pronoun.**

That's not your apple. It's mine ~~apple~~.

2 **Don't confuse theirs with *there's*.**

The apple is not mine. It's ~~there's~~ *theirs*.

3 **Possessive pronouns have one form. They do not change when the noun is plural.**

The apples are ~~mines~~ *mine*.

4 **In negative statements, use indefinite pronouns with *any*.**

I don't want to eat ~~nothing~~ *anything*.

Editing Task

Find and correct six more errors in this blog about a favorite place to eat.

Jessie's Snack Blog
Tuesday, March 8

BEST SANDWICHES IN TOWN

Everyone has a favorite sandwich shop in town, and the Snack Stop is definitely mine ~~favorite~~. I eat sandwiches a lot, and there's are the best. What do you think? Please leave a comment and let me know!

5 **COMMENTS:**

 I ate there once with my brother and sister, but I didn't like it. Everyone says the sandwiches are delicious, but ours sandwiches weren't good at all. Plus, my sister ordered dessert, but the server didn't bring her nothing. We had to remind him of our order. Then he charged my
10 brother for French fries, but the fries were mines.

  Wow. I remember the first time I ate at the Snack Stop. It was with my cousin. My sandwich was delicious, and so was hers sandwich. In fact, there wasn't nothing wrong with the whole meal.

5 Academic Writing

Descriptive Paragraphs

Brainstorm > Organize > Write > **Edit**

In Unit 18, you wrote paragraphs for the prompt below. In this unit (19), you will review, revise, and edit your paragraphs.

> Write about popular food in your country.

My Writing

Using Collocations

Collocations are words that writers often use together in a group, or chunk. There are many collocations to describe how food is prepared and served, such as the verb *be* + past participle + preposition:

The meat **is cooked on** a hot pan. It **is cooked with** onions and garlic.

Cambodian dishes **are served with** lots of vegetables. They **are** often **prepared with** coconut milk.

Remember to use *is* after singular count nouns and non-count nouns and to use *are* after plural count nouns.

Exercise 5.1 Applying the Skill

Write sentences with collocations about how your dishes are prepared or served. Use the chart below to help you.

The dish / The meat / The rice It	is	cooked with/on … boiled with/in …
The dishes / The vegetables / The eggs They	are	fried with/in … prepared with/in … served with/on …

1 _____
2 _____
3 _____
4 _____
5 _____

Exercise 5.2 Adding Collocations to Your Writing

Look at your paragraphs on page 241. Add collocations from Exercise 5.1 to at least two of your sentences.

Exercise 5.3 Revising Your Ideas

1. Work with a partner. Use the questions below to give feedback on the ideas in your partner's paragraphs.
   - Which details in your partner's paragraphs are the strongest?
   - Which details in your partner's paragraphs are unnecessary?
   - What types of details could your partner add to make the paragraphs stronger?
2. Make any necessary changes to your paragraphs.

Exercise 5.4 Editing Your Writing

Use the checklist to review and edit your paragraphs.

Did you write a paragraph about each dish?	
Did you include a topic sentence with the name of the dish and where it is from?	
Did you write about the ingredients?	
Did you write about the taste?	
Did you write about the food it is served with?	
Did you write a concluding sentence?	
Did you use count and noncount nouns correctly?	
Did you use quantifiers correctly?	
Did you use articles correctly?	
Did you use collocations to talk about how the dishes are prepared and what they are served with?	

Exercise 5.5 Writing Your Final Draft

Apply the feedback and edits from Exercises 5.3 and 5.4 to write the final draft of your paragraphs.

UNIT 20: Imperatives

Social Customs

1 Grammar in the Real World

ACADEMIC WRITING

Expository paragraph

A What do people do on the first day of a new job? Read part of a web article. What are two good things to do at a new job?

B Comprehension Check Complete the chart. Use the article to help you. Check (✓) *Yes* or *No*.

When you're at a new job, . . .	Yes	No
1 smile and introduce yourself to people.	☐	☐
2 interrupt people who are busy.	☐	☐
3 ask about your co-workers' families on your first day.	☐	☐
4 look down when you talk with people.	☐	☐
5 smile and be helpful.	☐	☐

C Notice Find these sentences in the article. Complete the sentences.

1 _____ "Good morning" or "Hi" and the person's name.

2 _____ at people when you talk to them.

3 _____ people who are very busy.

4 _____ and be helpful.

What do the verbs in 1–4 do? Circle the correct answers.

a describe people's habits   c describe the past

b give advice   d tell you what to do

Imperatives

Dos and Don'ts at a New Job

[1]**unspoken:** not said, even though somebody thinks or understands it

[2]**stare:** look directly at someone for a long time

[3]**interrupt:** stop something from happening for a short period, or start talking when someone else is already talking

[4]**uniform:** special clothing that shows you are part of an organization or job

It's easy to make mistakes when you go to work at a new job. There are unspoken[1] rules that people don't tell you. Here are some tips to help you avoid some common mistakes.

- **Be** friendly. When you arrive at your new job, **smile** and **introduce** yourself to people. **Say** "Good morning" or "Hi" and the person's name (if you know it).

- **Look** at people when you talk to them. It isn't polite to look down, but you shouldn't stare,[2] either.

- **Don't interrupt**[3] people who are very busy.

- When people at work know each other well, they sometimes talk about their families or their lives at home. **Don't do** this in the beginning. **Wait** until you know people a little. **Don't assume** that people want to talk about private things immediately, or at all.

In some workplaces, there are uniforms[4] or rules about clothes. If there are no rules, **notice** what other people wear. If they wear jeans or other casual clothes, then you can wear jeans, too.

Above all, **smile** and **be** helpful. **Show** that you want to learn and work hard.

Social Customs 257

2 Imperatives

Grammar Presentation

Imperatives tell people to do things. They can give instructions, directions, or advice.	*Be* friendly. *Don't interrupt* people who are very busy.

2.1 Statements

AFFIRMATIVE

Base Form of Verb	
Smile	and be helpful.
Look	at people when you talk to them.

NEGATIVE

Do + Not	Base Form of Verb	
Don't/ Do not	interrupt	people who are very busy.
	do	this in the beginning.

2.2 Using Imperatives in Writing

Imperatives are common in texts that tell people what to do and what not to do. They appear:	
• on public signs and advertisements	*Do not enter*. *Stand* behind the yellow line. *Buy* now and *save* $4.99.
• on forms and websites	Please *write* in CAPITAL LETTERS. *Log in*. *Enter* your password. *Search*. *Restart* your computer after you install a new program.
• in texts with instructions (like manuals, recipes, and labels)	*Add* hot water and *stir*. *Lift* here to open.
• in texts with advice (e.g., magazine articles, leaflets)	*Wait* until you know people a little. *Show* that you want to learn and work hard.

2.3 Using Imperatives in Speaking

A Imperatives are common in classrooms and demonstrations.	*Listen* to the conversation. *Don't open* your books. *Turn on* the computer and *enter* the password.
B You can use imperatives to give directions.	*Make* a left at the next traffic light. *Don't turn* right.

Imperatives

2.3 Using Imperatives in Speaking (continued)

C You can use imperatives in common social expressions or offers.

Have a good day!
Take care.
Have a cookie.

D You can use imperatives to warn people about dangers.

Watch out!
Be careful! There's a step there.

E When you know people well, you can use imperatives in everyday situations to ask for things or to give instructions or advice.

Call me later.
Don't forget your keys.
Don't worry.

When you don't know people well, don't use imperatives to tell them to do something. Even if you say *please*, you can sound rude.

F *Do not* is very strong and is not common in conversation. It is common to write it in formal situations, but do not use it in informal conversation.

Grammar Application

Exercise 2.1 Imperatives: Advice

A Give some advice about work. Use the negative or affirmative forms of the verbs in parentheses.

1 *Don't ask* (ask) about co-workers' lives at home when you are new.

2 _____ (take) a lunch break every day.

3 _____ (enjoy) long coffee breaks in the morning and afternoon.

4 _____ (eat) lunch with your co-workers.

5 _____ (socialize) with your co-workers after work if they invite you.

6 _____ (talk) about vacations or your weekend plans at work.

7 _____ (talk) about money or politics.

8 _____ (learn) from your mistakes.

B Pair Work Compare your answers with a partner. Are your imperatives the same? Discuss which advice is different.

Social Customs

C Over to You Write six sentences about work in a culture you know well. Use the imperative.

Don't ask about your co-workers' families.
Don't take too many breaks.
Have lunch with your boss when she invites you.

Exercise 2.2 Imperatives: Social Customs

A Jane is taking a work trip to Japan and India. Use the verbs in the box to give her some advice. You need to make the verb negative two times.

eat	give	take	wear
forget	keep	~~take off~~	wrap

1 _Take off_ your shoes.
2 _____ a small gift.
3 _____ your gift nicely.
4 _____ food with your left hand.
5 Also, _____ things to people with your left hand.
6 _____ your feet on the ground when you sit.
7 _____ nice clothes.
8 _____ to write a thank-you note later.

Do you take off your shoes?

Or wipe your feet?

B Over to You What are some social dinner customs you know? Write four imperatives about social dinner customs in a country you know well.

In the United States, bring flowers to the host(ess). Don't take your shoes off.

1 _____
2 _____
3 _____
4 _____

Imperatives

Exercise 2.3 Imperatives: Signs

A Look at the signs and complete the imperatives in the chart. Use the verbs from the box. Sometimes you need to make the verb negative. Then compare your answers with a partner.

| bring | drink | feed | ride | ~~throw~~ | turn | use | wear |

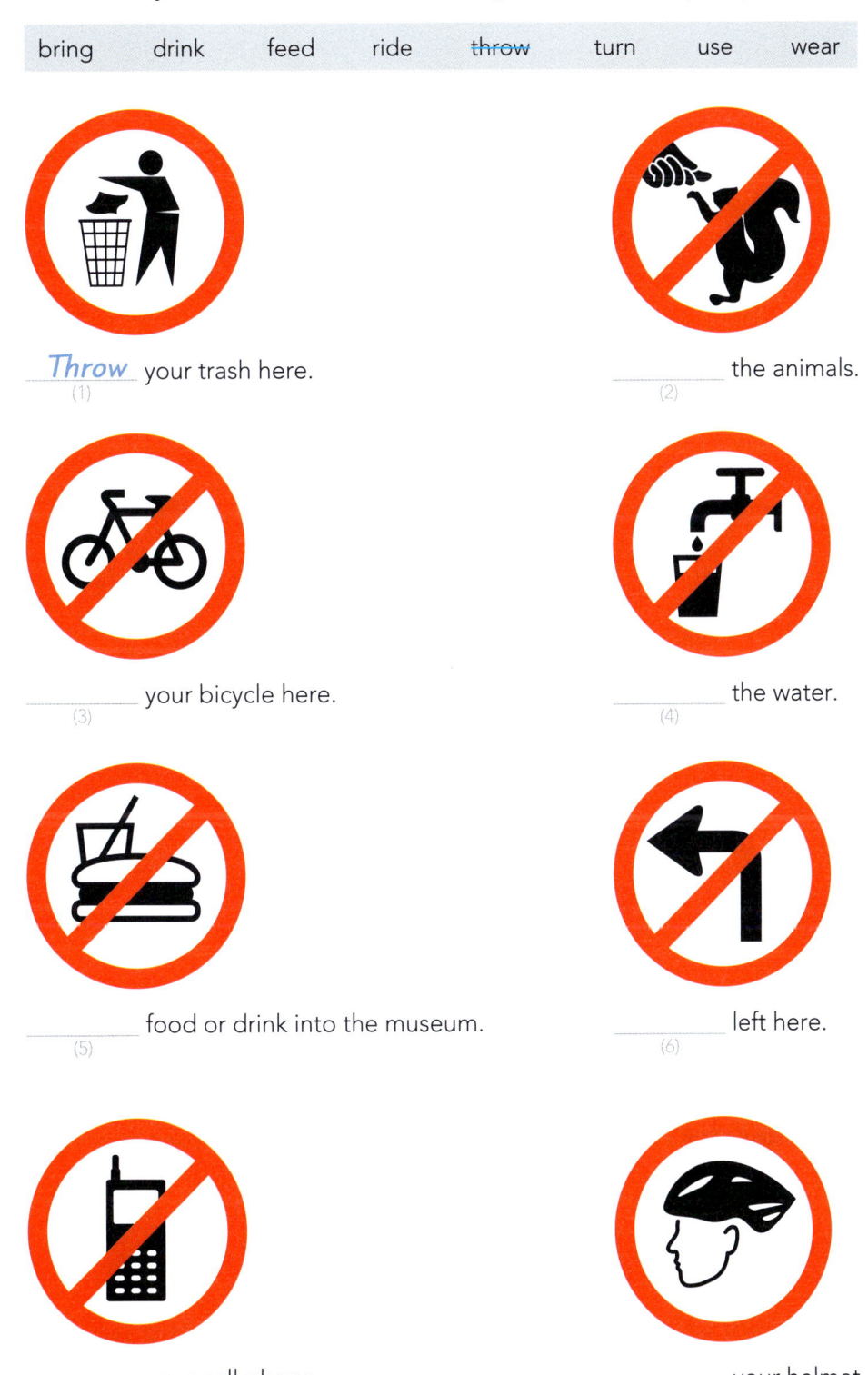

(1) _Throw_ your trash here.

(2) _____ the animals.

(3) _____ your bicycle here.

(4) _____ the water.

(5) _____ food or drink into the museum.

(6) _____ left here.

(7) _____ your cell phone.

(8) _____ your helmet.

Social Customs 261

B Pair Work With a partner, write a list of six signs you see every day. How many use imperatives?

Do not use elevators in case of fire.

1 _____
2 _____
3 _____
4 _____
5 _____
6 _____

C Over to You Write six signs for doors in your home and one for your classroom door. Make them funny. Then read your signs to a partner.

refrigerator door	
bedroom door	
front door	
living room door	
closet door	
kitchen door	
classroom door	

My sign for the refrigerator says, "Do not drink my soda!" What does your sign say?

Unit 20 Imperatives

Imperatives

Exercise 2.4 Imperatives: Directions

A Look at the map. Write down directions from Rogers College to Bob's Cafe. Use some of the imperative directions in the box below.

Common Directions

Take a right on . . .	Go straight on . . .	Go around the corner.	Cross the street.	Walk up the street two blocks.
Go past City Marketplace.	Cross Second Avenue.	Cross Coast Road.	Be careful!	Watch for cars!

Go straight on 4th Avenue.

_____

_____

_____

B Pair Work Write directions to a place in the neighborhood you are in. Read them to a partner. Switch roles. Guess your partner's place.

Social Customs

Exercise 2.5 Imperatives with *Always* and *Never*

> 🌐 **DATA FROM THE REAL WORLD**
>
> Research shows that people often use *always* and *never* in writing to make imperatives stronger.
>
> This is not common in conversation.
>
> **Always shake** hands when you meet someone new.
> **Never wear** shoes in someone's house.
> NOT *Never do not wear* shoes in someone's house.

A Complete the sentences from a brochure about visiting Brazil with *always* or *never*. Then listen to the student podcast.

WHEN YOU VISIT BRAZIL

1 _____Always_____ make eye contact when you speak with someone.
2 _____ arrive at a party early.
3 _____ bring your hostess a small gift.
4 _____ eat in class.
5 _____ ask your server for the check in a restaurant.
6 _____ tip your server.

B Over to You For each topic, write three pieces of advice for visitors to the country you are in now. Use *always* and *never* for strong advice. Read your sentences to a partner.

Advice for eating in restaurants:

1 _____
2 _____
3 _____

Advice for talking to people:

1 _____
2 _____
3 _____

Imperatives

Advice for going to a new college:

1. _____
2. _____
3. _____

3 Avoid Common Mistakes

1 **Use *don't* to form negative imperatives.**

   Don't
   ~~No~~ forget to do your homework.

2 **Remember to write *do not* as two words.**

   Do not   *Do not*
   ~~Donot~~ be late for class.   ~~Do n't~~ be late for class.

3 **Use an apostrophe to write *don't*. Put the apostrophe between the *n* and *t*.**

   Don't   *Don't*
   ~~Dont~~ send text messages during class.   ~~Do'nt~~ eat in the computer lab.

   Don't
   ~~D'ont~~ forget to save your work.

Editing Task

Find and correct nine more mistakes in these sentences about advice for college students in different countries.

   Don't
1. ~~Dont~~ be late for class.
2. No stand up when the teacher walks into the classroom.
3. Donot use the teacher's first name.
4. No forget to write the date your assignment is due.
5. Dont forget your homework assignment.
6. Do'nt copy another student's homework.
7. Donot buy or download essays on the Internet.
8. D'ont listen to your MP3 player in class.
9. No answer your phone in class.
10. Do n't send or read text messages in class.

Social Customs 265

4 Academic Writing

Expository Paragraph

Brainstorm > Organize > Write > Edit

In this writing cycle (Units 20-22), you are going to answer the prompt below. In this unit (20), you will look at an example of expository writing and then brainstorm ideas for your paragraph.

> *Write a paragraph about someone who is a role model to you. Explain why that person is a good role model.*

Exercise 4.1 Preparing to Write

Work with a partner. Ask and answer the questions.

1. If you admire someone, you respect that person a lot. You might even want to be like that person, that is, to have him or her as your role model. Think about people you admire. What makes their lives or achievements especially good?
2. Of all the people you have thought of, who do you admire the most? Why?
3. What can you do to be more like your role model?
4. If you succeed in being like your role model, how will the future be better for you and for other people?

Exercise 4.2 Focusing on Vocabulary

Read the sentences. Match the words in bold to the definitions.

1. Aisha runs at least ten miles (16 kilometers) every morning to **train** for the upcoming race.
2. It is important for a president to be **honest**. People must be able to trust the person leading their country.
3. Eugene was **brave** when he ran into a burning house to save an elderly woman. He could have died, but he did it anyway.
4. After five tries, 64-year-old Diana Nyad was finally able to **achieve** her goal of swimming from Cuba to Florida. It took her almost 53 hours to finish the 100-mile (160-kilometer) swim.
5. William graduated from college and then decided to follow his **dream** of opening a restaurant.

a _____ (n) something that you really want to do, be, or have in the future

b _____ (adj) not afraid of dangerous or difficult situations

c _____ (v) to prepare for a job, activity, or sport by learning skills or by exercise

d _____ (adj) truthful or able to be trusted; not likely to lie, cheat, or steal

e _____ (v) to succeed in doing something difficult

Role Models Reach Great Heights

It is easy to talk about how to be a good role model: Believe in yourself. Work hard. Help and respect others. Be **honest**. Do not just talk about what you want to do; do it. It is a lot harder to be a role model, but six **brave** women from Singapore became role models for their whole country.

In 2009, the Singapore Women's Everest Team (SWET) became the first group of women from Singapore to reach the top of the world's tallest mountain, Mount Everest. It took five years and a lot of hard work to prepare for the climb. Thirty women **trained** for the team, but at the end of the five years, only six were left. The six women had some important guidelines: Always train hard. Always believe in each other. Always work as a team. When some members were too tired to continue, other members helped them keep going.

Jane Lee was 25 years old and a co-leader of the team. She loves to set a difficult goal and then work hard to reach it. She has climbed all of the "Seven Summits"—the tallest mountains on each of the seven continents. She brings that same spirit of hard work to her studies. She completed her MBA from Yale University in 2013 and now works at a business-consulting company.

Sim Yi Hui was the other co-leader of SWET. She has also climbed many tall mountains, including one of the Seven Summits—Denali in Alaska. Like Lee, she enjoys difficult physical tasks. In 2011, she walked across the Gobi Desert in Mongolia. It took her 51 days. When she was on Everest, she showed a special kind of courage. She had a bad injury to her chest, but she was almost there. Should she continue? She made the difficult decision not to go to the top with her five teammates. It was the smart thing to do, but after she had planned so long and worked so hard, the decision was not easy. Her self-control and clear thinking are an inspiration to many people. Hui now works as an administrator at a university.

The women returned home as heroes and role models because of their strength and determination to **achieve** their **dream**. They are a part of the Singapore Women's Hall of Fame. They have inspired many others to follow their own dreams.

Exercise 4.3 Comprehension Check

Read the text on page 267. Circle the letter of the best answer to each question.

1 What is SWET?
   a a group of mountains
   b a team of mountain climbers
   c a prize for climbing mountains
   d a business-consulting company
2 What is true about both Jane Lee and Sim Yi Hui?
   a They both were injured and did not reach the top.
   b They both climbed all of the Seven Summits.
   c They both graduated from Yale.
   d They were both leaders of the Singapore team.
3 What can be most strongly inferred from the second paragraph?
   a The training was too difficult for many of the women who started on the team.
   b Many of the women who started on the team had never climbed a mountain before.
   c Lee and Sim told most of the women who started on the team to drop out.
   d Most of the women who started on the team didn't strongly believe in themselves.

Exercise 4.4 Noticing the Grammar

Work with a partner. Complete the tasks.

1 Underline the imperative verbs in paragraphs 1 and 2. How does the writer use this form?
2 Do you think imperatives are common in academic writing? Why or why not?

> **Balancing Facts and Qualities**
>
> A paragraph about a role model should explain why you admire that person. Your paragraph should include some basic facts about the person, such as name, nationality, age, and job, but these are not the main points. They only give background information. The main points for your paragraph should be the actions, qualities, and ideas that make your role model special.

Exercise 4.5 Applying the Skill

Look at paragraph 3 on page 267. Underline two basic facts about Jane Lee. Then draw circles around three sentences or phrases that talk about things to admire about her.

My Writing

Exercise 4.6 Brainstorming

Choose a role model to write about in your paragraph. Think of at least two basic facts and three things to admire about the person. Write them in the outline below.

My Role Model: _____

1 Basic facts

　A _____

　B _____

2 Things I admire

　A _____

　B _____

　C _____

Exercise 4.7 Using the Grammar

Work with a partner. Complete the tasks.

1 Make a list of six rules or guidelines that your role model would agree with. Write them below, using imperatives. Use verbs from the box to help you, or use your own verbs. The first one is done for you.

be　believe　do　help　respect　train　work

- *Do what you promise to do.*
- _____
- _____
- _____
- _____
- _____

2 Which three rules are the most important? Explain your choices to your partner.

UNIT 21 Ability and Possibility

Making Connections

1 Grammar in the Real World

ACADEMIC WRITING

Expository paragraph

A How do you stay in touch with friends and family? Read the article. Does technology help you stay in touch?

B Comprehension Check Answer the questions. Use the article to help you.

1. How does the Internet help people connect with each other?
2. Why is it easy to make a cat video?
3. Do you agree with the idea that people were lonely in the past? Why or why not?

C Notice Find these sentences in the article. Complete the sentences with *can*, *could*, or *could not*.

1. Fifty years ago, people _____ go online and watch funny cat videos.
2. Anyone with a smartphone _____ make a video.
3. In the past, people _____ share their lives in this way.
4. For example, a person from Morocco _____ team up with someone from Japan.

Ability and Possibility

TECHNOLOGY FOR MAKING CONNECTIONS

Fifty years ago, people **could not** go online and watch funny cat videos. However, today they **can**, and they do! There are more than 12,000 cat videos on YouTube, and a lot of people watch them. This happens because people **are able to** connect with strangers. Anyone with a smartphone **can** make a video. Anyone who sees it **can** share it.

In the past, people **could not** share their lives in this way. People **could** share ideas and information with friends, neighbors, and coworkers, but they **were not able to** connect with the rest of the world. Also, they **could not** make and post videos so easily.

Another way people connect with strangers is through computer games. In online games, players **can** be from different countries, but they **can** meet in the game. For example, a person from Mexico **can** team up with someone from Japan. They do not share personal information, but they **are able to** communicate like friends.

Cat videos and computer games are just two ways technology is changing friendship and community. Some people miss the face-to-face contact that they **were able to** have in the past. Others like the changes because they are never lonely.

2 Can and Could for Ability and Possibility

Grammar Presentation

Can and could express ability or possibility.

Anyone who sees it **can** share it.
People **could share** ideas and information with friends, neighbors, and coworkers.

2.1 Statements

AFFIRMATIVE

Subject	Can / Could	Base Form of Verb	
I You We They He / She / It	can could	use	e-mail.

NEGATIVE

Subject	Can / Could + Not	Base Form of Verb	
I You We They He / She / It	cannot can't could not couldn't	use	e-mail.

2.2 Yes/No Questions and Answers

Can / Could	Subject	Base Form of Verb	
Can Could	I you we they he / she / it	use	the computer?

Ability and Possibility

2.2 Yes/No Questions and Answers (continued)

AFFIRMATIVE ANSWERS

Yes	Subject	Can / Could
Yes,	I / you / we / they / he / she / it	can. / could.

NEGATIVE ANSWERS

No	Subject	Can / Could + Not
No,	I / you / we / theys / he / she / it	cannot. / can't. / could not. / couldn't.

2.3 Information Questions

Wh- Word	Can / Could	Subject	Base Form of Verb	
Who	can / could	I / you / we / they / he / she / it	ask	about the program?
What			do	on that website?
When			share	a video?
Where			use	our cell phones?
How			communicate	with each other?

2.4 Using Can and Could

A	Use *can* to talk about ability or possibility in the present.	I **can** use the Internet at the school library. Friends **can** post comments to each other.
B	Use *could* to talk about ability or possibility in the past.	I **could** use the Internet at my old school. My grandparents **could** only get the news through radio and television when they were young.
C	You can spell *cannot* as one word or as two words (*can not*), but it is usually spelled as one word (*cannot*). Spell *could not* as two words.	I **cannot** remember my password. I **can not** remember my password. We **could not** share with the public. NOT We ~~couldnot~~ share with the public. NOT I ~~couldnot~~ read the e-mail.
D	Use the contractions *can't* or *couldn't* in speaking, e-mails, and conversations but not in formal writing.	They **can't** remember the password. I **couldn't** read your e-mail. In the past, people **could not** share experiences in this way.

▸▸ Modal Verbs and Modal-like Expressions: See page A25.

Making Connections

Grammar Application

Exercise 2.1 *Can* and *Could* for Ability and Possibility

A Complete the sentences in the blog. Circle the correct words.

>> Serena's Blog

My New Life in the United States

When I was a student in Chile, I **can / (could)** (1) do everything easily. However, now I am a student at a community college in San Diego. When I first came here, I **cannot / could not** (2) do many things without help. In this post, I want to share my experience so other new students **can / could** (3) learn from it.

A few months ago, I **can't / couldn't** (4) find places. I got lost many times. Then I started using my GPS. Now I **can / could** (5) find everything on campus. Last week, I went to the computer center because I **cannot / could not** (6) login into my computer class. They told me to change my password. Now I always go there when I have a problem. I also like the student services building. Students **can / could** (7) play games and relax. They **can / could** (8) meet new people. Right now, I **cannot / could not** (9) speak English very well, so I want to join the International Club. Then I **can / could** (10) practice.

Food was another problem for me. I wanted food from my country, but I **cannot / could not** (11) find it in the cafeteria. Then my American roommate took me to a Chilean restaurant. It's not far, so I **can / could** (12) eat there a couple of times a week. I **can / could** (13) usually meet other Chilean people, so I feel happy.

Now, I **can / could** (14) say that I like my new life on campus!

Ability and Possibility

B Unscramble the words to make *Yes/No* questions and information questions with *can* and *could*.

1. Can / fit / your / phone / in your pocket / ?

    Can you fit your phone in your pocket?

2. Can / with your eyes closed / you / text / ?

3. check / your e-mail / can / When / you / ?

4. can / buy / I / a good computer / Where / ?

5. How / learn / I / to design websites / can / ?

6. five years ago / you / send / an e-mail / Could / ?

7. your parents / their passwords / remember / Can / ?

8. online / 50 years ago / Could / shop / people / ?

9. text messages / Who / 10 years ago / could / send / ?

10. make / you / Could / with your phone / a video / in 2005 / ?

11. you / Can / text / quickly / ?

12. How / communicate / could / people / 20 years ago / ?

C Pair Work Ask and answer the questions in B with a partner.

Making Connections   **275**

Exercise 2.2 Pronunciation Focus: Saying *Can* and *Can't*

Sometimes it's hard to hear the difference between *can* and *can't*.	
People usually do not pronounce the *a* in *can* very clearly.	*I can use a laptop* usually sounds like *I c'n use a laptop.* *Can I use your phone?* usually sounds like *C'n I use your phone?*
People always say the *a* in *can't* very clearly.	*I can't use a tablet.*[1] *He can't find his phone.*
In short answers, people always say the *a* in *can* and *can't* clearly.	*Yes, I can.* *No, I can't.*

[1]**tablet:** electronic reading device

A Listen and repeat the sentences.

1 I **can** use a laptop.
2 I **can't** use a laptop.
3 I **can** design a blog.
4 I **can't** design a blog.
5 He **can** find his phone.
6 He **can't** find his phone.

B Listen. Complete the chart. Check (✓) all the things you can do on the *Gen 5* and *Linkage* websites. Write an ✗ for everything you can't do.

	Gen 5 website	*Linkage* website
1 chat	✓	✗
2 join interest groups		
3 download songs		
4 send songs to friends		
5 find a job		
6 post pictures		

C Pair Work Look at the chart in B. Choose the website that is best for you. Share your reasons with a partner.

I like Gen 5. You can chat with Gen 5, but you can't chat with Linkage.

276 Unit 21 Ability and Possibility

3 Be Able To and Know How To for Ability

Grammar Presentation

Be able to expresses ability. Know how to expresses things we learned to do in the past.

Warren **is able to** edit movies on his phone.
I **know how to** post videos on the Internet. Someone taught me.

3.1 Be Able To: Affirmative Statements

Subject	Be	Able To	Base Form of Verb	
I	am / was	able to	send	text messages.
You We They	are / were			
He She It	is / was			

3.2 Be Able To: Negative Statements

Subject	Be + Not	Able To	Base Form of Verb	
I	am not / 'm not was not / wasn't	able to	send	text messages.
You We They	are not / aren't were not / weren't			
He She It	is not / isn't was not / wasn't			

3.3 Be Able To: Yes/No Questions

Be	Subject	Able To	Base Form of Verb	
Am / Was	I	able to	send	text messages?
Are / Were	you we they			
Is / Was	he / she / it			

Making Connections

3.4 *Know How To*: Affirmative Statements

Subject	Know	How To	Base Form of Verb	
I / You / We / They	know	how to	design	a website.
He / She / It	knows			

3.5 *Know How To*: Negative Statements

Subject	Do + Not	Know How To	Base Form of Verb	
I / You / We / They	do not / don't	know how to	design	a website.
He / She / It	does not / doesn't			

3.6 *Know How To*: Yes / No Questions

Do	Subject	Know How To	Base Form of Verb	
Do	I / you / we / they	know how to	design	a website?
Does	he / she / it			

3.7 Using *Be Able To* and *Know How To*

A You use *be able to* to express ability. It has the same meaning as *can / could*.	They **are able to** translate the menu with their phones. Mariko **wasn't able to** find the file.
B You use *know how to* to talk about things you learned to do.	Suri **knows how to** create a web page. My grandmother **didn't know how to** send e-mail until I taught her.

▸ Modal Verbs and Modal-like Expressions: See page A25.

Grammar Application

Exercise 3.1 Expressing Ability with *Be Able To* and *Know How To*

Complete the questions and answers about a class survey. Circle the correct words.

Ability and Possibility

A Class Survey On Technology Know-How!

By Ian Wright

Do my classmates and teacher know how to use different types of technology? I wanted to know, so I surveyed them to find out. Here are the questions I asked and the answers I got!

Q Mike, **do / does** Juan know how to use photo editing software?
(1)

A Yes, Juan **know / knows** how to use photo editing software.
(2)

Q **Do / Does** our classmates know how to use business networking sites?
(3)

A No, they **don't / doesn't** know how to use business networking sites.
(4)

Q Sam, **is / are** you able to design online games?
(5)

A No, I **am / are** not able to design online games.
(6)

Q Tony and Tara, **do / does** you know how to post a review?
(7)

A Yes, we **know / knows** how to post a review.
(8)

Q Sarah, **is / are** our teacher able to put tests online?
(9)

A No, our teacher **isn't / aren't** able to put tests online.
(10)

Q **Do / Does** our classmates **know / knows** how to create a group on social media?
(11)   (12)

A Yes, they **is / are** able to create a group on social media.
(13)

Exercise 3.2 Expressing Ability with *Be Able To* and *Know How To*

A Complete the sentences with the correct form of *be able to* or *know how to*. Use the words in parentheses.

Queta and her husband, Marco, live in Texas, but right now Marco has a new job in Nigeria. For Marco, flights to visit Queta and their daughter, Daniela, are very expensive. He _does not know_ (1) how he can find cheaper flights. Of course, Queta and Marco _____ (2) use video calling, but Marco _____ (3) to Daniela and Queta at night only because he is at work all day. However, Queta and Daniela _____ (4) talk at that time. That's because Marco's nighttime is their daytime. They _____ (5) to leave work or school at that time. Unfortunately, Marco _____ (6) to change the hours he works, so the family does not use video calling except on the weekends. Queta and Marco _____ (7) how to solve this problem. Living so far apart is difficult! But they _____ (8) send instant messages, and they can text or email photos, so for now this is an easy solution.

B Complete the conversation with the correct form of *can (not)*, *be (not) able to*, or *(not) know how to*. Sometimes there is more than one correct answer.

Jerry My phone bill is so expensive!

Mark That's because you still _____don't know how_____ (1) to use an app for phone calls.

Jerry No, I hate technology. Don't you?

Mark I like it when I _____ (2) save money.

Jerry Hmm. What is this app?

Mark I use TalkNow. I _____ (3) call anyone in the world for free!

Jerry OK, TalkNow, you say?

Mark Yes.

Jerry OK, but I _____ (4) download the app.

Mark Really? I _____ (5) believe that! Everyone _____ (6) download an app, even my six-year-old grandson.

Jerry Well, I _____ (7) .

Mark I'm sure your wife _____ (8) do it.

Jerry Probably, but I _____ (9) ask her for help. She's at work.

Mark OK, when _____ (10) I come over?

Jerry How about right now?

C Pair Work Work with a partner. Ask each other about some popular technology. Use *Yes/No* questions with *can*, *could*, *be able to*, and *know how to*.

A Do you know how to upload videos from your phone?
B Yes, I do.
A Are you able to edit videos on your phone?

Ability and Possibility

4 Avoid Common Mistakes

1 **There is only one form of *can* and *could*.**

He ~~cans~~ send e-mail. *(can)*

Ten years ago, she ~~coulds~~ only use a computer for typing reports. *(could)*

2 **Use the base form of the verb with *can* and *could*.**

Sue can ~~listens~~ to audio books on the bus. *(listen)*

Yesterday Sue could ~~listened~~ to music all day. *(listen)*

3 **Do not use *to* with the base form of the verb.**

I can ~~to~~ schedule a video conference.

4 **Use *could* to talk about ability in the past.**

Yesterday I ~~cannot~~ send an attachment. *(could not)*

Editing Task

Find and correct six more mistakes on Jenny's *Connected* page.

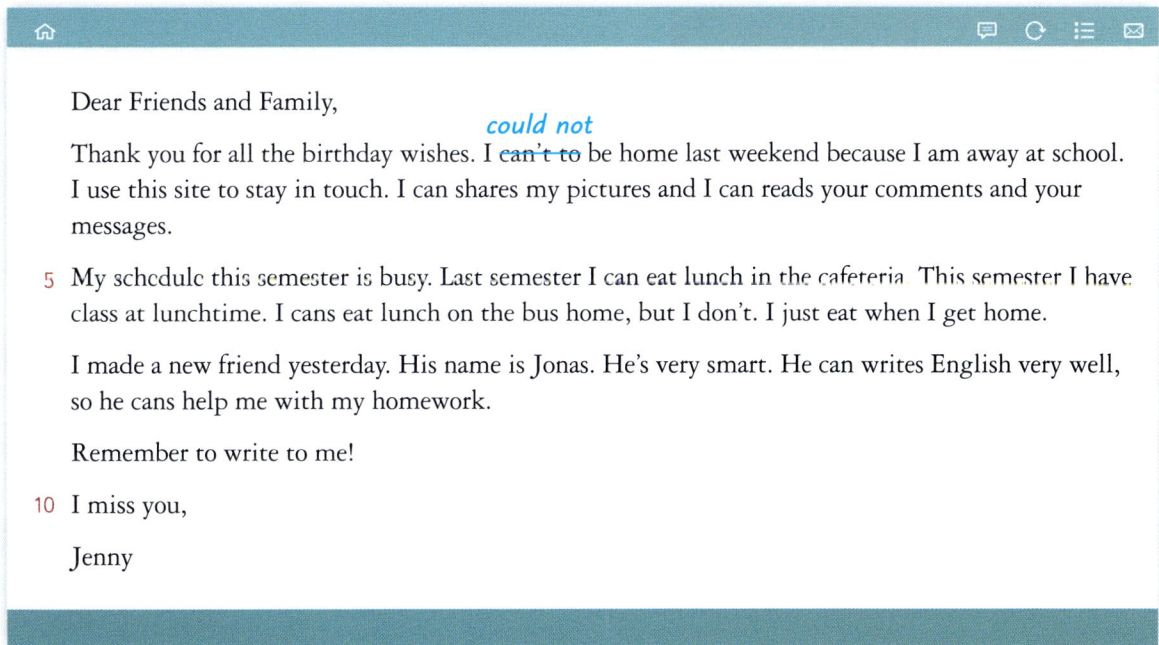

Dear Friends and Family,

Thank you for all the birthday wishes. I ~~can't to~~ *(could not)* be home last weekend because I am away at school. I use this site to stay in touch. I can shares my pictures and I can reads your comments and your messages.

5   My schedule this semester is busy. Last semester I can eat lunch in the cafeteria. This semester I have class at lunchtime. I cans eat lunch on the bus home, but I don't. I just eat when I get home.

I made a new friend yesterday. His name is Jonas. He's very smart. He can writes English very well, so he cans help me with my homework.

Remember to write to me!

10 I miss you,

Jenny

Making Connections 281

5 Academic Writing

Expository Paragraph

Brainstorm > Organize > Write > Edit

In Unit 20, you looked at an example of expository writing and then brainstormed ideas for the prompt below. In this unit (21), you will organize your information and notes.

> *Write a paragraph about someone who is a role model to you. Explain why that person is a good role model.*

Writing Concluding Sentences

If a text is only one paragraph long, the writer may end it with a **concluding sentence**. The concluding sentence usually summarizes the paragraph or refers to the main idea in different words. In a paragraph about a role model, the concluding sentence might summarize why the writer admires the person.

Look at the concluding sentence for a paragraph about a sports coach below:

Coach Smith taught me how to be a good team player in the game of life.

In longer texts like essays, body paragraphs flow into each other without concluding sentences. Only final paragraphs have concluding sentences.

Exercise 5.1 Applying the Skill

Circle the letter of the better concluding sentence for each paragraph about a role model. Discuss your answers with a partner.

1. In a paragraph about a role model who is strong and confident even though he has been very sick:
    a. He has shown me how to get over bad times and make the most of life.
    b. His experience has shown me the value of medical technology.

2. In a paragraph about the writer's father, a role model who has been very loving and supportive:
    a. Without my dad's help, I would not have achieved my dreams.
    b. For all these reasons, I like my dad.

3. In a paragraph about a role model who was one of the writer's teachers:
    a. She is truly an exceptional person and a great teacher.
    b. The lessons she taught me will stay with me for the rest of my life.

My Writing

Using Statements of Ability

A writer may need to explain what a role model is (or was) able to do. These statements may include *can*, *could*, *be able to*, and *know how to*.

Exercise 5.2 Applying the Skill

Think about the abilities of your role model. Write three sentences in each column using the verbs at the top. Each sentence should express a different ability.

can / could	be able to	know how to

Exercise 5.3 Organizing Your Ideas

Review the basic facts and qualities you brainstormed on page 269 and at the abilities you wrote about in Exercise 5.2. Use the guidelines to organize the information.

1. Write a topic sentence.
2. Write two facts (background information) about the person.
3. Write about three qualities or actions you admire.
4. Write about two of the person's abilities.
5. Write a concluding sentence.

UNIT 22

Requests and Permission

College Life

ACADEMIC WRITING

Expository paragraph

1 Grammar in the Real World

A Do you have an academic adviser? Read the academic adviser's web page. What are some things an academic adviser can help you with?

B Comprehension Check Answer the questions. Circle *Yes* or *No*. Use the article to help you.

1 Do students ask Henry different kinds of questions?   Yes   No
2 Does Henry discuss very personal problems?   Yes   No
3 Does Henry go to students' classes to talk about his work?   Yes   No
4 Can students find more common questions on the school's home page?   Yes   No

C Notice Find the student questions in the article. Complete the sentences.

1 _____ you help me choose the right classes for my major?

2 _____ you give me some advice, please?

3 _____ you give me information about tutors, please?

4 _____ you come to our class and talk about your work as an academic adviser, please?

What is the purpose of all these questions?

284

DEPARTMENT OF LANGUAGES

Hello,

My name is Henry Driscoll, and I am one of the academic advisers for the Department of Languages. My job is to help you with your educational and career goals. Students often come to my office to ask
5 questions. Here are some typical questions:

- **Can** you help me choose the right classes for my major?
- I want to take some courses in another department. **Could** you give me some advice, please?
- I need a tutor to help me with my English. **Can** you give me
10 information about tutors, please?
- **May** I come to your office to talk with you about a problem I have?
- I have a financial problem. **Can** you help me?
- I have a problem with my classes. **Can** you help me with it?

Often my answer is, "Sure! No problem. Of course I can help."
15 But sometimes I have to say, "Sorry, I **can't** help you with that" or "I'm sorry, I **can't** discuss that." For example, I **cannot** discuss questions about very personal issues, such as health or family problems. However, I **can** always refer[1] you to a person who can help you.

Here is my favorite question: "**Would** you come to our class and talk
20 about your work as an academic adviser, please?" To that question, the answer is always YES!

For more information and FAQs,[2] go to the school's home page at www.DCweb.cambridge.org.

---

[1]**refer:** send you to a different place or to a person who knows more about or can help more with a subject

[2]**FAQs:** frequently asked questions

2 Can, Could, and Would for Requests

Grammar Presentation

We use *can*, *could*, and *would* to ask people to do things.	**Can** you help me, please? **Could** you give me some advice? **Would** you please help me with my paper?

2.1 Can, Could, and Would for Requests

Can / Could / Would	Subject	Base Form of Verb	
Can Could Would	you	advise	me about the program?
		open	the door for me, please?
		come	to our class and talk about your work, please?

2.2 Using Can, Could, and Would to Make Requests

A Use *can*, *could*, and *would* to ask people to do something.	**Can** you meet me at 2:00 p.m. today? **Could** you give me some advice? **Would** you reserve a seat for me, please?
B *Could* and *would* are more polite than *can*. Use *could* and *would* in formal situations.	**Can** you give me a call tonight? **Could** you advise me about my project, please? **Would** you help me write my résumé, please?
C Use *please* when you ask a person you do not know well to do something.	Excuse me. Can you tell me the way to Mason Street, **please**?
Use *please* in formal situations.	Would you **please** come this way?
You can use *please* at the end of the sentence or after the subject.	Could you sign this document, **please**? Could you **please** sign this document?

▸ Modal Verbs and Modal-like Expressions: See page A25.

2.3 Answering Requests

A When you agree to a request, you can give a short answer.

"Can you come tonight?" "*Yes.*" / "*Yes, I can.*"

You can include the request in your answer.

"Can you help me?" "Yes, *I can help you.*"

Often we say other words of agreement instead of *yes*.

Informal Responses: *OK*, *sure*, *no problem*

Formal Responses: *of course*, *certainly*

"Could you please help me find the career adviser's office?"

"*Sure* I can."

"*Certainly*. Just follow that corridor. First door on the left."

B We use *cannot* or *can't* in negative answers to requests, even when the request uses *could* or *would*.

"Could you please give me your book?"
"No, I *can't*. I don't have it with me."
"Would you come to the meeting with us?"
"No, I *can't*. Sorry, I'm busy."

Can't is informal.

"Can you help me with this vocabulary word?"
"No, I *can't*. I don't know what it means."

Cannot is more formal.

"Could you help me with my health issues, please?"
"No, I *cannot* discuss health problems with you."

We often use *sorry* instead of *no*.

"Would you like to go out tonight?"
"*Sorry*, I can't. I have a lot of homework."
"Can you pass the dictionary?"
"*Sorry*, I *can't* reach it."

I'm sorry is more formal than *sorry*.

"Could you please tell me the time?"
"*I'm sorry*. I *can't*. I don't have a watch."

We often give a reason when we give a negative response to a request.

"Would you speak to our class tomorrow?"
"No, I'm sorry. *I can't*. *I'm in a conference all day*."
"Can you help me tonight?"
"Sorry, *I can't*. *I have to work*."

Grammar Application

Exercise 2.1 Using *Can*, *Could*, and *Would* in Requests and Answers

A Complete the sentences with *can*, *could*, *would*, or *can't*. Then listen to the conversations. Check your answers.

Elena I need to talk to Professor Baker. ___Can___(1) you tell me what building he's in?

Freda Yeah, sure. He's in the Ross Building. I'm going there now. Come on! So, what's up?

Elena Oh, it's just a problem about the exams. _____(2) you come with me to Professor Baker's office? Do you know where it is?

Freda Yeah, sure. I met with him last semester.

Elena When I finish with the professor, _____(3) we meet up again later?

Freda Yeah, good idea!

Elena Just one problem. I don't know what time the meeting finishes. _____(4) you wait for me in the cafeteria?

Freda No problem. I can do my homework.

Elena Hello, Professor Baker. Do you have a minute?

Prof. Baker Certainly. _____(5) you close the door, please?

Elena Of course. _____(6) you help me, please? I have an exam next Tuesday, and I have a family wedding on that day. _____(7) you write a letter to the exam professor about this?

Prof. Baker Oh, I'm sorry. I _____(8). A family wedding is not an excuse to miss an exam. That's the college's policy.

Elena Oh! Really?

Prof. Baker I'm very sorry. Those are the rules.

Elena Oh, well, OK. Thank you for your time.

B **Pair Work** Practice the conversations in A with a partner.

Requests and Permission

Exercise 2.2 Making and Answering Requests

A Change the imperatives to questions. Use *can*, *could*, or *would*. Sometimes there is more than one correct answer.

1 Help me write my résumé.
   Can you help me write my résumé?

2 Meet me at the cafeteria after class today.

3 Tell me the things that I need to put in the résumé.

4 Show me your résumé.

5 Advise me on the correct style for a résumé.

6 Correct my mistakes.

7 Help me arrange my résumé so it looks good.

8 Read my résumé and make sure it's OK.

B Pair Work Work with a partner. Ask and answer the questions in A. First, agree to the requests. Use *sure*, *no problem*, and *of course*. Then give negative answers. Use *sorry* and *I'm sorry*. Give a good reason for your negative answers. Take turns.

A Can you help me write my résumé?   A Can you help me write my résumé?
B Sure!   B Sorry, I can't help you. I'm really busy today.

College Life 289

3 Can, Could, and May for Permission

Grammar Presentation

We use *can*, *could*, and *may* to ask for permission to do things.	**Can** I make an appointment for tomorrow? **May** I please come in? **Could** I ask you a question?

3.1 Can, Could, and May for Permission

Can / Could / May	Subject	Base Form of Verb	
Can Could May	I	use	this pencil?
		leave	early today?
		ask	a question?

3.2 Using Can, Could, and May for Permission

A Use *can* in most situations.	**Can** I borrow your pen? **Can** I take a picture with your camera?
B *Could* is more polite than *can*.	**Could** we use Room 208 for our student meeting?
Use *could* with strangers and people you do not know well.	**Could** I study with you for the exam?
Use *could* in formal situations.	**Could** I talk to you for a moment?
C *May* is very polite.	Professor Wodak, **may** I interview you for the student newspaper, please?
Use *may* with people you do not know well in very formal situations.	**May** I use your pen for a moment?
D *Please* can make a request for permission more polite.	
Use *please* when you ask a person you do not know well for permission.	Can I use this telephone, **please**? May I use your pen for a moment, **please**?
Use *please* in formal situations. Use *please* at the end of the request or after the subject.	Doctor Takano, may I **please** ask a question about my project? May I ask a question about my project, **please**?

▸ Modal Verbs and Modal-like Expressions: See page A25.

3.3 Answering Requests for Permission

A	When you agree to a request for permission, you can give a short answer.	"Can I sit in this chair?" "*Yes*."
	You can include the request in your answer.	"Could I work in your group?" "*Sure*, you can work in our group!"
	Often we say other words of agreement instead of *yes*. Informal responses: *sure, no problem, go ahead* Formal responses: *of course, certainly*	"Can I see your homework?" "*No problem*!" "May I contact you by e-mail?" "*Of course*."
B	We often use *sorry* when we give a negative answer to a request for permission. People do not usually say *no*. They say *sorry* and give a reason.	"Could I see that?" "*Sorry*. It's not mine."
	I'm sorry is more formal than *sorry*.	"Can I speak to you for a moment?" "*I'm sorry*. I'm very busy. Maybe after class?"

Grammar Application

Exercise 3.1 Requests for Permission with *Can*, *Could*, and *May*

A Complete the requests. Circle the best answer.

1 To a friend: **(Can)/ May** I call you later?

2 To a professor: **May / Could** I leave early today?

3 To a stranger: **Can / May** I look at your bus schedule for a moment?

4 To a friend: **Could / May** I see your phone?

5 To a boss: **May / Could** I speak to you for a moment?

6 To a friend: **May / Can** we finish this tomorrow?

B Pair Work Practice saying and answering the requests in A with a partner. Give some affirmative answers and some negative answers.

A *Can I call you later?*
B *Sure. Call me anytime.*

A *Can I call you later?*
B *Sorry, I'm busy tonight. I can call you tomorrow.*

College Life 291

Exercise 3.2 More Requests for Permission

A Complete the chart. Who is the speaker? Where does the request take place? Use your own ideas.

	A student	A professor	A boss	A co-worker	Who?	Where?
1 Can I sit next to you, Joanna?					student	in class/ in a café
2 Could I please leave early today, Professor?						
3 May I have next Monday off, please? It's my birthday.						
4 Could I use your office for an hour today?						
5 May I use your telephone, please?						
6 Could I please make two copies of my report?						
7 Can I have one of your French fries?						
8 May I please talk to you about my schedule?						
9 Can I look at your project? There are problems with mine.						

B Pair Work With a partner, write answers to the requests in A. Practice saying and answering the requests.

A *Can I sit next to you, Joanna?*
B *Sure!*

A *Could I leave early today, Professor?*
B *I'm sorry. You left early yesterday.*

Exercise 3.3 Formal Requests for Permission

Complete the sentences with the words in parentheses. Reorder the words to make requests for permission.

Dear Professor Machado,

My name is Ricardo Yaka. I am the editor of the *English Now* newsletter. **May I interview you** (1) (I / interview / may / you) for about 15 minutes for this month's newsletter? _____ (2) (come / could / I / to your office / please) for the interview?

The newsletter often has articles about the lives of faculty members. We know that students like to read about their professors' college experiences.

_____ (3) (ask / I / may / you) about your college days? To make it easy for you, _____ (4) (can / you / I / please / send) a list of my questions?

The articles in our newsletters are informal, and many have photographs. _____ (5) (please / I / could / take) your picture? You can see a copy of the newsletter before the interview. _____ (6) (e-mail / I / may) it to you? The newsletter is very popular. About 200 students read the interviews every month, and more students read the newsletter on the Internet. _____ (7) (I / may / please / put) your interview on our website, too?

After you have read the questions, _____ (8) (visit / I / could / please) you at your office sometime this week?

Thank you very much. I look forward to your reply.

Kind regards,

Ricardo Yaka

Exercise 3.4 More Requests for Permission

Write a request for permission based on each situation.

1 You want to come in late for work tomorrow. Ask your boss.

   Could I come in late tomorrow, please? / May I please come in late tomorrow?

2 You want to use your best friend's pen. Ask him/her.

3 You want to change the channel on the TV at home. Ask a family member.

4 You want to hand in your homework one day late. Ask your teacher.

5 You want to speak to your boss after work today. Ask him/her.

6 You want to borrow your classmate's electronic dictionary. Ask him/her.

7 You want to charge your phone in the school office. Ask the secretary.

8 You want to use the atlas behind the reference desk in the library. Ask the librarian.

9 You want to borrow your roommate's bicycle. Ask him/her.

10 You want to get your professor's e-mail address. Ask him/her.

4 Avoid Common Mistakes

1 Use the correct word order for making requests.
Can you
~~You can~~ help me?

2 Use the base form of the verb after *can*, *could*, *may*, or *would*.
     help
Can you ~~to help~~ me?

3 Use *can*, *could*, or *would* to ask people to do something. Do not use *do*.
Would
~~Do~~ you come to my office, please?

4 Use *can*, *could*, or *would* to ask people to do something. Do not use *may*.
Could
~~May~~ you reserve a place for me, please?

Editing Task

Find and correct eight more mistakes in this e-mail about a college music show.

Hi Everyone,

The show is next week!

                    Can you
- Everyone: ~~You can~~ please make a list of the equipment you need?
- Gregori: You can tell me how many microphones we need?
5
- Jason: Could we to borrow your microphone, please? Thanks!
- Anna: We need a laptop from the computer lab. Can you to pick it up today?
- Jessie: May you contact Mr. Sparks about the lights?
- Hector: Your job is to get the chairs. You can please arrange that?
- Mari: Mr. Sanchez has the music playlist. Do you please contact him?
10
- Hong-yin: May we to borrow your projector, please?

Finally, may you all please come to the meeting at 2:00 p.m. tomorrow in Room 305?

Thanks!

Kazuo

5 Academic Writing

Expository Paragraph

Brainstorm > Organize > Write > Edit

In Unit 21, you learned about concluding sentences and organized ideas for the prompt below. In this unit (22), you will write, revise, and edit your paragraph.

> Write a paragraph about someone who is a role model to you. Explain why that person is a good role model.

Using Adjectives and Adverbs to Describe Challenges

Role models are often special because they can do difficult things. When writers describe role models, they often use adjectives and adverbs related to difficulty.

Exercise 5.1 Applying the Skill

Find and circle three phrases with adjectives or adverbs related to difficulty in the paragraph. The first one is done for you.

    Sim Yi Hui was the other co-leader of SWET. She has also climbed many tall mountains, including one of the Seven Summits—Denali in Alaska. Like Lee, she enjoys (difficult physical tasks). In 2011, she walked across the Gobi Desert in Mongolia. It took her 51 days. When she was on Everest, she showed a special kind of courage. She had a bad injury to her chest, but she was almost there. Should she continue? She made the difficult decision not to go to the top with her five teammates. It was the smart thing to do, but after she had planned so long and worked so hard, the decision was not easy. Her self-control and clear thinking are an inspiration to many people. Hui now works as an administrator at a university.

My Writing

Exercise 5.2 Writing Your Paragraph

Review the information you wrote in My Writing on page 283. Then write an expository paragraph about a role model. Include a topic sentence, background information, what you admire about the person, at least one of their abilities, and a concluding sentence.

Exercise 5.3 Revising Your Ideas

1 Work with a partner. Use the questions below to give feedback on the ideas in your partner's paragraph.
   - Which details in your partner's paragraph are the strongest?
   - Which details in your partner's paragraph are unnecessary?
   - What types of details could your partner add to make the paragraph stronger?

2 Use the feedback from your partner to revise your paragraph.

Exercise 5.4 Editing Your Writing

Use the checklist to review and edit your paragraph.

Did you write a topic sentence that includes your role model's name?	
Did you include some background facts about your role model?	
Did you explain the admirable qualities of your role model?	
Did you use imperatives correctly if you wrote about rules or guidelines?	
Did you use verbs of ability to discuss the person's abilities?	
Did you use adjectives or adverbs to describe difficulties in your role model's life?	
Did you end with a good concluding sentence?	

Exercise 5.5 Writing Your Final Draft

Apply the feedback and edits from Exercises 5.3 and 5.4 to write the final draft of your paragraph.

UNIT 23: Present Progressive

Body Language

ACADEMIC WRITING

Process paragraph

1 Grammar in the Real World

A What do you do during a conversation? Do you smile? Do you cross your arms? Do you nod your head? Do you make eye contact? Read the article about body language. Why is it important?

B Comprehension Check What can these gestures mean? Use the article to help you. Circle *a* or *b*.

1 A person is leaning toward you in a conversation.
   a He doesn't like what you are saying.   b He is interested.

2 Your friend is crossing her arms during an argument.
   a She doesn't agree with you.   b She is thinking about something else.

3 A person is touching her chin a lot during a discussion.
   a She is thinking.   b Maybe she's lying.

C Notice Complete these sentences. Use the forms of the verbs from the article.

1 Nod to show you _____ (listen).

2 Some experts say that when you keep your hands under the table, it can mean you _____ not _____ (tell) the truth.

3 However, a hand on the chin can just mean you _____ (think).

Look at the verb forms. How many parts does each verb have? What do they have in common?

Present Progressive

UNDERSTANDING BODY LANGUAGE

Body language is a crucial[1] part of face-to-face communication. Some experts[2] say that 93 percent of communication is nonverbal.[3] Of course, the meaning of body language varies from culture to culture. Even in one culture, experts do not always agree on the meaning of every gesture.[4] However, here are some things to remember for your next conversation, meeting, or interview. They apply mostly to communication in North America.

How **Are** You **Sitting**?

Lean[5] toward the other person to show you are interested in what he or she **is saying**. Nod to show **you are listening**.

Are You **Crossing** Your Arms?

Crossing your arms can seem defensive.[6] In an argument, it can mean you don't agree.

What **Are** Your Hands **Doing**?

Keep your hands out and open. Some experts say that when you keep your hands under the table, it can mean you **are not telling** the truth. However, a hand on the chin can just mean you **are thinking**.

Where **Are** You **Looking**?

Make eye contact. When you **are talking** to someone face-to-face, it is important to look at them. This shows that you **are listening** to them.

Learn to use positive body language. After all, what you *do* may communicate more than 90 percent of your message.

---

[1]**crucial:** extremely important
[2]**expert:** a person with a high level of knowledge or skill about a subject
[3]**nonverbal:** not spoken
[4]**gesture:** a movement of the body, hands, arms, or head to express an idea or feeling
[5]**lean:** move your body so it's bent forward
[6]**defensive:** wanting to protect or defend oneself

2 Present Progressive Statements

Grammar Presentation

The present progressive describes actions and events that are in progress now and around the present time. "In progress" means the action started before now but is not finished or complete.

*He **is not listening** to the professor.*
*We **are studying** body language in my psychology class.*

2.1 Affirmative Statements

Subject	Be	Verb + -ing
I	am	
You / We / They	are	talking.
He / She / It	is	

Contractions

I am → I'm
You are → You're
We are → We're
They are → They're
He is → He's
She is → She's
It is → It's

2.2 Negative Statements

Subject	Be + Not	Verb + -ing
I	am not	
You / We / They	are not	talking.
He / She / It	is not	

Contractions

I am not →	I'm not	
You are not →	You're not	You aren't
We are not →	We're not	We aren't
They are not →	They're not	They aren't
He is not →	He's not	He isn't
She is not →	She's not	She isn't
It is not →	It's not	It isn't

2.3 Spelling -ing Forms

A For most verbs, add -ing.

talk → talking
say → saying
go → going

B If the verb ends in a silent -e, delete e and add -ing.

live → living
make → making
write → writing

Present Progressive

2.3 Spelling -ing Forms (continued)

C	For *be* and *see*, don't <u>drop</u> the *e* because it is not silent.	be → be**ing** see → see**ing**
D	If the verb ends in *-ie*, change the *ie* to *y* and add *-ing*.	l**ie** → l**ying**
E	If the verb has one syllable and follows the pattern consonant – vowel – consonant (CVC), double the last letter and add *-ing*.	sit → sit**ting** put → put**ting** get → get**ting**
F	Do not double the consonant if the verb ends in *-w*, *-x*, or *-y*.	gro**w** → gro**wing** fi**x** → fi**xing** sa**y** → sa**ying**
G	If the verb has two syllables, ends in the pattern CVC, and is stressed on the last syllable, double the last letter and add *-ing*.	begin → begin**ning**
H	If the verb has two syllables and is stressed on the first syllable, do not double the last letter before adding *-ing*.	listen → listen**ing** travel → travel**ing** visit → visit**ing**

▶▶ Spelling Rules for Verbs Ending in *-ing*. See page A20.

2.4 Using Present Progressive

A	Use the present progressive for actions in progress as you write or speak. The action is not finished.	I **am writing** for information about . . . (in a letter) Look at that man. He**'s talking** to that woman, but he**'s** not **smiling**.
B	You can also use the present progressive for actions in progress "around now," at the present time.	I **am studying** psychology this semester. This week we**'re looking** at body language.
C	Use contractions in speaking. Do not use contractions in very formal writing.	He**'s taking** psychology this semester. I **am writing** to express my interest in this job. (in a letter)
D	You can use the present progressive with present time expressions like *now, right now, at the moment, this week/month, these days*.	Sorry, I can't talk. I**'m going** into class **right now**. I**'m working** two jobs **at the moment**.

Body Language 301

Grammar Application

Exercise 2.1 Present Progressive Verb Forms

A Complete the sentences below using the present progressive. Use contractions when possible.

1. The woman _is talking_ (talk).
2. She _____ (lean) toward the man.
3. He _____ (smile).
4. The man _____ (listen) to her.
5. They _____ (make) eye contact.
6. They _____ (get) along.
7. The man and woman _____ (not get along).
8. They _____ (not smile).
9. The woman _____ (not look) at the man.
10. She _____ (lean) away from him.
11. She _____ (not talk).
12. Maybe they _____ (have) an argument.

B Pair Work With a partner, describe some more things the people in A are doing. Use these verbs or your own ideas. Write affirmative and negative sentences for each picture.

| drink | eat | laugh | look | sit | talk |

Exercise 2.2 Statements

A What are the people doing before class? Use the words to write sentences about them. Use the present progressive.

1. Fatima / text her friend _Fatima is texting her friend._
2. Pedro / chew his pen _____
3. Carlos and Eun / not sit up straight _____
4. Ana and Kerry / talk _____
5. Lee and Tyler / not look each other in the eye _____
6. Yumi / not smile _____
7. Maria / stare at the door _____
8. The teacher / write on the board _____

302 Unit 23 Present Progressive

Present Progressive

B **Over to You** Look around your classroom. What are people doing? Write three affirmative sentences and three negative sentences about your classmates. Then compare your sentences with a partner.

Exercise 2.3 Vocabulary Focus: Time Expressions

There are many time expressions you can use with the present progressive. These are some:

(right) now	*at the moment*	*tonight*	*today*	*this morning / afternoon / evening*
this week	*this semester*	*this month*	*this year*	

You can put a time expression at the beginning or at the end of a sentence. You usually put a comma after the time expression if it is at the beginning of a sentence. If the time expression is just one word, you don't have to use a comma.

Right now, I'm typing a letter.

Julia is listening to her professor *at the moment*.

Today I'm studying for an exam.

Complete the e-mail. Use the present progressive form of the verbs in parentheses and an appropriate time expression (TE) from the box. More than one time expression can be correct.

Hi Josh,

How are you? How's college? I'm fine. I __'m sitting__ (sit) in a classroom __right now__ (TE).
(1) (2)
I _____ (wait) for class to start. _____ (TE), we _____
(3) (4) (5)
(study) communication. I _____ (enjoy) it. _____ (TE), I
(6) (7)
_____ (write) a paper on nonverbal communication. I _____ (take) a
(8) (9)
marketing class _____ (TE), too.
(10)

I _____ (not play) a lot of sports _____ (TE). I'm too busy!
(11) (12)
I _____ (work) in a grocery store. My parents _____ (plan) a trip to
(13) (14)
Mexico in the summer, and I _____ (save) some money to go with them.
(15)

What else is new? Oh, my cousin _____ (stay) with us.
(16)
I think he _____ (enjoy) his time with us.
(17)

OK. That's all for now. Class _____ (start).
(18)

Write to me soon,

Alex

Exercise 2.4 Negative Contractions

DATA FROM THE REAL WORLD

Research shows that in speaking, people usually use the negative forms *'s not* and *'re not*, especially after pronouns.

He / She / It's not . . . ingHe / She / It isn't . . . ing
You / We / They're not . . . ingYou / We / They aren't . . . ing

People often say *isn't* and *aren't* with names and nouns when it is difficult to add *'s not* and *'re not*.

Marcos **isn't** working. *(names and nouns)*
He**'s not** working. *(pronouns)*

Complete the conversation with negative contractions. Then listen and check your answers.

Carla Hey, Rod. You <u>*'re not studying*</u> (study) today?
(1)

Rod No, Chris _____ (come) to class today.
(2)

Carla You're doing a project together, right?

Rod Yes, with Jon, Lisa, and Cristina . . . but it _____ (go) well.
(3)
We _____ (get) along well, either.
(4)

Carla Really? Why not?

Rod Well, Chris _____ (do) his share of the work. He _____
(5) (6)
(read) the books, and he _____ (come) to meetings with the group.
(7)

Carla What do the others in the group think?

Rod They _____ (feel) too happy with him. In fact, they
(8)
_____ (speak) to him. We wrote a letter to the teacher about him.
(9)

Carla Maybe it's time to talk to him about it. I know he _____ (do)
(10)
a good job, but maybe there's a reason for it.

Rod I guess we _____ (give) him a chance to explain.
(11)

304 Unit 23 Present Progressive

3 Present Progressive Questions

Grammar Presentation

Present progressive questions ask about actions and events that are in progress now and around the present time.

Are you crossing your arms?
What are your hands doing?
What are you studying?

3.1 Yes/No Questions

Be	Subject	Verb + -ing
Am	I	
Are	you / we / they	working?
Is	he / she / it	

3.2 Short Answers

AFFIRMATIVE	NEGATIVE	
Yes, I **am**.	No, I**'m not**.	
Yes, you **are**.	No, you**'re not**.	No, you **aren't**.
Yes, we **are**.	No, we**'re not**.	No, we **aren't**.
Yes, they **are**.	No, they**'re not**.	No, they **aren't**.
Yes, he / she / it **is**.	No, he / she / it**'s not**.	No, he / she / it **isn't**.

3.3 Information Questions

Wh- Word	Be	Subject	Verb + -ing
Who	am	I	hearing?
What			feeling?
When	are	you / we / they	leaving?
Where			studying?
Why			laughing?
How	is	he / she / it	going?

Wh- Word as Subject	Be	Verb + -ing
Who	is	talking?
What		happening?

Body Language

3.4 Using Present Progressive Questions

A Use the present progressive to ask questions about actions in progress as you write or speak. The action is not finished.

Look at that man. **Is** he **talking** to that woman?

B Use the present progressive to ask questions about actions in progress at the present time (now) or "around now."

"**Are** you **studying** for an exam?" "Yes."
"What **are** you **doing**?" "**I'm studying**."

C The *Wh-* word is sometimes the subject.

"**Who**'s studying in the library now?"
"Jo and Marta."
"**What**'s going on?" "**We're studying**."

D You can use the present progressive with present time expressions like *now, right now, at the moment, this week/month,* and *these days* to ask questions.

Are you going into class **right now**?
Are you working two jobs **at the moment**?

E Time expressions always come at the end of the question, not at the beginning.

What are they talking about **right now**?
Is she crossing her arms **at the moment**?

Grammar Application

Exercise 3.1 Yes/No Questions and Answers

Write the questions and answers. Use the correct form of the verbs in parentheses.

Ashley: Hi, Jack. __Am__(1) I __disturbing__(1) (disturb) you?

Jack: No, _____(2) . Not at all.

Ashley: _____(3) you _____(3) (study)?

Jack: Yes, _____(4) . Well, kind of.

Ashley: Oh, _____(5) you _____(5) (watch) a movie?

Jack: No, _____(6) . It's a video for my French class.

Ashley: _____(7) the actors _____(7) (speak) French?

Jack: Yes, _____(8) . I think that guy _____(9) (say), "I love you."

Ashley: _____(10) you _____(10) (tell) me you can't understand it?

Jack: Well, yes. I only started my French class last week!

Present Progressive

Exercise 3.2 Forming Questions and Answers

A Unscramble the words to make present progressive questions.

1 notes? / you / are / taking

   Are you taking notes?

2 doing / what / your classmates / are / right now?

3 is / your teacher / what / saying?

4 to the teacher? / listening / who / is

5 right now? / happening / is / what / in class

6 are / up straight? / you / sitting

B Pair Work Ask and answer the questions in A with a partner.

4 Present Progressive and Simple Present

Grammar Presentation

The present progressive describes actions and events that are in progress now and around the present time. The simple present describes things that happen repeatedly or all the time.

I'm **studying** psychology right now.
I **take** four classes every semester.

4.1 Present Progressive and Simple Present

A Use the present progressive for actions and events in progress now.	I'm **writing** an essay about body language. Sorry, I can't talk. I'm **going** into class.
Use the simple present for repeated actions and events.	I **write** one essay every month. I **go** to school on Mondays and Wednesdays.

Body Language 307

4.1 Present Progressive and Simple Present (continued)

B	Use the present progressive for temporary events.	A friend **is visiting** this week. She**'s staying** with me.
	Use the simple present for permanent situations.	I **come** from Ohio, but my family **lives** in Texas.
C	Use the present progressive with present time expressions like *right now*, *at the moment*, and *today*.	I'm riding the train **at the moment**. (on the phone) **Right now,** I'm going to work.
	Use the simple present with frequency adverbs like *often*, *never*, *every week*, etc.	I **often** look at people on the subway and **watch** their behavior. Do you **usually** smile when you **meet** new people?

4.2 Non-active or Stative Verbs

A	Stative verbs describe states, not actions.	I **don't like** rude people. NOT I'm not liking rude people.
	These are some stative verbs: *love, know, want, need, seem, mean,* and *agree*. Use the simple present with stative verbs, not the present progressive.	What **do** you **know** about this? NOT What are you knowing? They **seem** upset. NOT They are seeming upset. Experts **don't agree** on the meaning of some gestures. NOT Experts are not agreeing on the meaning of some gestures.
B	Some verbs have a stative meaning and an action meaning.	STATIVE I **think** grammar is fun. (= an opinion) ACTION I**'m thinking** about my homework. (= using my mind) STATIVE The book **looks** interesting. (= appears) ACTION We**'re looking** at the book right now. (= using our eyes) STATIVE Do you **have** a dog? (= own) ACTION Are you **having** a good time? (= experiencing)
C	You can use *feel* with the same meaning in the simple present and the present progressive.	I **feel** tired today. OR I**'m feeling** tired today. How **do** you **feel**? OR How are you **feeling**?

▶▶ Stative (Non-Action) Verbs: See page A26.

Present Progressive

Grammar Application

Exercise 4.1 Statements

Complete the sentences about students in an English class with the present progressive or the simple present. Use the verbs in parentheses.

1. In our English class, I normally _sit_ (sit) up straight.
2. Right now, my friend José _____ (relax) in a comfortable chair.
3. Our classmate Maria _____ (cross) her arms a lot when she listens.
4. In conversations, I usually _____ (make) eye contact with my partner, Sara.
5. Sara often _____ (chew) on her pens and pencils when she's nervous.
6. Three other students _____ (chew) gum at the moment.
7. No one _____ (sit) quietly in class right now!
8. Our teacher usually _____ (stand) in class when she lectures.

Exercise 4.2 Vocabulary Focus: Some Common Stative Verbs

Possession	have, own
Feelings, wants, and needs	be, feel, hate, like, love, mind, need, want
Senses	hear, look (= seem), seem, sound, feel
Thought	agree, believe, know, mean, remember, think, understand

A Complete the questions with the present progressive or the simple present.

1. _Do_ you _own_ (own) a car?
2. _____ you _____ (look) for a new car right now?
3. _____ your voice _____ (sound) soft or loud?
4. _____ your last name _____ (mean) anything?
5. _____ you usually _____ (understand) movies in English?
6. _____ you _____ (read) anything interesting at the moment?
7. _____ you _____ (like) English grammar?
8. _____ you _____ (mind) working late on weekends?
9. _____ you _____ (feel) tired after school?

B Pair Work Ask and answer the questions in A with a partner.

Exercise 4.3 Present Progressive or Simple Present?

A professor is showing a video to the class. Complete the sentences using the present progressive or the simple present form of the verbs. Some sentences are negative.

Children and Body Language

The children in this animated video _are playing_ (1) (play). They _____(2) (not know) that we _____(3) (film) them. They _____(4) (look) busy, don't they?

These little girls _____(5) (not sit) on the floor. They _____(6) (look) at each other. They _____(7) (make) eye contact. They _____(8) (talk) about their friends. They _____(9) (seem) very happy together. _____(10) you _____(10) (agree)?

It _____(11) (seem) that little girls often _____(12) (talk) about their friends. They often _____(13) (tell) secrets, too. When little girls talk, they _____(14) (like) to look at their friends. On the other hand, little boys usually _____(15) (play) games. In general, they _____(16) (not look) at their friends. They often _____(17) (sit) side by side.

Present Progressive

5 Avoid Common Mistakes ⚠️

1 **To form the present progressive, use *be* and verb + *-ing*.**

   am   studying
I ^living in a dorm this semester.   I am ~~study~~ business administration.

2 **Check the spelling of the *-ing* verb form.**

    writing
I'm ~~writeing~~ a paper on psychology.

3 **Use present progressive for temporary and ongoing activities at the present time.**

    am writing
Right now, I ~~write~~ an essay on reality shows.

Editing Task

Find and correct nine more mistakes in this student's essay and progress report.

Talent Shows

                          are
Talent shows ^becoming a very popular form of entertainment these days. The contestants[1] in the shows trying to be famous. They sing every week. Millions of people watch these shows every week.

    People like the shows for a number of reasons. First, the shows have good music. For example, this season they are includeing a woman who sings opera. Second, viewers can vote for the winners every week. Third, the contestants in the shows come from ordinary backgrounds.

[1]**contestant:** someone who competes in a game show

Progress Report – Psychology 111

    In my group, we study one talent show this semester called *Do You Get It?* We are look at the body language of the contestants. We are try to see how it changes. I looking at hand gestures, and I am writeing a paper about the hand gestures of the losers. The paper goes well. I finding some interesting things to write about.

6 Academic Writing

Process Paragraph

> Brainstorm > Organize > Write > Edit

In this writing cycle (Units 23–26), you are going to answer the prompt below. In this unit (23), you will look at a reading about a process and at ways to brainstorm ideas for your writing.

Write a paragraph to describe the Sydney Triathlon.

Exercise 6.1 Preparing to Write

Ask and answer questions with a partner.

1. Do you take part in any physical activities such as running, swimming, or bicycling?
2. Do you watch any sporting events like the Olympic Games?
3. What makes athletic competitions difficult?
4. Why do people participate in competitions even though they are difficult?

Exercise 6.2 Focusing on Vocabulary

Read the sentences and choose the best definition for the words in bold.

1. In January 2015, the Hong Kong Marathon had over 73,000 **participants**.
    a. people who take part in an activity
    b. people who organize an activity
2. The **course** was so long that most officials drove cars to get from the starting line to the finish.
    a. an area used for sporting events, such as a race
    b. an area where players get together after they finish a sport
3. It takes about six hours to **climb** Mount Fuji in Japan. Many people try to reach the top just before the sun rises.
    a. wait for something to start
    b. go up something or onto the top of something
4. There was an **accident** during the car race yesterday. One car hit another, but neither driver was hurt.
    a. something bad that happens that is not intended and that causes injury or damage
    b. something that someone does in order to hurt another person
5. In order to stay **in shape**, you should eat foods that are good for you, exercise, and stay active.
    a. interesting because you like different things
    b. in good health; strong
6. One of the most **challenging** games is table tennis, which is also called Ping-Pong. Players must be strong, quick, and able to focus on the ball for long periods of time.
    a. easy to learn
    b. difficult in a way that tests your ability

Present Progressive

Tough Guy: A Race to the Limit

1 Right now, people all over the world are training for one of the most difficult races on Earth: the Tough Guy competition. Every January, more than 3,000 people take part in the Tough Guy race in the United Kingdom. **Participants** run, swim, and **climb** across a 9-mile (15-kilometer) course. But this is not a normal race. These runners have to crawl through tunnels, run across a field of stinging plants, and jump over fire. What's more, the competition takes place in the middle of winter, so often participants run in temperatures as low as 21 °F (-6 °C).

2 Diagram 1 shows an example of the Tough Guy **course**. First, participants run for 0.6 miles (1 kilometer) along a muddy road. Next, they crawl under low nets on the ground. After that, the runners jump of a high platform into a lake and swim for another 0.6 miles (1 kilometer). Then they reach the field of fire. While they are running across a field, they jump over small bonfires. Next, participants must crawl through a long tunnel. It is partly underwater. Finally, the runners run 1.2 miles (2 kilometers) through nettles (plants with sharp parts) before they reach the finish line.

3 Clearly, the competition is very dangerous, and every year there are **accidents**. Injuries like broken bones and cuts are common. The race is very hard: one-third of participants do not finish it. Runners have to be healthy and **in shape**. The organizers change the event every year and are always adding new things. This means that the competition stays exciting and **challenging**, so people go back year after year. It is also the first race like it in the world, and it is becoming more and more popular. As a result, many new participants are signing up for the race. They travel from all around the world to take part, including the U.S., Australia, and China. There is still time to sign up for next year's race. What are you waiting for?

Diagram 1

Body Language   313

Exercise 6.3 Comprehension Check

Read the text on page 313. Work with a partner. Ask and answer the questions.

1 Where does the Tough Guy competition take place? _____
2 In what month is the competition held? _____
3 What is the first part of a Tough Guy race? _____
4 What is the last part of the race? _____
5 How do the organizers keep the race exciting and challenging? _____

Exercise 6.4 Noticing the Grammar

Complete the tasks. Compare your answers with a partner's.

1 Underline all the present progressive verbs in the text.
2 In paragraph 1, when does the writer use the present progressive? What about the simple present?
3 When you write about a process, do you usually use the present progressive or the simple present for each step?

Using Line Diagrams

When writers describe a process, they explain the order of events. They show what happens first, what happens second, and so on. Before writers describe a process, they think about the events that are part of it. This helps the writer collect information for the description. Notice Diagram 1 on page 313. The order of events there can be put into a line diagram, as shown below.

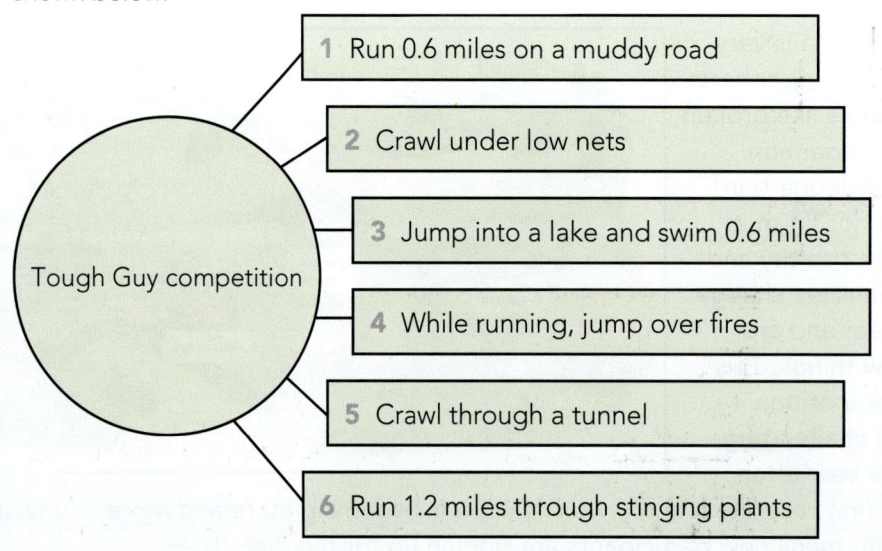

314   Unit 23 Present Progressive

Present Progressive

Exercise 6.5 Applying the Skill

Complete the line diagrams. Think about the process in each circle. Fill in each blank box with a missing step from the process.

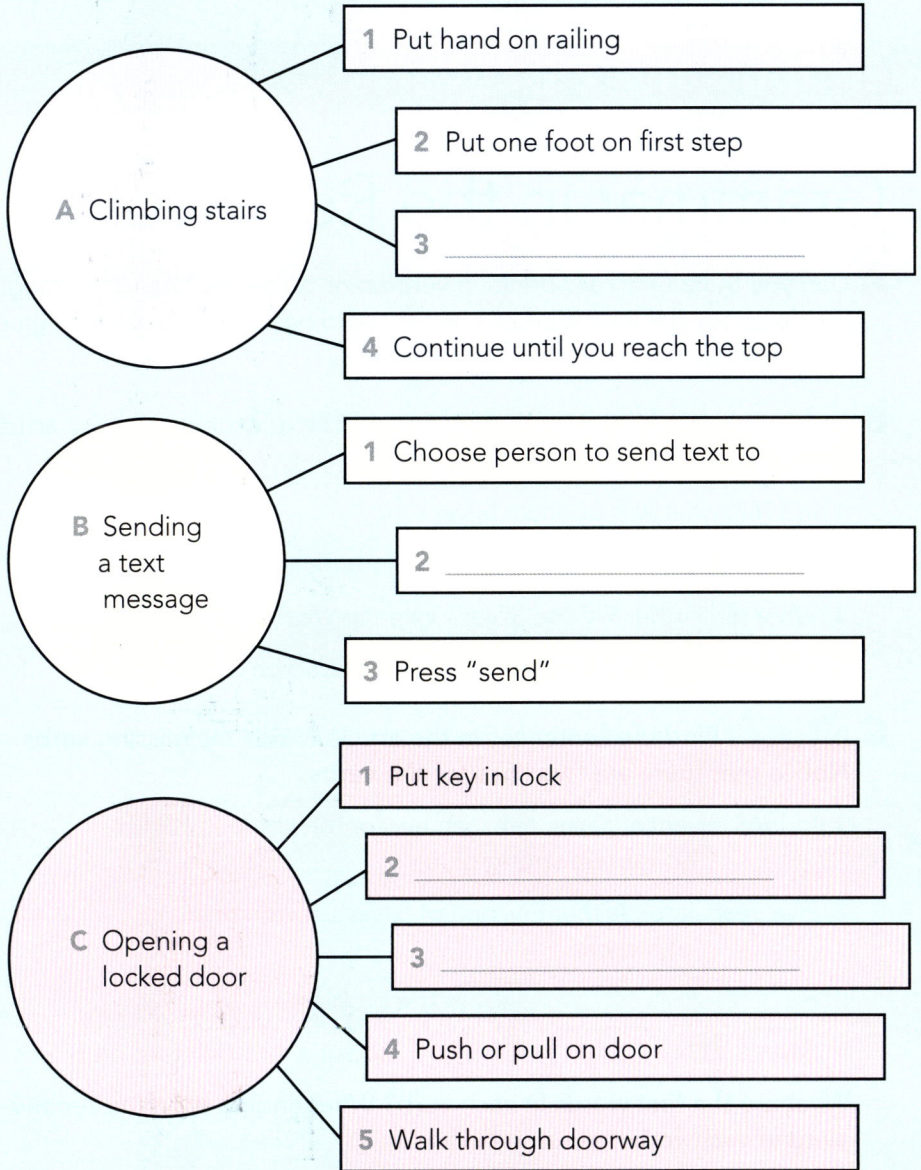

A Climbing stairs
1. Put hand on railing
2. Put one foot on first step
3. _____
4. Continue until you reach the top

B Sending a text message
1. Choose person to send text to
2. _____
3. Press "send"

C Opening a locked door
1. Put key in lock
2. _____
3. _____
4. Push or pull on door
5. Walk through doorway

My Writing

Exercise 6.6 Writing Sentences

Look at the line diagrams you completed for climbing stairs, sending a text message, and opening a locked door. Choose one of the processes. Write a complete sentence for each step in the line diagram for the process you choose.

Body Language

UNIT 24

Past Progressive and Simple Past

Inventions and Discoveries

1 Grammar in the Real World

ACADEMIC WRITING

Process paragraph

A Can you think of an accidental invention or discovery? Read the magazine article about the invention of Post-its. Who had the idea of using glue with bookmarks?

B Comprehension Check Answer the questions. Use the article to help you.

1. In 1968, what was Spencer Silver's job?
2. What did he make?
3. What did Arthur Fry use Silver's invention for?
4. What product did the company make based on Silver's and Fry's ideas?

C Notice Find the sentences in the article. Write the missing verbs. Notice that there are two lines for the verbs.

1. In 1968, Spencer Silver, a researcher for the company 3M, _____ _____ to make a strong glue.
2. Five years later, Arthur Fry, one of Silver's coworkers, _____ _____ in a choir.
3. He _____ _____ about the problem.
4. Silver and Fry _____ _____ to solve two different problems.

What are the first words in each verb? What ending is on the second word in each verb?

316

A Great Invention

In 1968, Spencer Silver, a researcher[1] for the company 3M, **was trying** to make a strong glue, but he actually invented a very weak glue. The glue stuck[2] things together, but they could separate easily. Silver showed the invention to his company's management, but they weren't interested. They didn't see a use for it.

Five years later, Arthur Fry, one of Silver's co-workers, **was singing** in a choir. The bookmarks[3] that he put in his songbook **were** always **falling** out whenever he opened the book. He **was thinking** about the problem, remembered Silver's glue, and had the idea to use it on his bookmark. The weak glue worked. Fry could stick the notes on the page and easily take them off again. He gave his co-workers samples of the notes, and they were very popular. So finally Fry's company decided to make the new product.

In 1980, Post-its were in stores nationwide. Marketing of the invention was easy. Everyone wanted to buy the small sticky notes. Today the whole world uses Post-It notes. Most people do not realize that this invention was just a lucky accident: Silver and Fry **were trying** to solve two different problems, and Fry saw the connection. Thanks to Fry, we now have a product that we can't live without!

[1]**researcher:** a person who studies a subject in order to discover new information about it
[2]**stuck:** simple past of stick
[3]**bookmark:** something you can put between pages in a book to show where you stopped reading

2 Past Progressive

Grammar Presentation

The past progressive describes things that were in progress at a specific time in the past.	Arthur Fry **was singing** in a choir. I **was studying** psychology last semester.

2.1 Statements

AFFIRMATIVE

Subject	Past of *Be*	Verb + *-ing*
I He She It	was	working.
You We They	were	

NEGATIVE

Subject	Past of *Be* + Not	Verb + *-ing*
I He She It	was not wasn't	working.
You We They	were not weren't	

2.2 Yes/No Questions — Short Answers

Past of *Be*	Subject	Verb + *-ing*
Was	I he she it	working?
Were	you we they	

AFFIRMATIVE

	Subject	Past of *Be*
Yes,	I he she it	was.
	you we they	were.

NEGATIVE

	Subject	Past of *Be* + Not
No,	I he she it	was not. wasn't.
	you we they	were not. weren't.

2.3 Information Questions

Wh- Word	Past of Be	Subject	Verb + -ing
Who	was	I / he / she / it	studying?
What	was	I / he / she / it	doing?
When	was	I / he / she / it	researching?
Where	were	you / we / they	working?
Why	were	you / we / they	experimenting?
How	were	you / we / they	feeling?

Wh- Word as Subject	Past of Be	Verb + -ing
Who	was	talking?
What	was	happening?

▶▶ Spelling Rules for Verbs Ending in -ing: See page A20.

2.4 Using Past Progressive

A Use the past progressive to talk about an event in progress at a specific time in the past.

In 2010, I **was working** in a science lab.
"**Were** you **studying** in the cafeteria at lunchtime?"
"No. I **was studying** in the library."

B Use information questions to ask about events in progress at a specific time in the past.

Why **were** the researchers **working** all night?
What **was** Lucy **wearing** at the party?
Who **were** you **talking** to this morning?

C Use the full negative forms when writing in class.

The machine **was not working**.

Use negative contractions in everyday speaking.

I **wasn't working** yesterday afternoon.

Grammar Application

Exercise 2.1 Past Progressive Statements

A Complete the sentences with the past progressive form of the verb in parentheses.

1 I _was looking_ (look) the Web the other day, and I found out some interesting information about inventions.

2 In 1968, another scientist, Spencer Silver, _____ (try) to make a strong glue, but he made a very good weak glue. Arthur Fry, a co-worker, put the glue on small pieces of paper and used the sticky papers at work. Soon the other co-workers _____ (use) the sticky papers, too. The sticky papers became Post-its.

Inventions and Discoveries **319**

3 In 1945, a scientist named Percy Spencer _____ (experiment) with microwave energy. He _____ (stand) too close to a machine when it melted a peanut candy bar in his pocket. The machine became the first microwave oven.

4 In 1930, Ruth Wakefield _____ (make) cookies for customers at her restaurant. She put small pieces of chocolate in the cookies and called them chocolate chip cookies. Soon Wakefield's customers _____ (ask) her for the cookie recipe, and it is now on bags of chocolate chips.

5 In 1853, George Crum, a chef at a New York restaurant, _____ (feel) unhappy with a customer. The customer _____ (refuse) to eat his potatoes because they were too thick. So Crum cut the potatoes into thin slices and fried them, and they became the first potato chips.

B Pair Work Ask and answer *Wh-* questions with *Who* as the subject about the inventors in A. Use the past progressive.

A Who was feeling unhappy with a customer?
B George Crum was feeling unhappy because a customer wasn't eating his food.

🌐 DATA FROM THE REAL WORLD

The past progressive is used most commonly with verbs of speaking and thinking, such as *talk, think, say, wonder,* and *ask*.

What **were** you **talking** about at breakfast?
Fry **was thinking** about bookmarks.
He **was wondering** how to keep them inside his songbook.
They **were asking** about the accident last night.

The past progressive is also used with verbs that describe everyday actions, such as *do, try, look, get, come, work, sit, walk, take, watch, read, make, drive,* and *wear*.

Silver **was trying** to invent a strong glue.
He **was working** all day Thursday, so he missed class.
Were you **watching** TV at 8 o'clock last night?
Ruth Wakefield **was making** cookies.

320 Unit 24 Past Progressive and Simple Past

Exercise 2.2 Commonly Used Verbs

Write sentences with the commonly used verbs to describe what the people were doing at 7:15 p.m. yesterday evening.

1 José *was driving home from school.*
(drive / home from school)

2 Thomas _____
(think / about his children)

3 Lorna _____
(watch / TV)

4 Gabi and Jim _____
(sit / in a restaurant)

5 Liz _____
(try / to park her car)

6 Kevin and Selena _____
(look / at some photos)

7 Peter _____
(work / at his computer)

8 Clara _____
(talk / to a friend on the phone)

Exercise 2.3 Yes/No Questions and Information Questions

A Read Joe's schedule for yesterday. Write questions about him. Use the words in parentheses with the verbs in the past progressive.

> 9:00 a.m.: in class – take notes!
> 11:30 a.m.: study English in the library
> 12:30 p.m.: have lunch at Chinese restaurant
> 1:30 p.m.: meet classmates at park to practice English
> 3:00 p.m.: work at computer store
> 7:00 p.m.: call Mom about Dad's birthday
> 11:00 p.m.: work on business project

1 (what / Joe / do / at 9:00 a.m.?) <u>What was Joe doing at 9:00 a.m.?</u>
2 (he / eat / lunch at 11:30 a.m.?) <u>Was he eating lunch at 11:30 a.m.?</u>
3 (what / he / study?) _____
4 (his friends / meet / him at 12:30 p.m. for lunch?) _____
5 (where / his classmates / meet / him?) _____
6 (what / he / do / at 3:00 p.m.?) _____
7 (what / he / do / at 7:00 p.m.?) _____
8 (who / he / talk / to last night?) _____
9 (he / work / on his project / at 11:00 p.m.?) _____

B Pair Work With a partner, practice asking and answering the questions in A. Then write and ask two more questions.

A What was Joe doing at 9:00 a.m.?
B He was taking notes in class.

A Where was Joe having lunch?
B He was having lunch at a Chinese restaurant.

C Pair Work Create your own schedules for a day last week. Do not show your partner. Ask and answer questions to find out what your partner was doing.

A Were you working in the afternoon?
B Yes, I was.

A What were you doing at 7:00 p.m.?
B I was doing my homework.

3 Time Clauses with Past Progressive and Simple Past

Grammar Presentation

A time clause tells when the main clause happened.

MAIN CLAUSE — TIME CLAUSE
He called me on his phone *while he was walking home yesterday.*

3.1 When or While + Event in Progress

A *When* refers to a particular time or period that something was in progress.

I met Joanna.
↓
——— I was living in Houston. ———→
I met Joanna *when I was living* in Houston.

B *While* means at the same time, or during the time that an event was in progress.

The phone rang three times.
↓ ↓ ↓
——— We were having dinner. ———→
The phone rang three times *while we were having dinner.*

3.2 Time Clauses with Past Progressive

Time Clause (with Past Progressive)		Main Clause (Simple Past)
When While	he was working,	he discovered the cure.

Main Clause (Simple Past)	Time Clause (with Past Progressive)	
He discovered the cure	when while	he was working.

3.3 Time Clauses with Simple Past

Time Clause (with Simple Past)	Main Clause (Past Progressive)
When he discovered the cure,	he was working.

Inventions and Discoveries   323

3.3 Time Clauses with Simple Past *(continued)*

Main Clause (Past Progressive)	Time Clause (with Simple Past)
He was working	**when he discovered the cure.**

3.4 Using Time Clauses with Past Progressive or Simple Past

A You can use a time clause with *when* or *while* and the past progressive to talk about an event that was in progress when a second event happened.

EVENT IN PROGRESS — SECOND EVENT
While Tim was thinking about the problem, he had an idea.

SECOND EVENT — EVENT IN PROGRESS
Mr. Crum invented chips **while he was working in a restaurant**.

Use the simple past for the second event in the main clause.

EVENT IN PROGRESS — SECOND EVENT
When we were sitting in the library, **the alarm went off**.

SECOND EVENT — EVENT IN PROGRESS
I met an old friend when I was walking home.

B You can also use a time clause with *when* and the simple past to talk about a second event that happened while another event was already in progress.

EVENT IN PROGRESS — SECOND EVENT
She was driving home **when she saw the accident**.

Use the past progressive for the event that was already in progress (in the main clause).

SECOND EVENT — EVENT IN PROGRESS
When my friend arrived, **I was watching TV.**

C Don't forget to use a pronoun in the second clause if the subject is the same in both clauses.

Marie was talking about her problem when **she** thought of a solution.

When **Marie** thought of a solution, **she** was talking about her problem.

D Remember that a time clause can come before or after the main clause.

MAIN CLAUSE — TIME CLAUSE
It started to rain **while we were walking in the park.**

MAIN CLAUSE — TIME CLAUSE
José was taking a test **when his cell phone rang.**

Use a comma when the time clause comes first.

TIME CLAUSE — MAIN CLAUSE
While we were walking in the park, it started to rain.

TIME CLAUSE — MAIN CLAUSE
When his phone rang, José was taking a test.

Grammar Application

Exercise 3.1 Past Progressive and Simple Past

Complete the sentences in the article. Use the past progressive or the simple past form of the verbs in parentheses.

Sometimes unexpected things happen, and someone invents or discovers something. The discovery of gravity – the force that pulls all the stars and planets to each other in the universe – is an example of this. In 1666, Isaac Newton, an English scientist, __was sitting__ (sit) (1) in his garden when an apple _____ (fall) from an apple (2) tree. Newton got the idea of gravity from that one moment.

Another story is about James Watt, who was born in 1736. Some people say that while James Watt _____ (look) at a (3) boiling tea kettle, he _____ (get) the idea for a (4) steam engine.¹

In 1799, French soldiers _____ (work) in Egypt (5) when they _____ (find) a stone with writing on it. (6) This was the famous Rosetta Stone. The stone helped people learn how to read Egyptian writing.

In 1908, while a German woman _____ (make) a (7) cup of coffee, she _____ (discover) that paper worked (8) as an excellent filter for coffee and water. She invented coffee filters.

In 1895, a German scientist _____ (experiment) (9) with electricity when he _____ (notice) that one piece (10) of equipment _____ (create) some strange green (11) light around some objects. While he _____ (work), he (12) noticed that the stripes of light – or rays – _____ (go) (13) through paper but not thicker objects, and through humans but not through bones. By 1900, scientists everywhere _____ (14) (work) with the new rays, and doctors _____ (use) X-rays (15) to take pictures of people's bones.

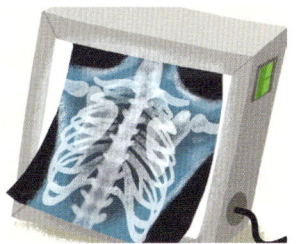

It's amazing that all these inventions and discoveries _____ (happen) by accident! (16)

¹**steam engine:** an engine that makes something move because steam goes through it

B Now listen and check your answers.

C Pair Work Ask three questions using *What was/were . . . doing?* about the events in A. Ask and answer the questions with a partner.

  A *What was the German woman doing?*
  B *She was making a cup of coffee.*

Exercise 3.2 Past Progressive and Simple Past with *When* and *While*

A Combine the ideas in the stories about unexpected events using the past progressive and simple past. Circle *when* or *while*.

Alice needed some money. She didn't know where she could get some. One day, she __was walking__ (1) (walk) down the street __when/while__ (2) she _____ (3) (find) a $100 bill. She was able to pay her phone bill and buy groceries at the supermarket.

__When/While__ (4) Eric _____ (5) (write) a paper for school, he _____ (6) (receive) an e-mail from a stranger in France with the same last name. __When/While__ (7) Eric _____ (8) (read) the e-mail and _____ (9) (learn) about the man's family history, he _____ (10) (realize) that they were cousins.

Julia and Susan went to a party. They _____ (11) (look around) to see who they knew __when/while__ (12) they _____ (13) (see) their co-worker John. They _____ (14) (smile) and _____ (15) (wave) at him, but he _____ (16) (not wave) back. The next day, __when/while__ (17) they _____ (18) (work), they _____ (19) (see) him walk into the office. He said he wasn't at the party. It was his twin brother!

B Pair Work With a partner, tell stories about unexpected events. Take turns. Use *when* and *while* with the simple past and past progressive.

  A *What were you doing when it started to rain yesterday?*
  B *I was waiting for the bus.*

4 Avoid Common Mistakes ⚠️

1. **Form the past progressive by using *was / were* + verb + *-ing*.**

   Some strange things ~~happening~~ *were* happening in the laboratory.   We were ~~study~~ *studying* in the library.

2. **With the subjects *I, he, she, it*, or a singular noun, use *was* in the past progressive.**

   The professor ~~were~~ *was* asking some questions about the experiment.

3. **With the subjects *you, we, they*, a plural noun, or a compound subject, use *were* in the past progressive.**

   The scientists ~~was~~ *were* trying to find a solution to the problem.   Diana and I ~~was~~ *were* working in the library.

4. **In information questions, use question word order after the *Wh-* word in the past progressive.**

   What ~~you were~~ *were you* doing at 5 o'clock yesterday?

Editing Task

What were you doing when . . . ? We asked some people to remember what they were doing on special days. Find and correct ten more mistakes in the questions and answers.

Person	Question	Answer
Juno (30 years old)	What ~~you were~~ *were you* doing when Barack Obama became president?	I watching TV all day.
Elsa (71 years old)	What was you doing when the first men landed on the moon?	I was listen to the radio, and I talking to a friend on the phone.
Pamela (18 years old)	What you doing at 2:00 p.m. on your birthday?	I were having lunch with some friends.
Andrea (37 years old)	What was you and your husband doing at midnight last New Year's Eve?	We dancing at a party at a friend's house.
Helen (52 years old)	What you were doing at 4:00 p.m. last 4th of July?	My family and I was having a picnic.

5 Academic Writing

Process Paragraph

Brainstorm > **Organize** > Write > Edit

In the Unit 23, you learned about the events in a process and brainstormed ideas for your writing. In this unit (24), you will use transition words to organize your writing.

Write a paragraph to describe the Sydney Triathlon.

Ordering Events in a Process

When writers describe a process, they usually write about events in the order that they happen. **Transition words** help show the order of events. Some useful transition words are *first, second, next, then,* and *after that.*

First, the participants run through mud. **Then**, they crawl under nets. **After that**, they swim in a lake.

Transition words usually come at the start of a sentence and are followed by a comma.

Exercise 5.1 Applying the Skill

Rewrite each sentence about last year's Tough Guy race. Add the transition words in parentheses, and change the verbs to the simple past. The first one is done for you as an example.

1. The participants run for 0.6 miles along a muddy road. (first)
   First, the participants ran for 0.6 miles along a muddy road.

2. They crawl under low nets on the ground. (next)

3. The runners jump off a high platform into a lake and swim for another 0.6 miles. (after that)

4. They reach the field of fire. (then)

5. While they are running across a field, they jump over small bonfires. (finally)

Describing a Process Diagram

Writers often describe processes that are shown in diagrams. They notice the parts of the diagram to see the steps in the process.

Past Progressive and Simple Past

Exercise 5.2 Applying the Skill

Look at the diagram of the Sydney Triathlon. Label the diagram with the following words: *bike route*, *bridge*, *central library*, *running route*, *swim route*, and *tunnel*. Use the key to help you.

My Writing

Exercise 5.3 Organizing Your Writing

Look at the diagram of the Sydney Triathlon again. Complete each sentence about the order of events. Use the words in the box to help you.

| bike | finish | run | start | swim |

1 First, _____

2 Next, _____

3 Then, _____

4 After that, _____

5 Finally, _____

Inventions and Discoveries 329

UNIT 25
Subject and Object Pronouns; Questions About Subjects and Objects

Fast Food or Slow Food

1 Grammar in the Real World

ACADEMIC WRITING

Process paragraph

A How many times a week do you eat dinner at home? Read the article. What do you eat when you are in a hurry?

B Comprehension Check Answer the questions. Use the article to help you.

1 What is different about American eating habits today?
2 Why are Americans cooking less at home?
3 What changes is one chef making to recipes?
4 Why is another chef visiting American towns?

C Notice Read the sentences from the article. Answer the questions about the words in bold.

1 "Nowadays, Americans are eating more unhealthy food, and **they** are getting heavier because of **it**."

   Who does *they* refer to? What does *it* refer to?

2 "For example, one chef recently wrote a new healthy-eating cookbook. **He** adapted the recipes for popular high-calorie dishes and made **them** healthier."

   Who does *he* refer to? What does *them* refer to?

3 "Another chef is visiting towns in the United States to help people think about their diets. **She** wants the people in these towns to change the way **they** eat."

   Who does *she* refer to? Who does *they* refer to?

Subject and Object Pronouns; Questions About Subjects and Objects

SHOULD YOU CHANGE THE WAY YOU EAT?

Eating habits in the United States are now different from what **they** were 40 years ago. Nowadays, Americans are eating more unhealthy food, and **they** are getting heavier because of **it**. Also, because their schedules are busy, Americans do less cooking at home, and many of **them** often eat at fast-food restaurants. The food at these restaurants can be high in fat and calories,[1] and some of **it** is made from processed,[2] or pre-cooked, ingredients.[3] This means that many Americans are eating less natural, less healthy food.

Some chefs are not happy about these new eating habits, and **they're** working to change **them**. **They** are promoting healthy food and encouraging Americans to be more careful about what **they** eat. For example, one chef recently wrote a new healthy-eating cookbook. **He** adapted the recipes[4] for popular high-calorie dishes and made **them** healthier. This means that now people can cook their favorite meals and **they** get only half the calories. Another chef is visiting towns in the United States to help people think about their diets.[5] **She** wants the people in these towns to change the way **they** eat. **She** also wants children to eat healthy food, so **she** is encouraging schools to create healthy lunch plans for **them**.

[1]**calorie:** a unit for measuring the amount of energy food provides
[2]**processed:** treated with chemicals that preserve or give food extra taste or color
[3]**ingredient:** one part of a mixture
[4]**recipe:** a set of instructions for how to prepare and cook a kind of food
[5]**diet:** the food and drink a person has every day

Fast Food or Slow Food   331

2 Subject and Object Pronouns

Grammar Presentation

Pronouns refer to nouns. There are different pronouns for subjects and objects.

Rachel usually makes lunch for *Diego*.
$\quad\quad\quad$ (= RACHEL) $\quad\quad\quad\quad\quad$ (= DIEGO)
However, yesterday *she* decided to take *him* to a restaurant.

2.1 Subject and Object Pronouns

Subject Pronouns	Object Pronouns
I	me
you	you
he	him
she	her
it	it
we	us
they	them

▶▶ Subject and Object Pronouns: See page A18.

2.2 Using Subject and Object Pronouns

A The subject in a sentence is the person or thing doing the action. Subject pronouns replace nouns that are the subject of a sentence.

$\quad\quad\quad$ SUBJECT $\quad\quad\quad\quad\quad\quad\quad\quad$ SUBJECT
$\quad\quad\quad\quad\quad\quad\quad\quad\quad\quad\quad\quad\quad\quad\quad$ PRONOUN
Our chef wrote a cookbook. *He* included many new recipes.

$\quad\quad\quad\quad\quad\quad\quad\quad\quad\quad\quad\quad\quad\quad$ SUBJECT
$\quad\quad\quad$ SUBJECT $\quad\quad\quad\quad\quad\quad\quad\quad\quad\quad$ PRONOUN
Americans cook less at home. *They* often eat at restaurants.

B The object in a sentence is the person or thing receiving the action. Object pronouns replace nouns that are the object in a sentence or the object of a prepositional phrase.

$\quad\quad\quad\quad\quad\quad\quad\quad\quad\quad\quad\quad$ OBJECT
$\quad\quad\quad\quad\quad\quad\quad$ OBJECT $\quad\quad\quad\quad\quad$ PRONOUN
I remember *James*. I met *him* in the cafeteria.

$\quad\quad\quad\quad\quad\quad\quad\quad\quad\quad\quad\quad\quad\quad\quad\quad\quad$ OBJECT
$\quad\quad\quad\quad\quad\quad\quad\quad$ OBJECT $\quad\quad\quad\quad\quad\quad\quad\quad$ PRONOUN
My sister loves *hamburgers*. My mom often makes *them*. She wants *children* to eat healthy food. She is making healthy lunch plans for *them*.

C A pronoun can refer to one or more noun phrases.

I grow *carrots and tomatoes*.

They taste good.

Subject and Object Pronouns; Questions About Subjects and Objects

2.2 Using Subject and Object Pronouns (continued)

D	When talking about yourself and another person, put yourself last. Use the correct pronoun. (SUBJECT = *I*; OBJECT = *me*)	*Eric and I* eat vegetables. Martha told *Eric and me* about the new store.
E	Use a pronoun after the noun is introduced.	*My brother* eats fast food. *He* likes fries. NOT ~~He~~ eats fast food. ~~My brother~~ likes fries.

Grammar Application

Exercise 2.1 Choosing Pronouns

A Complete the sentences with the correct subject or object pronoun for the underlined words.

1. These days, many <u>people</u> are eating better. **(They)/ Them** are choosing healthy foods.
2. For example, instead of ice cream, some people order frozen <u>yogurt</u>. **It / He** doesn't have as many calories.
3. <u>My friends and I</u> love hamburgers, but **we / us** make <u>turkey burgers</u> because **they / them** are healthier!
4. I really don't like <u>vegetables</u>, but **they / them** are good for **I / me**.
5. My friend <u>Marco</u> loves pizza. I made one for **he / him** with just a little cheese and a lot of vegetables. **He / Him** loved it!
6. <u>Marco and I</u> ate <u>vegetable pizza</u> twice last week. **It / They** tasted great and made **we / us** happy!

B Pair Work Discuss these questions with a partner.

1. What food do you like to eat?
2. What food is good for you?
3. What food isn't good for you?

A *I love to eat pasta. How about you?*
B *I love it, too, but I need to eat more vegetables.*

Fast Food or Slow Food

Exercise 2.2 Using Subject and Object Pronouns

A Complete the sentences using the correct subject pronoun or object pronoun for the underlined words. Use some of the pronouns in the chart.

Subject	I	you	he	she	it	we	they
Object	me	you	him	her	it	us	them

COLLEGE NEWS

Cobalt University Cafeteria: Now Serving . . . Vegetables!

By Yuki Tanaka

The university cafeteria is offering a new menu to give students healthy options for their meals. <u>Students</u> often eat unhealthy food. __They__ (1) don't usually have time to cook, so _____ (2) eat in either fast-food restaurants or in the cafeteria. To help _____ (3) eat healthier food, the school asked nutritionists[1] to create a healthy menu for the cafeteria. <u>Nutritionists</u> found that if _____ (4) can offer quick <u>food</u> that is both healthy and tasty, students will enjoy eating _____ (5). Nutritionists also know that <u>students</u> perform better if _____ (6) eat healthy <u>food</u> because _____ (7) gives _____ (8) energy and nutrients[2] – two things that are very important to a busy student.

I surveyed some students about the new menu yesterday. One student said, "My <u>roommates and I</u> just had <u>breakfast</u> here, and _____ (9) loved _____ (10)." Another student reported, "<u>We</u> asked for better food in the cafeteria, and the school listened to _____ (11). This is great news for everyone."

Check out the new <u>menu</u> as soon as you can! It's long, and you can order many things from _____ (12). For example, there are all kinds of salads, sandwiches, vegetarian choices, and smoothies. Students can even order sushi. _____ (13) is delicious!

[1]**nutritionist:** an expert on the subject of how the body uses food
[2]**nutrient:** something that plants, animals, and people need to grow

B Pair Work Compare your answers with a partner. Discuss any differences in the pronouns you chose.

Subject and Object Pronouns; Questions About Subjects and Objects

3 Questions About the Subject and the Object

Grammar Presentation

Subjects are the people or things that do the action in a sentence. Objects receive the action in a sentence. *Wh-* questions with *who* or *what* can ask about the subject or the object.

"**Who** made this sandwich?"
   SUBJECT
"**Rachel** made it."
"**What** did you eat?"
             OBJECT
"I ate **a salad**."

3.1 Questions and Answers About the Subject

QUESTIONS			ANSWERS			SHORT ANSWERS	
Who / What	Verb		Subject	Verb		Subject	Form of *Do*
Who	eats ate	fast food?	**My sister**	eats ate	fast food.	**My sister**	does. did.
What	makes made	the food good?	**The spices**	make made	it good.	**The spices**	do. did.

3.2 Questions and Answers About the Object

Who / What	Form of *Do*	Subject	Verb		Subject	Verb	Object
Who	does did	James	see	in the cafeteria?	**He**	sees saw	**Rachel.**
What	do did	the students	eat	for lunch?	**They**	eat ate	**tacos.**

3.3 Asking and Answering Questions About Subjects and Objects

A Use *who* to ask about people.

"**Who** ate lunch with you?" "Kevin did."
"**Who** did you take to lunch?" "I took Kevin."

B Use *what* to ask about things.

"**What** smells good?" "The food does."
"**What** did you eat for lunch?" "I ate a sandwich."

Fast Food or Slow Food   335

3.3 Asking and Answering Questions About Subjects and Objects (continued)

C	Answer questions about the subject with the subject and *do / does / did*.	"Who wants dessert?" "I **do**." "Who likes sushi?" "Carla **does**." "Who went with you?" "Su-bin **did**."
D	You can answer questions about the object with just the object.	"Who did you see in the cafeteria?" "**Carla**." "What did you eat for lunch?" "**A sandwich**."
E	Use *who* in object questions.	"**Who** did you eat with?" "I ate with my mom."
	Whom is rarely used nowadays and is very formal.	~~With whom~~ did you eat?
F	🌐 In conversation, subject questions are four times more common than object questions.	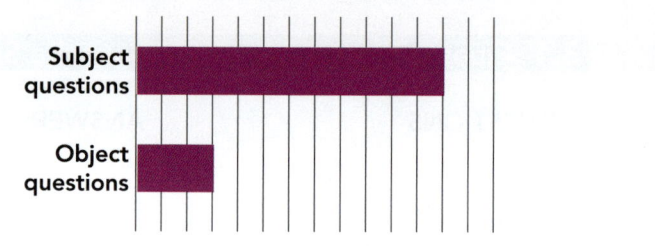

Grammar Application

Exercise 3.1 Using *Who* and *What*

A Complete the questions using *Who* or *What*.

Ana Maria is a writer for the university e-newsletter. She is curious about the eating habits of students. She interviewed several students on campus.

Ana Maria	Hi! My name is Ana Maria. __What__ did you eat for lunch today?
	(1)
Philip	I ate a garden salad.
Ana Maria	_____ did you eat with?
	(2)
Philip	I ate with my roommate here, Mike.
Ana Maria	Hi! _____ did you have for lunch?
	(3)
Mike	I had a chicken sandwich and fresh tomato soup.
Ana Maria	Thanks! Excuse me, can I ask you some questions?
	_____ usually cooks your dinner?
	(4)
Maya	My mom usually does.
Ana Maria	_____ is your favorite dish?
	(5)
Maya	It's definitely my mom's orange chicken. It's great.
Ana Maria	Thanks so much!

336 Unit 25 Subject and Object Pronouns; Questions About Subjects and Objects

Subject and Object Pronouns; Questions About Subjects and Objects

B Listen to the interviews in A. In each answer, underline the subject or object that Ana Maria's question asks about. Some questions may ask about more than one subject or object.

Ana Maria   Hi! My name is Ana Maria. What did you eat for lunch today?

Philip   I ate a <u>garden salad</u>.

Exercise 3.2 Forming Questions About Subjects and Objects

A Look at the restaurant receipts below for these students' lunches. Write questions about them. Use the underlined words in the answers to help you.

Ricardo's Lunch

BILL'S BURGER BAR

1 cola	$2.50
1 large fries	$4.25
1 double cheeseburger with tomatoes and mushrooms	$14.00
1 large chocolate milkshake	$6.99
Subtotal	$27.74
Tax	$2.13
Total	**$29.87**

Kai Lin and Clara's Lunch

The Garden Room

1 hot tea	$4.00
1 bottle of water	$4.50
2 large garden salads	$24.00
1 baked potato	$8.00
Subtotal	$40.50
Tax	$3.24
Total	**$43.74**

1. *Who ate fast food?*   <u>Ricardo</u> ate fast food.
2. _____   He ate <u>a double cheeseburger</u>.
3. _____   Kai Lin ate with <u>Clara</u>.
4. _____   He drank <u>a milkshake</u>.
5. _____   <u>Clara</u> had a baked potato.
6. _____   Kai Lin had <u>a bottle of water</u>.
7. _____   <u>Kai Lin and Clara</u> had a healthier lunch.
8. _____   <u>Ricardo</u> spent less money.

B **Pair Work** Write three more questions about the receipts. Then ask and answer the questions with a partner.

A Who drank a cola?
B Ricardo did.

Fast Food or Slow Food   **337**

C Group Work Think about your last meal. Ask four classmates about their last meals, and tell them about your meal. Then enter their information in the chart and report to the class.

A What did you have for lunch, Paulo?

B I had a chicken sandwich and some chips.

A Who did you eat with?

B I ate lunch alone.

Who	What
1 Paulo	1 chicken sandwich and chips
2	2
3	3
4	4
5	5

Paulo had a chicken sandwich and chips. He ate alone. He said his lunch was great!

4 Avoid Common Mistakes

1 Do not confuse subject and object pronouns.

My friends and ~~me~~ *I* eat together at school.

She
~~Her~~ never eats breakfast.

2 Use the correct gender in pronouns: *he / him* for males and *she / her* for females.

He
Mr. Jack eats salad for lunch. ~~She~~ is concerned about his health.

3 Use a pronoun after the noun is introduced.

Henry   *He*
~~He~~ makes a tasty vegetable pot pie. ~~Henry~~ uses sweet potato, mushrooms, carrots, and cheese.

Editing Task

Find and correct the mistakes in Nicole and Alison's blog about fast food.

Fast Food Blog

Hi! Welcome to our Fast Food Blog!

Who eats fast food? So many of ~~we~~ *us* do.

My sister and me started this blog because a lot of our friends and family members had unhealthy diets. We wanted to help they make
5   healthier choices. We also wanted to give other people information to help they make better choices about their diet.

Alison had the idea to start a blog. He told me about her idea, and I liked it. Then my
10 friend James helped Alison and I design the site. Thanks, James!

If you have questions about fast food or about healthy eating, just post your question or e-mail it to we. Alison and me read the questions every day
15 and try to answer them.

He sent us our first question. John wrote this: "Why do so many Americans eat fast food?" Well, John, some people eat it because them have very busy schedules. Other people eat it because it's affordable. But, of course, lots of people just eat fast food because them like it! We do, too! Alison and me just want to remind people that
20 TOO MUCH fast food is not a good idea!

We hope that helps.

5 Academic Writing

Process Paragraph

Brainstorm > Organize > **Write** > Edit

In Unit 24, you learned about ordering events in a process and planned a paragraph to answer the prompt below. In this unit (25), you will learn how to choose relevant information, and then you will write your paragraph.

> Write a paragraph to describe the Sydney Triathlon.

Exercise 5.1 Reviewing the Process

Look at the diagram of the Sydney Triathlon. Number the parts of the race from 1 to 5 to show the order of events.

_____ ride a bike over the bridge

_____ ride a bike through the tunnel

_____ run along the road

_____ swim in the harbor

_____ ride a bike near the central library

Key
- 1 mi (1,500 m) – swim (1 lap)
- 25 mi (40 km) – bike (3 laps)
- 6.2 mi (10 km) – run (2 laps)

Change-over point

START

FINISH

Removing Unrelated Information

Good writers are careful about choosing the most important information. They remove any information that is not related to the main idea of a paragraph or an essay. For example:

The race starts out near the Smith Tower. ~~The tower is made mostly of steel and is a popular attraction for tourists.~~ Then, the race goes along several roads in the downtown area.

The writer mentions the Smith Tower because it is related to the main idea, the race and where it goes. The second sentence is not about the race, so the writer removed it.

340 Unit 25 Subject and Object Pronouns; Questions About Subjects and Objects

Exercise 5.2 Applying the Skill

Read the writing prompt and the paragraph. Then complete the tasks.

Write a paragraph to describe how to do the high jump.

    The high jump is an Olympic sport that is practiced in many countries. Athletes competed in over 30 venues during the 2012 London Olympic Games. First, the high jumper runs toward the bar. It is important to run very fast. The high jump is the most popular sport in Russia. Second, the high jumper jumps. I was on the track-and-field team at school. The high jumper must jump from the right foot and keep their arms close to their sides. Next, the high jumper twists their body so that their back is to the bar. They must lift their head and feet and keep them high above the bar. The high jump is a really interesting sport. After that, the high jumper lands. They must be careful to land safely on the mat. Derek Drouin from Canada won the gold medal in the men's high jump at the 2016 Olympic Games in Rio, and Ruth Beitia from Spain won the gold for the women's high jump. Finally, the high jumper stands up, takes a bow, and leaves the mat.

1. Cross out the information in the paragraph that is not about the main idea. Remember that the main idea is often in the first sentence.

2. Compare your answers to a partner's. Explain your choices.

My Writing

Exercise 5.3 Writing Your Paragraph

Look again at your description of the Sydney Triathlon diagram on page 329 and your ordering of events in the process on page 340. Write a paragraph describing the triathlon. Since the same course is usually used every year, use the present tense in your paragraph. Most of your verbs will be in the simple present, but some may be in the present progressive.

Start your paragraph with a topic sentence about the overall process of the triathlon. Write supporting sentences about the triathlon in the correct order. Use transition words to show the time order.

UNIT 26

Infinitives and Gerunds

Do What You Enjoy Doing

ACADEMIC WRITING

Process paragraph

1 Grammar in the Real World

A Can a teenager change the world? Read this article from a magazine for teens. How did Tavi's interest in fashion change her life?

B Comprehension Check Match Tavi's age with the event that took place in her life.

1. Tavi started writing a blog. _____
2. She tried acting for the first time. _____
3. She decided to turn her blog into a magazine. _____

a age 11
b age 15
c age 18

C Notice Find similar sentences in the article. Complete the sentences with the verb in parentheses. Use the article to help you with the form of the verb.

1. Like most young women, Tavi enjoyed _____ (learn) about style and fashion.
2. At the age of 12, Tavi decided _____ (start) an online blog.
3. Fashion editors discovered the blog, and invited Tavi _____ (go) to fashion shows.
4. Tavi did not expect _____ (become) a celebrity.
5. Tavi tried _____ (act) a few years later.

WRITER, EDITOR, AND ACTRESS – All Before Age 20

A lot of teenagers **like to share** their pictures and opinions online. A lot of young women **like to experiment** with fashion. Tavi Gevinson **loved to do** both. She also **enjoyed shopping** for unusual clothes. Her interests in social media and fashion went beyond a free-time activity. Her interests helped her become a famous fashion blogger by the time she was only 11 years old!

Tavi began her career as a writer and editor in 2008 with her fashion blog *Style Rookie*. She **enjoyed posting pictures** of unusual outfits and writing about fashion trends. She **wanted to post online** for fun, and she **did not expect to become** famous.

Soon her blog became very popular, and people **began to read** her opinions. Editors from international fashion magazines discovered her blog. They **started to invite** Tavi to fashion shows.

At 15 Tavi **decided to change** her blog. She started a magazine for teens called *Rookie* about pop culture, fashion, and social issues. Soon it **began to get attention** and many girls wrote to Tavi about their hopes and dreams. *Rookie* **continues to publish** art and writing from celebrities, journalists, and the magazine's online readers.

At 18 Tavi **wanted to do** something different. She was interested in theater, so she got a part in a New York play. Again she was successful. Tavi **continues to act** and she continues to run her magazine. What's next? Someday she **hopes to write** a book.

2 Infinitives

Grammar Presentation

An infinitive is *to* + the base form of the verb: *to design, to play, to do, to be.* Infinitives follow some verbs.

She <u>liked</u> **to share** pictures and opinions online.
She <u>wanted</u> **to do** it for fun.

2.1 Verb + Infinitive

Subject	Verb	Infinitive	
Teenagers	like	to share	online.
Tavi	loved	to experiment	with fashion.
People	started	to read	her blog.
Tavi	wanted	to do	something different.
She	continues	to write and act.	

2.2 Using Infinitives

A You can use an infinitive after these verbs: *want, need, like, love, hate, prefer.*

Tavi **wanted to start** a magazine.
She **needed to learn** about style.
Young people **like to share** pictures online.
Tavi **loves to write** articles.
Some people **hate to post** online.
I **prefer to take** photographs.

B You can use an infinitive after these verbs: *plan, decide, expect, hope.*

How does she **plan to develop** her magazine?
She **decided to act** in plays.
She never **expected to become** famous.
She **hopes to help** teenagers.

C You can use an infinitive after these verbs: *begin, start, continue.*

She **began to get** letters from young women.
People **started to invite** Tavi to fashion shows.
Her business **continues to grow**.

Infinitives and Gerunds

2.2 Using Infinitives (continued)

D You can use an infinitive after these verbs: *learn, refuse, try.*

She **learned to create** layouts.
She **refused to sell** her business.
Someone **tried to buy** her company in 2006.

▶▶ Verbs + Gerunds and Infinitives: See page A26.

2.3 Using Infinitives with *Would Like*

A *Would like* is a polite way to say *want*.

Tavi **would like to write** a book someday.
(= She wants to . . .)

Use an infinitive after *would like*.

They **would like to design** a website.

B People usually use *I'd like, she'd like,* or *they'd like* in speaking.

I'd like to learn more about business, too.

C Notice the difference between *I'd like to* and *I like to*.

I'd like to play chess online. (Person doesn't play yet.)
Sometimes **I like to play** chess online. (Person plays sometimes.)

D To ask someone if they would like to do something, say or write, "Would you like + infinitive . . . ?"

"**Would you like to read** more about Tavi?"
"Yes, I'd like to know more."

Grammar Application

Exercise 2.1 Infinitives

A It's the first day of computer class, and Professor Sullivan asked how his students and their friends use technology. Complete the sentences with infinitives from the boxes.

| buy | chat | ~~check~~ | reply | spend | write |

Jaime I like **to check** my e-mail before class.
(1)

Ana My friend Paulo refuses _____ clothes in stores. He only shops online.
(2)

Rosa My friends and I don't like _____ to e-mail. We prefer _____ on social networking sites.
(3)
(4)

Clarissa I love _____ time on the Internet.
(5)

Alejandro I recently started _____ a blog.
(6)

Do What You Enjoy Doing 345

do	miss	send	explore	watch

Sam I love _____(7)_____ text messages to friends.

Rafael I watch TV on my cell phone on the bus. I don't want _____(8)_____ my favorite shows. I can watch them online anytime.

Sun-mi I like _____(9)_____ the Web. I bookmark all my favorite sites.

Susan I try _____(10)_____ the latest videos on YouTube when I have time.

Hiroshi I like _____(11)_____ everything my classmates said. I'm on my computer 24/7!

B Over to You Make the sentences in A true for you. Then compare with a partner.

A *I like to check my e-mail before class. How about you?*
B *Well, I like to check my e-mail in the evenings.*

Exercise 2.2 Pronunciation Focus: Saying *To: Want To, Would Like To*

In natural speech, people say *to* quickly. It can sound like /tə/ or /tə/.	*Children like to play on computers.* *She wanted to share her pictures.*
Want to often sounds like "wanna."	**CONVERSATION** *What do you want to do?* *Do you want to go?*
Do not use "wanna" in writing and formal speaking.	**FORMAL SPEAKING** *In this presentation, I want to talk about three problems.*
People say '*d* softly in *I'd like to*.	*I'd like to join that new social networking site.*

A Listen and repeat the sentences in the chart above.

B Listen to the conversation. Check (✓) the topics they talk about.

☐ careers ☐ family
☐ computers ☐ friends
☐ hobbies ☐ teaching
☐ school ☐ working with children

Infinitives and Gerunds

C Complete the conversation with the verbs + infinitives from the box. Then listen to the conversation and check your answers.

| 'd like to be | hope to have | like to work | need to stay | want to have |
| 'd like to work | like to spend | need to do | ~~want to do~~ | want to teach |

Vic What do you _want to do_ (1) as a career?

Bryan I _____ (2) a teacher. You know, I really _____ (3) elementary school. I _____ (4) with children. How about you?

Vic Well, I _____ (5) my own business one day.

Bryan Really? So, what kind of business do you _____ (6)?

Vic Well, I _____ (7) with computers somehow. Computers are my hobby right now. I actually _____ (8) time in front of a screen.

Bryan So, how do you do that? I mean, what do you _____ (9)?

Vic I guess I _____ (10) in college another year and develop my computer skills.

D Pair Work With a partner, talk about what you would like to do or want to do on the Internet this week. Use these verbs: *chat, download, listen to, look for, read, reply, send, watch, write.* Say *to* quickly.

3 Gerunds

Grammar Presentation

A gerund is the base form of the verb + *-ing*: *going, watching, working.*

Gerunds follow some verbs.

She enjoyed **writing** about fashion.
She keeps **working** her magazine.

3.1 Verb + Gerund

Subject	Verb	Gerund	
I	stopped	taking	a web design course.
They	finished	reading	the new blog posts.
Tavi	enjoyed	shopping	with her friends.
She	continues	writing	for the magazine.

Do What You Enjoy Doing 347

3.2 Using Gerunds

A You can use a gerund after these verbs: *enjoy, stop, avoid, miss, finish, keep, imagine.*

Tavi **enjoyed working** with teenagers.
She **stopped going** to school.
Sal **avoided taking** computer classes because he was afraid of computers!
I **miss listening** to music on my MP3 player.
They **finished working** on the new design yesterday.
She **kept developing** her website every day.
Can you **imagine being** famous at 15?

B Don't confuse the present progressive with verb + gerund. The present progressive uses the verb *be* + base form of verb + *-ing*.

VERB + GERUND
She **enjoys developing** the website.

PRESENT PROGRESSIVE
She **is developing** a website right now.

3.3 Verbs + Gerund or Infinitive

A You can use either a gerund or an infinitive after these verbs: *like, love, hate, prefer, begin, continue, start.*

The meaning is exactly the same.

She **started to play** with web designs.
She **started playing** with web designs.

 Verbs + Gerunds and Infinitives: See page A26.

DATA FROM THE REAL WORLD

You can use some verbs with gerunds or infinitives. Research shows that some verbs use gerunds more often and some verbs use infinitives more often.

People use an infinitive more often with *like, love, hate, prefer,* and *continue.*

People use a gerund more with *start*. They use an infinitive or a gerund equally with *begin.*

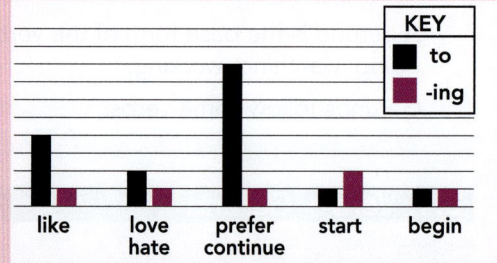

Grammar Application

Exercise 3.1 Gerunds

A Complete the questions with gerunds. Use the verbs in the box. Sometimes more than one answer is correct.

| do | e-mail | learn | play | read | ~~use~~ | visit | write |

Chad is writing an essay on students and their computer use. He created this online survey for students around campus to complete. He hopes to get some useful information.

My Own Survey

☐ 1 When did you start _using_ a computer?
☐ 2 Do you enjoy _____ new computer programs?
☐ 3 Do you like _____ games online?
☐ 4 Do you like _____ social media?
☐ 5 Do you enjoy _____ your friends?
☐ 6 Do you prefer _____ the news online or in a newspaper?
☐ 7 Do you always back up your files when you finish _____ a report or an essay?
☐ 8 What do you dislike _____ on your computer?

B Pair Work With a partner, ask and answer the questions from Chad's survey. You can add extra information.

A When did you start using the software?
B Only about two years ago.

A What did you start using it for?
B I needed to write papers for school.

Exercise 3.2 Gerunds or Infinitives

A Circle the correct form of the verbs in this article. Sometimes both are correct.

Sarah Amari never expected (**to make**)/ making money from her hobby, but now she runs a successful business. Sarah always enjoyed **to take / taking** photographs. She also liked **to edit / editing** them on her computer. She continued **to work / working** on her photographs until she liked the result. She never expected **to give / giving** them to people. Then one day a friend said she wanted **to use / using** one of Sarah's photographs. She planned **to put / putting** it on a birthday card. This gave Sarah an idea. She decided **to make / making** greeting cards with her photographs. She learned **to design / designing** her own website, and then she started **to sell / selling** her cards online. She kept **to add / adding** new cards for different holidays and celebrations. The business continues **to grow / growing**. Sarah is doing something she loves.

B Complete the sentences with a gerund or an infinitive. Sometimes both are possible.

Monica and Jenna are new community college friends and are getting to know each other.

Monica Jenna, how do you stay in touch with your friends? Do you like _to text_ (text) them?
(1)

Jenna Not really. I prefer _____ (chat) on a social
(2)
networking site. I like _____ (read) their news
(3)
and I enjoy _____ (check) out all their photos.
(4)

Monica I like that, too. I also enjoy _____ (read) my
(5)
friends' updates on my phone. I have a great cell phone plan, so I can text as much as I want.

Jenna Cool. But can you imagine _____ (live) without computers?
(6)

Monica No! I love the Internet, too. I miss _____ (check) messages when
(7)
I'm in class or at work.

Jenna Hey, I hear there's a new social networking site called *Hands Around the World*. Do you want _____ (join) it?
(8)

Monica Not really. I can't continue _____ (check) all those sites.
(9)
I have too many friends online already.

Jenna I do, too. But I love _____ (meet) new people. There's a big world
(10)
out there, and you never know what interesting people you can meet.

Monica Be careful, Jenna. Don't start _____ (give) people too much
(11)
information about yourself.

Jenna Don't worry. I avoid _____ (say) too much about myself online.
(12)

Monica Good. You have to be careful these days. Let's meet again after class so we can start _____ (study).
(13)

Jenna OK. See you then.

C Pair Work Ask and answer these questions with a partner.
1 What Internet sites do you like visiting?
2 What social media do you prefer to use? Why?
3 Do you enjoy texting? How often do you text?
4 Do you like meeting new friends online?

Infinitives and Gerunds

Exercise 3.3 Vocabulary Focus: *Go + Gerund*

You can use *go* + a gerund for some sports and leisure activities.	I **go dancing** every weekend. I **went dancing** last week. I would like to **go swimming** soon.

go bowling	go fishing	go running	go skating
go camping	go hiking	go shopping	go skiing
go dancing	go jogging	~~go sightseeing~~	go swimming

Pair Work Complete the questions with the verbs + gerunds from the box above. (You do not need to use all the verbs + gerunds above.) Then ask and answer the questions with a partner. Make the questions true for you.

1 Do you usually _go sightseeing_ on vacation?
2 Do you and your friends ever _____?
3 Do you like to _____ on the weekend?
4 How often do you and your friends _____?
5 Did your family _____ last year?
6 Do you or your friends _____ every week?
7 Would you like to _____ with your friends or family?
8 Would you like to _____?

4 Avoid Common Mistakes

1 **Don't use a base form when you need an infinitive or gerund.**

Eliza hopes ^to finish college soon.　　　　I enjoyed ~~meet~~ meeting you.

2 **Learn which verbs take an infinitive.**

I want ~~having~~ to take my own business.　　Joe needs ~~taking~~ to have one more computer class.

3 **Learn which verbs take a gerund.**

I enjoyed ~~to learn~~ learning about website design.　　Ashley keeps ~~to work~~ working hard on her business.

4 ***I would like to / I'd like to* means "I want to do this." *I like to* means "I do this now and I enjoy it."**

~~I like to~~ I'd like to go to college next year.

5 **In writing, use *want to*. Never write *wanna*.**

I ~~wanna~~ want to work in the summer.

Editing Task

Find and correct six more mistakes in this student's e-mail to her professor.

To: Professor Carter
Subject: Marketing Classes

Dear Professor Carter,

I enjoyed ~~to go~~ *going* to your class last week. I plan getting a job in marketing when I graduate, so I really enjoy to listen to your lecture. I like to come to your class on Thursdays next semester because I can't attend your Monday class. I hope get a job on Monday nights, but I don't wanna miss any classes. I also like to attend your marketing and technology class next semester. May I come and talk to you about this?

Thank you,

Grace Sanchez

5 Academic Writing

Process Paragraph

Brainstorm > Organize > Write > **Edit**

In Unit 25, you learned about removing unrelated information and then wrote a paragraph to answer the prompt below. In this unit (26), you will review, revise, and edit your process paragraph.

> *Write a paragraph to describe the Sydney Triathlon.*

My Writing

Using Gerunds to Add Information

Writers often use **gerunds** to add information or opinions about the steps in a process.

Look at the sentence pairs about two Olympic running events. The first sentence introduces a step in the event. The second sentence adds the writer's opinion about that step.

The 100-meter race **starts** with a gun shot. **Starting** fast is very important for a good race.

The marathon usually **finishes** inside a stadium. **Finishing** in front of thousands of people is a dream for most runners.

In both examples, the gerund is the subject of the second sentence.

Exercise 5.1 Applying the Skill

Look at your paragraph. Use a gerund to add information or an opinion about at least one part of the Sydney Triathlon. Make sure the information or opinion is relevant to the paragraph.

Exercise 5.2 Revising Your Ideas

1. Work with a partner. Use the questions below to give feedback on the ideas in your partner's paragraph.

   - Which of your partner's ideas seem strongest to you?
   - Which of your partner's ideas need to be explained more clearly?
   - What could your partner add or remove to make the ideas easier to understand?

2. Make any necessary changes to your paragraph.

Exercise 5.3 Editing Your Writing

Use the checklist to review and edit your paragraph.

Did you write about the general process of the Sydney Triathlon?	
Did you correctly identify the events in the process?	
Did you put the events in the correct order?	
Did you use transition words to show the order of the events clearly?	
Did you remove any unrelated information?	
Did you use the correct verb forms?	
Did you use subject and object pronouns correctly?	
Did you use gerunds to add information or opinions about the steps in a process?	

Exercise 5.4 Writing Your Final Draft

Apply the feedback and edits from Exercises 5.2 and 5.3 to write the final draft of your paragraph.

UNIT 27
Future with *Be Going To*, Present Progressive, and *Will*
The Years Ahead

ACADEMIC WRITING

Opinion paragraph

1 Grammar in the Real World

A What are your plans after graduation? Read this article from a college newsletter. Are any of these students doing something you would like to do?

B Comprehension Check Answer the questions. Use the newsletter to help you.

1. What are three different things the students at Greenlough College plan to do after graduation?
2. What is one reason Sarah Woodley is going to Chile to teach English?
3. What does the Teach for America program do?
4. How did José Marquez get his new job?

C Notice Read the sentences. Look at the underlined verb in each sentence. Is the sentence about something now or in the future? Check (✓) the correct box.

	Now	Future
1. Sarah Woodley <u>is moving</u> to Chile to teach English.	☐	☐
2. George Guzmán <u>is going to</u> take a special course.	☐	☐
3. I <u>will be</u> nervous teaching kids for the first time.	☐	☐

Future with *Be Going To*, Present Progressive, and *Will*

What's Next?

Every June, thousands of students graduate from college. What are these new graduates' plans and hopes for their future? Several graduates recently shared their plans with us.

Sarah Woodley, who is getting a degree in English, **is moving** to
5 Chile to teach English. "I really want to experience living in a different culture. I'**m going to enjoy** learning Spanish while I teach English. I'm also **going to enjoy** helping people!"

Tara Stout **is joining** the Teach for America program. It's a program that places new college graduates in city schools across the country to
10 teach for two years. Tara says, "I know I **will be** nervous teaching kids for the first time, but teaching is my dream. This is a perfect way to begin!"

José Marquez **is graduating** with an associate's degree in graphic design.[1] "I used the career center here at Greenlough, and I found a job at an advertising company as a junior designer. I'**m starting** right after
15 graduation. I **will certainly put** all of my training in this field to good use! I'm expecting terrific results."

Finally, George Guzmán, also an English major, **is going to take** a special course in publishing[2] this summer. "I really want to become an editor.[3] Meeting people in publishing **will help** a lot. I'm sure I'**ll find** a
20 good job."

We are so excited for all of these graduates and their classmates. Congratulations and good luck, graduates!

[1]**graphic design:** using pictures and diagrams, especially made by a computer, to make advertisements, posters, logos, etc.
[2]**publishing:** the business of making books, magazines, and newspapers
[3]**editor:** a person who corrects and makes changes to texts such as books and magazines

2 Future with *Be Going To* or Present Progressive

Grammar Presentation

We can talk about the future using *be going to* or the present progressive.	*Sarah **is going to enjoy** learning Spanish.* *José **is starting** his new job right after graduation.*

2.1 Statements with *Be Going To*

AFFIRMATIVE

Subject	Be	Going To	Base Form of Verb	
I	am	going to	get	a job.
You / We / They	are			
He / She / It	is			

NEGATIVE

Subject	Be + Not	Going To	Base Form of Verb	
I	am not	going to	get	a job.
You / We / They	are not			
He / She / It	is not			

2.2 Yes/No Questions with *Be Going To*

Be	Subject	Going To	Base Form of Verb	
Am	I	going to	get	a job?
Are	you / we / they			
Is	he / she / it			

▸ Short Answers with *Be Going To*: See page A13.

2.3 Information Questions with *Be Going To*

Wh- Word	Be	Subject	Going To	Base Form of Verb	
Who	am	I	going to	interview	tomorrow?
What	are	you / we / they		do	after graduation?
When				leave	for New York?
Where				work	after college?
Why	is	he / she / it		move	to Canada?
How				pay	his loans?

3.4 Using *Will* to Talk About the Future (*continued*)

Wh- Word as Subject	*Be*	*Going To*	Base Form of Verb	
Who	is	going to	get	a job after college?
What			happen	after school?

2.4 Statements with Present Progressive

AFFIRMATIVE

Subject	*Be*	Verb + *-ing*	
I	am	moving	next week.
You / We / They	are		
He / She / It	is		

NEGATIVE

Subject	*Be* + *Not*	Verb + *-ing*	
I	am not	moving	next week.
You / We / They	are not		
He / She / It	is not		

▶▶ Spelling Rules for Verbs Ending in *-ing*: See page A20.
▶▶ Present Progressive (Contractions): See page A8.

2.5 *Yes / No* Questions with Present Progressive

Be	Subject	Verb + *-ing*	
Am	I	moving	tomorrow?
Are	you / we / they		
Is	he / she / it		

Short Answers	
Yes, you **are**.	No, you**'re** not.
Yes, we **are**.	No, we**'re** not.
Yes, they **are**.	No, they**'re** not.
Yes, he / she / it **is**.	No, he**'s** / she**'s** / it**'s** not.

2.6 Information Questions with Present Progressive

Wh- Word	*Be*	Subject	Verb + *-ing*	
Who	am	I	**interviewing**	tomorrow?
What	are	you / we / they	**doing**	after graduation?
When			**leaving**	for New York?
Where			**working**	after college?
Why	is	he / she / it	**moving**	to Canada?
How			**paying**	his loans?

Wh- Word as Subject	*Be*	Verb + *-ing*	
Who	is	**getting**	a job after college?
What		**happening**	after school?

2.7 Using *Be Going To* and Present Progressive

A	Use *be going to* when you talk about plans or intentions for the future.	She**'s going to** apply for a job in a software company. (intention)
B	Use the present progressive for arrangements already made for the near future.	She**'s applying** for a job in a software company tomorrow. (arrangement already made)
C	Use *be going to* when you feel certain about something in the future based on evidence in the present.	The sky is very dark. It**'s going to** rain. I love my classmates. I**'m going to** miss them.
D	Use full forms when writing in class.	They **are graduating** next week.
E	Use contracted forms in everyday speaking and informal writing.	I**'m going to** rewrite my résumé.

Grammar Application

Exercise 2.1 *Be Going To*

A A group of college students is talking about summer plans. Complete the conversation with *be going to* + the verb in parentheses. Use contractions when possible.

Laurie I **'m going to travel** (travel) around Europe with my backpack for the summer!
(1)

Daniela Great! My sister and I _____ (join) a volunteer group to help city kids. What about you, Luke?
(2)

Luke I _____ (look) for a job right away.
(3)

Imelda Laurie, you _____ (do) the same thing as me! I _____ (go) to Europe, too.
(4)
(5)

Matthew It sounds like all of you _____ (do) some fun things. Not me. I _____ (work) at the bakery all summer. How about you, Fiona?
(6)
(7)

360 Unit 27 Future with *Be Going To*, Present Progressive, and *Will*

Future with *Be Going To*, Present Progressive, and *Will*

Fiona My mother _____ (be) here from Ireland
(8)
next month. She _____ (take) me to San
(9)
Francisco! I can't wait.

Ruth Hey, maybe we can see you in San Francisco,
Fiona. My friend Anna and I _____ (rent)
(10)
a camper and drive across the United States.

Yolanda I wish I could join you! I _____ (not go)
(11)
anywhere! I _____ (stay) home and relax!
(12)
It all sounds great!

B Pair Work Write information questions about the friends in A. Then ask a partner for the answers. Write the answers.

A *Where's Laurie going to travel this summer?*   B *She's going to go to Europe.*

1 _____   _____

2 _____   _____

3 _____   _____

Exercise 2.2 Future Use of Present Progressive

A Complete the sentences using the present progressive form of the verbs.

Ruth and Anna are in Arizona. Fiona is in New York waiting for her mother to arrive. Ruth and Fiona are texting each other. They want to meet up in San Francisco.

Ruth How are you? **Is** your mom **coming** (come) today?
(1)   (1)

Fiona I'm fine. She _____ (arrive) this evening.
(2)

Ruth We're in Arizona. We _____ (go) to the Grand
(3)
Canyon tomorrow. The weather is going to be beautiful,
so we _____ (meet) the tour group at 7:00 a.m.
(4)

The Years Ahead   **361**

Fiona Have a great time! Mom and I _____(5)_____ (leave) for San Francisco on Friday. When _____(6)_____ you _____(6)_____ (get) there?

Ruth Probably by Saturday afternoon. Where _____(7)_____ you _____(7)_____ (stay)?

Fiona At the Golden Gate Bridge Hotel. Call us when you arrive. We _____(8)_____ (go) to the aquarium early on Sunday. I hope you can join us.

B Pair Work Ask *Yes/No* and information questions to find out your partner's plans for the next few weeks. Use the time expressions in the box. Use the present progressive in your questions.

| at (5:00 p.m.) | at lunchtime | next (Monday) | this weekend | tomorrow | tonight |

A Are you staying in town this weekend?
B No, I'm going to New Jersey.

A What are you doing tonight?
B I'm playing basketball with some friends.

Exercise 2.3 *Be Going To* or Present Progressive

A Listen to the speech and complete the sentences with *be going to* or the present progressive form of the verb in parentheses.

Welcome, students, and thank you for coming today!

As you know, we're all here because of your efforts to help Redview Community College become a better place of learning! With your help, we now have enough money to begin improvements.

First, we **'re replacing** (replace) all the old computers in the library with new ones.
(1)
The technician _____(2)_____ (come) in on Monday to begin work. The librarian _____(3)_____ (order) new reference materials. They _____(4)_____ (be) here by next semester.

362 Unit 27 Future with *Be Going To*, Present Progressive, and *Will*

We _____ (expand) our recycling program. I _____ (meet) with some people from the environmental studies program this afternoon to finalize the details.

The biggest news is that we _____ (build) a new student center. It _____ (have) a food court, a large bookstore, and conference rooms for student groups to meet in. We think that the builders _____ (start) next week. Unfortunately, it _____ (not be) ready until next year.

I hope you're looking forward to the great new services on campus! Thank you, once again, for all of your help!

B Pair Work Look at the speech again with a partner. Discuss which items in the speech are (a) plans or intentions for the future, or (b) definite plans already made for the near future.

A *I think that replacing the old computers is a definite plan.*
B *I agree. It says, "The technician is coming on Monday." That's also definite.*

C Group Work Write three information questions about the speech. Use present progressive and *be going to* + verb. Ask your group. Write the answers.

A *What is the librarian ordering for the library?*   B *She's ordering new reference materials.*

1 _____
2 _____
3 _____

3 Future with *Will*

Grammar Presentation

| We can use *will* to talk about facts in the future or to make predictions. | I **will be** 25 next year.
 The economy **will grow** next year. |

3.1 Statements

AFFIRMATIVE

Subject	Will	Base Form of Verb	
I You We They He / She / It	will 'll	have	a healthy life.

NEGATIVE

Subject	Will + Not	Base Form of Verb	
I You We They He / She / It	will not won't	have	a healthy life.

3.2 Yes/No Questions

Will	Subject	Base Form of Verb	
Will	I / you / we / they / he / she / it	have	a healthy life?

Short Answers

Yes, I / Yes, you / Yes, we / Yes, they / Yes, he / she / it	will.	No, I / No, you / No, we / No, they / No, he / she / it	won't.

3.3 Information Questions

Wh- Word	Will	Subject	Base Form of Verb	
Who		I / you / we / they / he / she / it	meet	at the interview tomorrow?
What			do	in your training program?
When	will		return	your documents?
Where			find	information about careers?
Why			travel	to South America?
How			build	new apartments?

3.4 Using *Will* to Talk About the Future

A	Use *will* for predictions and expectations about the future.	The economy **will grow** next year.
B	Use *will* for things that are certain in the future. You could also use *be going to*, but *will* is more common in academic writing.	Next year **will be** the city's 150th anniversary. Next year **is going to be** the city's 150th anniversary.
C	Use *will* for an immediate decision about a future action, often with *I'll* or *we'll*.	(to a server in a restaurant) **I'll have** the chicken salad, please. I have to go. **I'll call** you this evening. Bye.
D	Do not use *will* for arrangements already made in the near future. Use the present progressive.	I'm sorry, I'm busy this evening. **I'm meeting** Andrea. NOT I'll meet Andrea.
E	Do not use *will* for plans and intentions. Use *be going to*.	**I'm going to** buy a new laptop, so I'm looking at prices on the Web. NOT I'll buy a new laptop.

3.4 Using *Will* to Talk About the Future (*continued*)

F We often use *I think, I suppose,* and *I guess* before statements with *will*. *I guess* is informal.

I think it **will cost** about $250.
I guess it **won't happen** until next year.

G Use full forms when writing in class.

The building **will not be** ready until 2028.

H Use contracted forms in everyday speaking and informal writing.

She**'ll be** 28 on her next birthday.

Grammar Application

Exercise 3.1 *Will* and *Will Not* for Predictions

A Complete the sentences about life in 2030 using *will* or *will not* and the verb in parentheses.

Science Tomorrow
By Scott Lupine

One of my favorite things to do is to think about how life will be in the future. Here are some of my ideas about a "green" future in the year 2030.

1 Cars and trucks __will run__ (run) on clean hydrogen[1] power.
2 All used products _____ (be) recycled.
3 People _____ (make) energy in their homes.
4 People _____ (grow) their own fruit and vegetables.
5 We _____ (not use) oil for energy.
6 We _____ (store) body heat to warm a building.
7 We _____ (get) all our power from the sun, wind, and water.
8 We _____ (change) garbage into energy.
9 We _____ (not pay) high prices for alternative energy.[2]

[1]**hydrogen:** a very light gas that is one of the chemical elements
[2]**alternative energy:** energy from a natural source, like wind, water, and the sun, that doesn't hurt the environment

B Over to You How many of the predictions in A do you think will be true? If you think the statements will *not* be true, change them. Explain your answers.

I think we will continue to use oil. There will still be some in the world.

Exercise 3.2 Be Going To and Will

A Write sentences with *be going to* or *will*. In one sentence, either one is possible.

Mia — I / move to a new apartment. (going to)
1. *I'm going to move to a new apartment.*

Debra — When / that be? (will)
2. _____

Mia — Next week. The landlady / give me the key soon. (going to)
3. _____

Debra — I / help you move. (will)
4. _____

Mia — Great. I / need all the help I can get. (will / be going to)
5. _____

Debra — Then I think I / call Roberto and Ivan to help you, too. (will)
6. _____

Mia — That / make it much easier for me. Thanks. (will)
7. _____

Debra — Let's celebrate, then. You / love having your own place! (going to)
8. _____

B Over to You Moving is a big change in life. Are you going to make any changes in the near future? Write sentences about the change. Then tell a partner about it.

I'm going to quit my job soon. Then I'll look for another one.

Exercise 3.3 Pronunciation Focus: Information Questions with Will

When people speak quickly and informally, they often use the contraction *'ll* instead of *will* after a *Wh-* word.	**Who'll** turn garbage into energy? **What'll** we do without oil? **How'll** we use body heat to warm a building? **When'll** we have cleaner cars and trucks?

Listen and repeat the questions in the chart above.

4 Avoid Common Mistakes

1 Use the present progressive for arrangements already made for the near future. Do not use *will*.

                             is meeting
Trudy is busy this evening. She ~~will meet~~ Alex.

2 Use *be going to* for plans and intentions. Do not use *will*.

am going to
I ~~will~~ apply to graduate school. Can you give me any advice?

3 The form in *be going to* statements is *am / is / are* and the *-ing* form of the verb *go*.

  is
She ˄ going to do volunteer work.

4 Use *will*, not the simple present, for predictions.

                         will
Many more countries ˄ have a female president in the next 10 years.

              will become
The earth ~~becomes~~ warmer over the next 30 years.

5 Use question word order in information questions about the object.

       are you
What ~~you are~~ going to do during the vacation?

Editing Task

Find and correct eight more mistakes in this e-mail.

Hi Nuala,

  am meeting
I ~~will meet~~ with a career adviser next week, and I going to discuss my future. What can I tell him? My dream is to work in television or the movies. I think I going to apply to a media studies program. I going to take a special course or something. I going to talk to some people who know about careers in TV soon. I think they give me some good advice.

Can we talk about this? What you are doing on Monday? I go away on the weekend, but I be back Monday morning. I'll call you then.

Thanks,

Fandi

5 Academic Writing

Opinion Paragraph

Brainstorm > Organize > Write > Edit

In this writing cycle (Units 27–30), you are going to answer the prompt below. In this unit (27), you will read about the advantages and disadvantages of video games and then brainstorm ideas for your writing.

"The Internet wastes our time. It does not help us do more work." Do you agree or disagree?

Exercise 5.1 Preparing to Write

Ask and answer questions with a partner.

1. How do you use the Internet? For schoolwork? For entertainment? For something else?
2. Do you think you use the Internet more than most people do? Less? About the same? Explain.
3. Some people say their lives are much easier because of the Internet. Do you agree?
4. Some people say that spending a lot of time on the Internet has had bad effects on their lives. What do you think those effects could be?

Exercise 5.2 Focusing on Vocabulary

Read the definitions. Complete the sentences with the correct form of the words in bold.

affect (v) to influence someone or something; to cause change

creative (adj) good at thinking of new ideas or creating new and unusual things

download (v) to copy computer programs, music, or other information electronically from the Internet to your computer

educational (adj) providing education, or relating to education

imagination (n) the part of your mind that creates ideas or pictures of things that are not real or that you have not seen

improve (v) to get better or to make something better

interactive (adj) allowing the user to exchange information with a system or computer program

Future with *Be Going To*, Present Progressive, and *Will*

1. There are a lot of apps you can _____ onto your phone to help you learn a new language.

2. I like to watch _____ videos so I can learn something new. I just watched one about the history of airplanes.

3. The children's museum has a/an _____ exhibit. Kids can feed and touch unusual animals there.

4. Gabriela took a class to _____ her computer skills. Now she can type faster and find information on the Internet more easily.

5. Reading, telling stories, and having new adventures can help kids to develop their _____.

6. Art students are very _____. In my program, they use new software to make some really interesting and beautiful designs.

7. Spending too much time on your smartphone may _____ your health in negative ways. It can hurt your eyes and give you a headache.

Video Games: **Benefits** and **Dangers**

1. Around the world, people are spending more and more free time playing video games. In the U.S., 72% of teens play video games regularly, and children as young as five play an average of 42 minutes per day. It is likely that video games are going to become an even more important part of our lives in the future. This information tells us that the benefits and dangers of video games must be carefully considered.

2. For many people, video games are fun and **educational**. They have interesting art and exciting stories. Video games make you think in a **creative** way, and you have to move your hands and eyes quickly. This can **improve** the way a young person's brain works. Teachers are using video games in classrooms to help their students learn. Video games also make people use their **imagination** by drawing, telling stories, and building things. Video games are going to be even more creative and **interactive** in the future!

3. However, a recent study suggests that video games can also be bad for us. Many games are free, which means that young people might **download** violent or scary games. This can **affect** children negatively, and some of the children may become more violent after playing games. In addition, many people play games for hours every day and do not know when to stop. People who spend too much time playing video games are going to have problems at school and work.

4. In conclusion, it seems clear that the benefits and dangers of video games must be carefully considered. On the one hand, they can be educational and help people to be more creative. On the other hand, many people spend too much time on games. However, video games are going to be popular for a while. In the future, it will be important to limit the time we spend looking at screens and spend more time with our friends and family.

The Years Ahead

Exercise 5.3 Comprehension Check

Read the text on page 369. Write *T* (true) or *F* (false) next to the statements. Correct the false statements.

_____ 1 In the United States, young children play video games for more than an hour each day.

_____ 2 There are good and bad things about video games.

_____ 3 According to writer, video games are going to become less popular in the future.

Exercise 5.4 Noticing the Grammar

Work with a partner. Complete the tasks.

1 Highlight the present progressive verb form in the first paragraph. Is it about the present or the future?

2 Underline *be going to* in the text. Why does the writer use *be going to*? What does it refer to?

3 Circle *will* in the text. Why does the writer use *will*? What does it refer to?

Recognizing Advantages and Disadvantages

When writers express opinions, they often state both the **advantages** and **disadvantages** of a topic. Even if a writer's opinion is mostly positive, including some disadvantages can make the text fair and honest.

How can you tell if a statement is about an advantage or disadvantage? Vocabulary is one way. Writers can use words like *benefit*, *positive*, and *improve* to write about advantages. They use words like *problem*, *danger*, and *negative* to write about disadvantages.

The structure of the text is another clue. Writers may describe advantages in one paragraph and disadvantages in a different paragraph.

Exercise 5.5 Applying the Skill

1 Write the number of the paragraph in the text on page 369 that contains the main idea. Then write the sentence that expresses the main idea.

   a Video games have some advantages.

   Paragraph: _____

   Sentence: _____

   b Video games have some disadvantages.

   Paragraph: _____

   Sentence: _____

2 Cross out the advantages and disadvantages of video games below that are not in the text.

+	−
− are creative	− can cause problems at school/ work
− improve the way people think	− are boring
− teach people about money	− can take up too much time
− are fun	− can be unsuitable for children
− can help people exercise	− can cause problems between parents/children

Exercise 5.6 Brainstorming Advantages and Disadvantages

Work with a partner. Complete the tasks.

1 Discuss the advantages and disadvantages of video games in the text. Do you agree with the writer? Why or why not?

2 Think of at least two more advantages and two more disadvantages of video games.

My Writing

Exercise 5.7 Brainstorming Ideas

1 Think about how people use the Internet. For example:
   • How much time do they spend online? What do they do during that time?
   • What are the advantages of spending time online? What are the disadvantages?

2 Make a list of your ideas in your notebook. Do not try to organize your thoughts. Just write down as many thoughts as possible. You can review and organize later.

3 Compare your list with a partner. Add any new ideas to your list.

What to Do after Brainstorming

After you brainstorm, put away your list. After at least 30 minutes, take out your list and review it. Make notes on your list. Cross out ideas that do not seem useful. Add any new ideas that you have. Use "+" and "-" signs to indicate positive and negative points. Draw boxes and arrows to show which ideas belong together. This is a step toward the next stage of the writing process, organizing.

Exercise 5.8 Applying the Skill

Follow the steps above to review your list of ideas from Exercise 5.7.

UNIT 28

Will, May, and Might for Future Possibility; Will for Offers and Promises

Will We Need Teachers?

ACADEMIC WRITING

Opinion paragraph

1 Grammar in the Real World

A How do you think schools will be different in 2050? Read this article from an education magazine. How many changes did you predict?

B Comprehension Check Answer the questions about the article.
1. What is a virtual classroom?
2. Why can students in virtual classrooms live in different countries?
3. How will the teacher's job probably change?
4. In your opinion, will the combination of humans and technology make learning more or less enjoyable?

C Notice Find these sentences in the article. Complete the missing part of the verbs.
1. Professional workers _____ to update career skills.
2. They _____ be able to attend a traditional university.
3. Your teacher _____ human.
4. You _____ a talk by a famous human professor and then interact with the bot for your assignments.

Will, May, and *Might* for Future Possibility; *Will* for Offers and Promises

Virtual[1] Education

The year is 2050. As a 21st century worker, you **will need** to update your skills, so you take a class. What can you expect?

First, tomorrow's students **will be** different.
5 Professional workers **will need** to update career skills. More students **may have** jobs and families.

Second, education **will change**. People **won't attend** a traditional university. Universities and private companies **will offer** online courses to
10 students from all over the world. You **might be** in a class with ten thousand other students.

Third, your teacher **might not be** human. A teacher bot[2] **will type** and talk like a person. It **may even have** a name, but it **will be** an intelligent
15 machine communicating through the Internet. You **may watch** a talk by a famous human professor and then send the bot your assignments.

Finally, the learning environment will change. You **will put on** a headset to "go to class." In this virtual
20 classroom, you **will see**, hear, and **feel** like you are at a museum or maybe a traveler inside a human body.

One thing **may not** change. You **will probably still enjoy** the company of human classmates. Research shows that the best education still happens
25 in a social environment.

---

[1]**virtual:** through the use of a computer
[2]**bot:** An automated computer program

Will We Need Teachers?

2 May and Might; Adverbs with Will

Grammar Presentation

| You can use *may* or *might* and a base form of a verb to talk and write about what is possible in the future. | *Students **may** not need to buy books.*
*Everyone **might** take classes online.* |

2.1 Statements with May and Might

Subject	May / Might	Not	Base Form of Verb	
I You We They He She	**may** **might**	(not)	go talk	to a different kind of school in the future. to classmates all over the world.
It			be	the future of education.

2.2 Using Will, May, and Might

A You can use *will* when you are 100 percent certain about something.	*By 2050, there **will** be new ways to learn.*
B Use *may* or *might* when you are less than 100 percent certain.	*Students **may** do all of their work online.*
They have a similar meaning, but *may* sounds a little more certain than *might*.	*Your teachers **might be** bots.*
C You can use *may* or *might* to answer questions with *be going to* or *will*.	*"Are you going to enroll in an online course?"* *"I **might**. I **might not**. I'm not sure yet."*
D You can use *might*, but not *may*, with *Wh-* words to ask questions about possibility. These questions are not very common.	*What **might** machines be able to do in 2050?*
E Use the full negative forms *might not* and *may not*. Don't use contractions.	*Students **may not** have to sit in classrooms at all.* *Teachers **might not** be human.*

Will, May, and *Might* for Future Possibility; *Will* for Offers and Promises

2.2 Using *Will*, *May*, and *Might* (continued)

F	Don't confuse the adverb *maybe* and *may be*.	I *may* be in college this time next year.
	Maybe usually comes before the subject.	*Maybe* I'll go to college next year.

▶▶ Modal Verbs and Modal-like Expressions: See page A25.

DATA FROM THE REAL WORLD

You can use *may* and *might* in speaking and writing. *Might* is more common in conversation. *May* is more common in writing. *May* sounds more formal.

2.3 Using Adverbs with *Will* for Levels of Certainty

A You can use these adverbs *after* will, *between* will and not, or *before* won't.

100% certain	certainly, definitely, surely
less than 100% certain	likely, probably, possibly

Online learning *certainly won't* replace the classroom.
They *will surely* do all of their work online for most classes.
Class materials *will likely* be online.
Students *will probably not* use books.
Some teachers *will possibly* be robots.

B *Probably* is the most frequent of these adverbs. You can also use it in writing, but it is more common in speaking.

I'll *probably* take the online course next term.
Jake *probably won't* because his computer broke.

Grammar Application

Exercise 2.1 *Will*, *May*, and *Might*

A Listen to the conversation. Complete the text with *will* (*not/won't*), *may* (*not*), or *might* (*not*). Use contractions when possible.

Carla   So what are your plans for the fall? Are you going to college?

Sharon   Actually, I ___*might not*___ go to a college. But I think I _____
(1)   (2)

probably enroll in an online program.

Carla   Oh, really? Like a degree online?

Will We Need Teachers?

Sharon Yeah, or maybe just a few courses. The thing is that my family is definitely going to move this year. So with an online program, I probably _____(3) need to change schools.

Carla That's smart. You can study from anywhere. Do you know what you're going to take?

Sharon I think so. I like chemistry, so I _____(4) definitely take chemistry.

Carla Oh, so you're interested in science?

Sharon Yeah. And I _____(5) take biology, too. I _____(6) definitely take Spanish.

Carla Awesome! But why Spanish?

Sharon Well, my family's going to move to California, so I thought Spanish _____(7) be useful.

Carla Well, let me know how it goes.

Sharon Sure. I _____(8) definitely keep in touch. I _____(9) be online all the time!

B Pair Work Answer the questions. Compare your answers with a partner.

1 What are Sharon's plans?

2 Why is she making these plans?

3 What is she going to study?

4 How certain or sure is Sharon about her plans? Write her plans in the correct section of the chart.

SHARON'S PLANS	
Certain	**Not Sure**
	attend a college

Will, May, and *Might* for Future Possibility; *Will* for Offers and Promises

Exercise 2.2 More *Will, May,* and *Might*

A Complete the sentences with *will (not)/won't, may (not),* or *might (not)*. Give your own opinion. Sometimes there is more than one correct answer.

Classrooms of the Future
What do you think classrooms of the future will look like?

1 Many students ____may not____ go to traditional universities.
2 They _____ not meet in classrooms.
3 Students _____ have classmates at different ages.
4 Classrooms _____ have equipment for experiments.
5 Some classrooms _____ be virtual.
6 Students _____ use classrooms to make things.
7 Students _____ collaborate with classmates.
8 Classes _____ be more interesting.

B Pair Work Discuss your sentences about classrooms of the future with a partner. Do you agree?

A *I wrote, "Students may go to class one or two days a week."*
B *I don't agree. I think we won't go to class at all.*

C Over to You Complete the sentences with *will (not)/won't, may (not),* or *might (not)*. Give your own opinion. Then discuss with a partner.

Schoolwork and Exams
What do you think schoolwork and exams will be like in the future?

1 Students ____will not____ need to take handwritten notes in lectures.
2 Students _____ do more activities online.
3 They _____ write in books.
4 They _____ go to libraries.
5 Exams _____ be different.
6 Students _____ need to memorize facts for exams.
7 People _____ need a keyboard because they will be able to talk to their computers.
8 Computers _____ teach and grade students' work.
9 Teachers _____ be in the same classroom as the students.
10 Students _____ have paper books.
11 Computers _____ be very small and light.
12 Students _____ only speak with other students online.

Exercise 2.3 Adverbs with *Will*

A Write sentences about your opinion with the words below. Use *will* or *will not/won't* and an adverb of certainty from the box.

certainly	definitely	likely
certainly not	definitely not	likely not
possibly	probably	surely
possibly not	probably not	surely not

1 Teachers / give all their classes from home.

<u>Teachers will probably not give all their classes from home. / Teachers probably won't give all their classes from home.</u>

2 Teachers / be bots.

3 Teachers / need to prepare for their classes.

4 They / check exercises.

5 Computer software / check students' work.

6 Teachers / spend more time with each student.

7 They / need to speak English.

8 Computer software / translate from any language.

B Pair Work Compare your sentences with a partner. Do you have the same ideas? What other ideas do you have about teachers in the future? Think of three more ideas.

A *I think teachers probably won't teach all their classes from home.*
B *Well, I think some teachers will. Some teachers will probably give classes in classrooms, too.*

C Over to You Write sentences about your future. Use *may*, *will*, or *might* with an adverb (*certainly*, *definitely*, *surely*, *likely*, *probably*, *possibly*). Use the topics below.

1 school plans   *I'll probably enroll in an online degree program.*
2 place to live   _____
3 subject of study   _____
4 learn another language   _____
5 start a business or find a job   _____
6 your own idea   _____

D Pair Work Ask and answer questions with a partner about your plans.

A *Are you going to go to a four-year college next year?*
B *I might. I'll definitely study somewhere.*

3 Offers and Promises

Grammar Presentation

This is an offer:
I'll help you with your homework tonight.

This is a promise:
I'll call you. **I won't forget.**

3.1 Making Offers

A You can use *I'll* to make an offer.	"Where is the cafeteria?" "**I'll** show you. **I'll** take you there."
B You can also offer other people's help using *will*.	"My computer's not working." "My sister **will** help you. She knows all about computers."

Will We Need Teachers?

3.2 Making Promises

| You can use *I'll*, *I will*, or *I won't* to make promises. | **I'll** send my comments on your assignment today. I **won't** forget. "Will you marry me?" "Yes, **I will**!" |

Grammar Application

Exercise 3.1 Offers and Promises

A Complete the conversation. Use Pat's offers of help and Chris's promises. Add *I'll*.

PAT'S OFFERS	CHRIS'S PROMISES
~~lend you $10~~ look at the homework with you drive you home show you	help you with your math homework pay you back make you dinner

Chris: I don't have any money for lunch.
Pat: _I'll lend you $10._ (1)
Chris: Thanks! _____ tomorrow. (2)
Chris: Where's the computer room? I'm lost.
Pat: _____ (3)
Chris: I can't carry all my books home. They're so heavy.
Pat: _____ (4)
Chris: Great! Are you hungry? It's already 6:00 p.m.
_____ (5)
Chris: I'm having trouble with my English homework.
Pat: _____ (6)
Chris: How can I thank you? I know. _____ (7)

B **Pair Work** Practice the conversation in A with a partner. Add more details.

A I don't have any money for lunch. I left my wallet at home. I was in a hurry this morning.
B I'll lend you $10 for lunch. Would you like to have lunch together?
A Sure, thanks. I'll pay you back tomorrow.

Avoid Common Mistakes

1 *Maybe* and *may be* have different meanings.
May be is the verb *may* + base form of the verb *be*. *Maybe* is an adverb. Use it before the subject.

~~may be~~ → *may be*
Books ~~maybe~~ rare in the future.

~~May be~~ → *Maybe*
~~May be~~ people will stop using books.

2 Use *might* or *may* to talk about possibility in the future. Avoid using *can* for predictions about the future.

may / might
Some students ~~can~~ prefer to go to a regular class.

3 Use *will* to talk about certainty in the future. Avoid using *can*.

will
Everyone ~~can~~ study in a virtual classroom in the future.

Editing Task

Find and correct 10 more mistakes in this education article.

The Future of Education

The Internet ~~can~~ *will* change education completely in the future. May be colleges will not be buildings with people and furniture, but complex websites. Teachers maybe characters in virtual worlds like *Second Life*. In the future, students can "travel" to different countries using their computers. They can walk around the world's famous museums without leaving home. May be students will go back in time. They can possibly "talk to" famous people from the past, like George Washington. History students can watch or be part of historic events. We can buy artificial brains so we won't have to go to school at all! There maybe many changes to education, but learning can definitely never stop.

5 Academic Writing

Opinion Paragraph

Brainstorm > **Organize** > Write > Edit

In Unit 27, you read about the advantages and disadvantages of video games and then brainstormed ideas for your writing. In this unit (28), you will look carefully at the writing prompt and plan a topic sentence.

> "The Internet wastes our time. It does not help us do more work." Do you agree or disagree?

Understanding a Question or Prompt

Before you answer a question, it is important to understand exactly what the question asks you to do. You can do this by thinking carefully about the question. If there is more than one part, look at each part of the question. You can then decide what to write in order to answer the question completely.

Exercise 5.1 Applying the Skill

Read the writing prompts. Then choose the best way (*a* or *b*) to answer each prompt.

1. How does the Internet waste our time? How does it help us do more work? _____

2. "The Internet wastes our time more than it helps us do work." Do you agree or disagree? _____
   a. Give your opinion about whether the Internet wastes our time or helps us do more work. Give examples to support your argument.
   b. Describe the ways the Internet wastes our time or helps us do more work. Give examples to support your argument.

Exercise 5.2 Organizing Details

Read the sentences about the Internet. Then write the numbers in the correct column of the chart on page 383.

1. You can get help from different websites.
2. If you have a computer problem, it might take a long time to fix.
3. You spend a lot of time on social media sites.
4. You can read newspapers from around the world.
5. People can work from home sometimes.
6. You can spend hours playing video games.
7. You can watch educational videos.
8. You might not spend enough time with people.

The Internet helps us	The Internet wastes our time

Exercise 5.3 Adding Details

Work with a partner. Complete the tasks.

1. Add two more details to each column in Exercise 5.2.
2. Highlight the three advantages and disadvantages that you agree with the most, and discuss them with another pair.

Writing a Topic Sentence for an Opinion Paragraph.

The **topic sentence** tells you the main idea of a paragraph. The topic sentence has two parts: the **topic** and the **main idea**. The topic tells what the paragraph is about. The main idea gives the topic a focus. In an opinion paragraph, the main idea is the writer's opinion about the topic.

TOPIC   MAIN IDEA

The Internet has many advantages.

From this topic sentence we can expect the paragraph to discuss the Internet's advantages. All of the sentences that follow will support this positive opinion.

Exercise 5.4 Applying the Skill

Circle the topic and underline the main idea in each topic sentence. Does the writer have a positive or negative opinion of the topic?

1. Social media sites make it easy to keep in touch with your friends.
2. Smartphones can be expensive.
3. Information on the Internet is not reliable.

My Writing

Exercise 5.5 Understanding the Writing Prompt

Complete the sentences about the writing prompt at the top of page 382.

1. The writing prompt expresses the idea that the Internet is harmful because _____
   _____
2. My paragraph will _____ with this idea and explain my reasons.

Exercise 5.6 Writing Your Topic Sentence

Write a topic sentence for your opinion paragraph.

UNIT 29 Suggestions and Advice

Study Habits

1 Grammar in the Real World

ACADEMIC WRITING

Opinion paragraph

A What are two ways that you study? Read the web article about study tips. How many different suggestions does the writer give?

B Comprehension Check Answer the questions.
1. What should you do if you live in a noisy place and need to study?
2. Why might you want to eat a snack before you study?
3. How do you set a study goal?
4. Should you check your e-mail while you study? Why or why not?
5. How could you ask a friend to study with you?

C Notice Answer the questions. Use the article to help you.
1. Write the two verbs that come after the bold words in the third paragraph.

   a _____ b _____

2. What verb form are the words in item 1? _____

3. Which is used most in the text: *should*, *might*, or *ought to*?
   _____

4. Find the form "*why don't you …*" in the last paragraph. Is it asking for a reason or making a suggestion? _____

384

Suggestions and Advice

Study to Learn, Learn to Study
By Amy Chin, Communications Major

By the time we get to college, we think we know how to study. Then the first time we get a test back with a low grade, we wonder what happened. Research shows that many students study ineffectively.[1] Here are a few suggestions about how to study more effectively.

First, it's important to find the right place to study. You **ought to** study in a quiet place. If you live with other people, you **should** probably try to study when no one else is at home. If your roommates are noisy, you **might want to** go to the library to study. If you have to study in a noisy place, try listening to soft music with earphones.

Once you find a quiet place, you **should** make sure you're not hungry. You **might want to** eat a small snack before you study so you can concentrate better.

Next, set a study goal. Look at your task and decide how much you want to accomplish[2] during this study session. For example, **should** you read all four chapters now? Maybe you **ought to** read two now and the other two later. You **should** set a realistic goal and work to reach it. Setting a study goal will help you focus on the task you need to do, but it's easy to get distracted.[3] You **should** not check e-mail, text, or surf the Web while you study.

If you have to learn a lot of facts or study for a math test, you **might want to** study with a friend. Just say, "**Let's** meet after class and review our notes."

Why don't you try these suggestions for a month? You will definitely see results!

---

[1] **ineffectively:** in a way that doesn't get the results you want; not effectively

[2] **accomplish:** do or finish something successfully

[3] **distracted:** when someone's attention is taken away from what they are doing or should be doing

2 Suggestions and Advice

Grammar Presentation

> You can make suggestions or give advice with *should, ought to, might want to, why don't,* and *let's*.
>
> You **should** probably write new words in a vocabulary journal.
> You **ought to** listen to these suggestions!
> You **might want to** write sentences with each new word.
> "**Why don't we** study together?"
> "Yes! **Let's** study math first."

2.1 Statements with *Should, Ought To, Might Want To,* and *Let's*

AFFIRMATIVE

Subject	Modal / *Might Want To*	Base Form of Verb	
I You We They It He She	**should** **ought to** **might want to**	stay	inside in this weather.
			late.

NEGATIVE

Subject	Modal / *Might Want To*	Base Form of Verb	
I You We They It He She	**should not** **ought not** **might not want to**	stay	outside in this weather.
			late.

LET'S

Let's (Let + us)	(Not)	Base Form of Verb	
Let's	not	read	the chapter together.
		study	alone tonight.

Suggestions and Advice

2.2 Questions with *Why Don't You / We*

Why Don't	Subject	Base Form of Verb		Answers
Why don't	you / we	study	in your room?	OK. That's a good idea.
		go	to the library now?	I can't.

2.3 Using *Should, Ought To, Might Want To, Why Don't You / We,* and *Let's*

A	*Might want to* is softer and more polite than *should* or *ought to*.	You **might want to** take Ms. Novak's writing class.
B	Use *maybe, probably,* or *I think* with *should* and *ought to* to soften the suggestion or advice.	**Maybe** we **should not** listen to loud music while we study.
	In affirmative statements, *probably* can come before or after *should*.	We **should probably** study together. We **probably should** study together.
	In negative statements, *probably* comes before *should not*.	We **probably should not** study together.
	Maybe and *probably* always come before *ought to*.	We **probably ought to** go to the movies later. **Maybe** we **ought to** go to the movies later.
C	Use the expression *Why don't you / we …* to make suggestions or give advice in a soft, polite way.	(SUGGESTION) **Why don't we** study together on Tuesday night? (ADVICE) **Why don't you** keep a vocabulary journal?
D	Use the expression *Let's …* to make suggestions that include you and the listener. *Let's = Let us*	**Let's** study at the library. **Let's** not stay up late the night before our test.

 Modal Verbs and Modal-like Expressions: See page A25.

DATA FROM THE REAL WORLD

We and *you* are the most common subjects for suggestions and advice.

Should is the most common form used for suggestions and advice. *Ought to* is very rare. *Ought not to* is also very rare.

Might is usually followed by *want to* when making suggestions or giving advice.

We **should** keep a vocabulary journal.
You **ought to** study for the test.

You **should** learn a new word every day.

You **might want to** review for the vocabulary test.

Study Habits

Grammar Application

Exercise 2.1 Suggestions and Advice

A The students in an English class are having some vocabulary problems. Give advice for each student. Use the words in parentheses and *should* (*not*), *might want to*, or *ought to*. Sometimes there is more than one correct answer.

Problem	Advice
1 Marissa doesn't read well because she doesn't know a lot of words.	*She ought to read more.* (she / read more)
2 Veronica wants to learn a lot of new words quickly.	_____ (she / practice new words every day)
3 Petra wants to remember how to use new words.	_____ (she / write sentences with the new words)
4 Ricardo is afraid to try new words.	_____ (he / practice using the words with a friend)
5 Eniko and Irina want a fun way to practice vocabulary.	_____ (they / do crossword puzzles)
6 The whole class wants a good way to learn new words.	_____ (they / create a picture in their minds that shows the meaning of each word)

B Pair Work With a partner, write three suggestions for learning new words. Use your own experience or ideas from the unit. Then share your ideas with the class.

A *Let's write new words on cards and practice them.*
B *We might want to tape the cards on a wall to practice.*

Exercise 2.2 More Suggestions and Advice

A Listen. Complete the class discussion with the missing words.

Professor Taking good notes is an important part of being a successful student. Let's hear some advice from students about how they take notes.

Teresa Some teachers speak very quickly. You __*should*__ (1) ask these teachers if you can record the class. Then you can listen to the notes again in your home. You _____ (2) record the class without the teacher's permission.

Amadou You _____ (3) attend a workshop on note taking. That can be very helpful. I know it helped me.

Suggestions and Advice

Alex   Find a student with good notes, and ask him or her if you can copy the notes. You _____(4)_____ offer to buy that student coffee or a snack. _____(5)_____ you _____(6)_____ suggest a time to meet once a week to trade notes. If you aren't sure how to suggest this, here are some ways: "_____(7)_____ we get together on Thursdays to trade notes?" or "_____(8)_____ meet in the student union."

Professor   Thank you for your suggestions. I _____(9)_____ add here that you _____(10)_____ just copy the notes. You _____(11)_____ compare their notes with yours. Try to figure out what's different.

B Pair Work Use the information in A to give your partner suggestions or advice about taking notes. Take turns.

A   *Why don't you ask the teacher's permission to record the class?*
B   *That's a good idea.*

A   *You should attend a workshop on note taking.*
B   *I'll look for one.*

C Over to You Many people give us advice and suggestions. What is some advice that you received recently? Was it helpful?

3 Asking for and Responding to Suggestions and Advice

Grammar Presentation

Use Yes/No and information questions to ask for suggestions and advice.

"**Should** I register for a writing class?"
"**That's a good idea.**"
"**When should** I register for class?"
"**Why don't you** register next week?"

3.1 Yes/No Questions to Ask for Suggestions and Advice

Should	Subject	Base Form of Verb		Answers
Should	I / we	take	a math class?	That's a good idea.
		meet	you in the student union?	I think it's closed.

Study Habits   **389**

3.2 Information Questions to Ask for Suggestions and Advice

Wh- Word	Should	Subject	Base Form of Verb		Answers
What	should	I / you / we / they / he / she / it	bring	to class?	I don't know.
Where			meet	you?	Let's meet at the library.
Who			ask	for help?	Ask Professor Li.
When			tell	the boss?	As soon as possible.
How			study	for the test?	She ought to study one chapter at a time.
Why			be	difficult?	Because the teacher gives hard tests.

3.3 Responding to Questions for Suggestions and Advice

A For a strong, <u>positive</u> response to a Yes/No question for suggestions or advice, use:
Yes. / That sounds great. / Definitely. / Absolutely.

"*Should* we eat lunch before our class?"
"Yes. **That sounds great**!"
"**Definitely**!"
"Oh, **absolutely**!"

B If you are <u>uncertain</u> about the answer to a Yes/No question, use:
Maybe. / Probably. / I'm not sure.

"*Should* we eat lunch before our class?"
"**Maybe**."
"**Probably**. Let's check my schedule."
"Oh. **I'm not sure**."

C For a strong, <u>negative</u> response to a Yes/No question for suggestions or advice, use:
That's not a good idea.

Why don't we + different idea

I'd like to, but + reason

"*Should* we eat lunch before our class?"
"**That's not a good idea.** We don't have enough time."
"**Why don't we** eat after class?"
"**I'd like to, but** I have to study."

D Respond to information questions with: probably / maybe / why don't you

Using *should* alone is stronger.

"What class *should* I take next semester?"
"You should **probably** take a writing class."
"**Maybe** you should take a writing class."
"**Why don't you** take a writing class?"

Suggestions and Advice

 DATA FROM THE REAL WORLD

What should I / we . . . ? and *Where should we . . . ?* are the most common information questions used to ask for suggestions / advice.

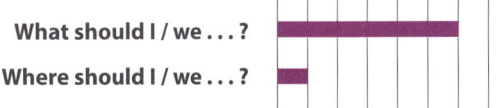

Grammar Application

Exercise 3.1 Responding to Questions for Advice

A Complete the conversation. Use the cues to help you.

Jill: Hi, Sandra! I'm so glad to see you! Could you help me with something? I need to find an apartment. I know you know a lot about the area. ___Should___ (1) (Yes/No question) I rent a place near school?

Sandra: ___Yes. Absolutely!___ (2) (a strong positive response) It's so much easier to live near school.

Jill: _____ (3) (Wh- questions) I look to find an apartment for rent? Can I look in the local paper?

Sandra: Yes. You _____ (4) (uncertain answer) look in the paper or online. That's a good place to start.

Jill: Great! Do you have any other advice?

Sandra: Yes, you _____ (5) (strong response) ask about utilities. Sometimes things like electricity, heat, and air-conditioning are included in the rent.

Jill: Oh, right. _____ (6) (Yes/No question) I also ask about deposits?

Sandra: _____ (7) (strong positive response)!

Jill: Thanks, Sandra. You're a great friend!

B Pair Work Write a conversation with suggestions/advice for <u>one</u> of the situations below. Use the conversation in A to help you. Then share with another pair.

1. **Two Classmates:** One classmate just started college in the United States and needs advice on study habits.

2. **Graduating Student and Job Coach:** A student is looking for advice on how to begin a job search / get a job.

3. **College Freshman and College Senior:** A freshman wants advice on courses, restaurants, bookstores, etc.

Situation 1
A *My English is not very strong. What should I do to improve my vocabulary?*
B *Well, first you should definitely keep a vocabulary journal. …*

Study Habits 391

Exercise 3.2 Asking for and Giving Advice

A Respond to the situations below. Ask for advice or give advice.

1 You want to ask your friend for advice about how to fix your computer.
   What should I do first?

2 You are not sure which movie to go to. Ask a friend for advice.

3 A friend asks for advice on how to take notes. What do you say?

4 You are not sure where to buy school supplies. Ask a friend for advice.

5 Your teacher asks for advice on what cell phone to buy. What do you say?

6 A classmate is about to do something that is not a good idea. What advice do you give?

7 A classmate needs help with his math homework. What advice do you give?

8 You want to learn more English vocabulary. Ask your teacher for advice.

B Pair Work Compare your answers with a partner. Did you use any of the same expressions to ask for or give advice?

C Over to You Think of two problems or situations this week that you will need advice on. Write your questions here, asking for advice.

1
2

4 Avoid Common Mistakes

1 Use the base form of the main verb after *should*.

He should ~~eats~~ *eat* lunch before class.
We should ~~to~~ study after class.

2 After *ought*, use *to* + the base form of the main verb.

He ought *to* eat lunch.

3 The subject comes after *should* and *might* in information questions.

Where ~~I~~ should *I* meet you?

4 Put *probably* and *maybe* before *ought to*.

We *probably* ought to ~~probably~~ go to the library.

5 In negative statements, *probably* comes before *should not*.

Tim *probably* should not ~~probably~~ call tonight.

Editing Task

Find and correct the mistakes in this conversation between two classmates.

Julia   Monica, I need help studying! How ~~I~~ should *I* tell the professor?

Monica   Don't worry. I can help. First, we should shares class notes.

Julia   When we should meet at the library? After class today?

Monica   Sure, but we ought to probably meet in the cafeteria. I'll want to eat something.

5 **Julia**   OK. We should eats dinner while we study. What I should bring?

Monica   Just your notebook. You should not probably bring the big textbook – I don't think we'll need it.

Julia   You should to be ready for a lot of questions from me! I have so many!

Monica   As long as you are ready to learn, I'm happy to help! When we're done, we
10   ought see a movie!

Julie   That sounds great! See you later!

Monica   See you then, Julie. We should to study together more often!

5 Academic Writing

Opinion Paragraph

Brainstorm > Organize > **Write** > Edit

In Unit 28, you organized details and wrote a topic sentence to answer the prompt below. In this unit (29), you will learn ways to introduce and support your opinion, and then you will write your paragraph.

> "The Internet wastes our time. It does not help us do more work." Do you agree or disagree?

Exercise 5.1 Stating Your Opinions

Complete the sentences with your opinions about spending time on the Internet.

1. Spending time on the Internet _____
2. Spending time on the Internet _____
3. Spending time on the Internet _____

Using Phrases to Introduce Opinions

In academic writing, some useful phrases for expressing your opinion are *I think that, I believe that, It seems to me that, In my opinion, I agree that,* and *I disagree that.*

Opinion: Video games are bad for people.

I think/believe that video games are bad for people.
It seems to me that video games are bad for people.
In my opinion, video games are bad for people.
I agree/disagree that video games are bad for people.

Exercise 5.2 Applying the Skill

Rewrite the sentences in Exercise 5.1. Use a different opinion phrase in each one.

1. _____
2. _____
3. _____

Suggestions and Advice

Supporting an Opinion

After you state your opinion, you need to give reasons, facts, or examples to support it.

Opinion: In my opinion, video games are bad for people.

Reason: Some experts believe that people can become more violent after they play violent video games.

Reason: Video games and equipment are also expensive, and it is easy to waste money on them. Example: For example, my friend spent $1000 on a TV, a video game system, and four games.

Reason: Finally, people who spend too much time playing video games may not get enough exercise and can become unhealthy.

Exercise 5.3 Applying the Skill

Look at your sentences in Exercise 5.2. Support each sentence with a fact, reason, or example.

1 _____

2 _____

3 _____

Exercise 5.4 Making Suggestions and Giving Advice

Work with a partner. Use the questions below to give feedback on your partner's sentences in Exercise 5.3.

1. How clear is your partner's opinion?
2. How strong are your partner's supporting sentences?
3. What other fact, reason, or example should your partner add to each statement?

My Writing

Exercise 5.5 Writing Your Paragraph

Look at your notes and topic sentence on pages 371 and 383. Write an opinion paragraph that answers the writing prompt at the top of page 394. Include the topic sentence, reasons and examples to support your opinion, and a concluding sentence.

Study Habits

UNIT 30

Necessity and Conclusions

Getting What You Want

1 Grammar in the Real World

ACADEMIC WRITING

Opinion paragraph

A How much does your school cost each year? How do you pay for it? Read the article about scholarships.

B Comprehension Check Answer the questions. Use the article to help you.

1 Is college expensive in the United States?
2 Are there many scholarships available for students?
3 How early should you start your applications?
4 Who can help you with your application?
5 What do you need to give your teachers for their recommendations?

C Notice Read the sentences. Decide if the actions are *necessary* or *not necessary*. Circle *necessary* or *not necessary*.

1 Many students **need to** apply for scholarships to lower their education costs.   necessary   not necessary

2 You **don't have to** feel stressed about being able to complete a good application.   necessary   not necessary

3 Eligible students **must** search for scholarships that are appropriate for them.   necessary   not necessary

4 You **need** to ask your adviser for help.   necessary   not necessary

Applying for a SCHOLARSHIP[1]

As a student, you **must** agree that college is expensive in the United States. Many students **need to** apply for scholarships to lower their education costs. Here are a few tips on how to complete a good scholarship application.

There are many scholarships available every year, but students **have to** search for them. Search online with keywords like *scholarship* or *grant*.[2] There are also scholarships for people with specific skills, backgrounds, and ethnicities.[3] Eligible[4] students **must** search for scholarships that are appropriate for them.

You **need to** ask your adviser for help. He or she knows a lot about scholarships and can help you complete your application. Ask your adviser to help you create a schedule for each step in the application. Think of a time line for when you **must** finish each step. Try to have everything ready one week before you send your application.

You should start your scholarship applications early, about six months before they are due. Your application will take time to complete because you will **need to** request letters of recommendation[5] from teachers and a transcript[6] from your school. Your school will need time to send the transcript to the scholarship organization, and your teachers will need time to write the recommendations. When you ask a teacher for a recommendation, give him or her a deadline. All students must send their applications out on time, so be persistent and remind your teachers of the due dates.

You **don't have to** feel stressed about being able to complete a good application. With a little hard work and care, you can send out a good scholarship application and lower your school costs.

---

[1]**scholarship:** money given to a person to help pay for his or her education

[2]**grant:** a sum of money that a university, government, or an organization gives to someone for a purpose, such as to do research or study

[3]**ethnicity:** shared national, racial, or cultural origins of a group, often with the same language

[4]**eligible:** having the necessary qualities

[5]**recommendation:** a letter or statement saying someone is good or suitable for something, like a job, school, or scholarship

[6]**transcript:** an official, written copy of someone's grades at an institution

2 Necessity and Conclusions with *Have To, Need To, Must*

Grammar Presentation

Have to, *need to*, and *must* express an obligation or necessity. *Must* also expresses a conclusion we can make about something.

Students **need to** apply for scholarships. (= It is necessary.)
Students **do not have to** feel stressed about completing their application. (= It is not necessary.)
As a student, you **must** know that college is expensive in the United States. (CONCLUSION Students know that college is expensive in the United States.)

2.1 Statements with *Have To* and *Need To*

AFFIRMATIVE

Subject		Base Form of Verb	
I / You / We / They	have to / need to	write	an essay.
He / She / It	has to / needs to	search	online.

NEGATIVE

Subject			Base Form of Verb	
I / You / We / They	do not / don't	have to / need to	write	an essay.
He / She / It	does not / doesn't		search	online.

2.2 Statements with *Must*

AFFIRMATIVE

Subject		Base Form of Verb
I / You / He / She / It / We / They	**must**	know.

NEGATIVE

Subject			Base Form of Verb
I / You / He / She / It / We / They	must	not	know.

2.3 Using *Have To*, *Need To*, and *Must*

A *Have to*, *need to*, and *must* talk about things that are important or necessary to do.

Students **need to** send an application.

Necessity and Conclusions

2.3 Using *Have To*, *Need To*, and *Must* (continued)

B Using *must* in conversation can seem rude.	She **needs to** make a schedule. She **must** make a schedule. (Sounds rude.)
C In conversation, *must* usually expresses conclusions.	Today is Monday, so tomorrow **must** be Tuesday.
D *Have to* can also express conclusions. *Need to* <u>never</u> expresses conclusions.	Today is Monday, so tomorrow **has to** be Tuesday. NOT ~~Today is Monday, so tomorrow needs to be Tuesday~~.
E *Do not have to* or *do not need to* means it is not necessary. There is no obligation.	Tom **doesn't have to** pay for school. He **does not need to** pay for school.
Must not means it is forbidden. *Mustn't* is <u>very</u> rare.	Students **must not** forget to send in their application on time.

▸▸ Modal Verbs and Modal-like Expressions: See page A25.

2.4 *Yes/No* Questions with *Have To* and *Need To* and Short Answers

Do / Does	Subject	Have to / Need to	Base Form of Verb	
Do	I you we they	**have to** **need to**	write	an essay?
Does	he she it			

Yes / No	Subject	
Yes,	I you we they	do.
No,		do not / don't.
Yes,	he she it	does.
No,		does not / doesn't.

2.5 Information Questions with *Have To* and *Need To* and Responses

Wh- Word	Do / Does	Subject		Base Form of Verb
When	do	I you we they	**have to** **need to**	send the application?
	does	he she it		

Getting What You Want   399

2.5 Information Questions with *Have To* and *Need To* and Responses *(continued)*

Subject	Do / Does (Not)		Base Form of Verb
I / You / We / They	do not / don't	have to / need to	send the application next month.
He / She / It	does not / doesn't		

Note: Using *must* in questions is very rare.

Grammar Application

DATA FROM THE REAL WORLD

These are some of the most frequent verbs used with *have to*, *need to*, and *must* in speaking and writing:

be	go	get	take	know	talk	give
do	have	make	look	say	come	work

Exercise 2.1 Necessity and Obligation

A Complete the sentences with the correct form of *have to*, *need to*, or *must*.

Driver's Licenses in Canada and the United States

In the U.S. and Canada, states and provinces have different rules for getting a driver's license.

1 Drivers ___have to___ (have to) get a license in their state of residence. They can go to their local DMV (Department of Motor Vehicles*).

2 Generally, a person _____ (have to) be 16 to 18 years old to have a license. This depends on the state or province.

3 A driver _____ (need to) show documents to prove his or her identity.

Necessity and Conclusions

4 An acceptable document _____ (need to) have your name and address.

5 Foreigners can drive in the U.S. and Canada. Drivers _____ (not/have to) be U.S. or Canadian citizens.

6 Foreign drivers _____ (have to) have an international driver's license.

7 Some states require new drivers to take a driving class. In most states in the U.S., new drivers _____ (have to) pass an exam in order to get a license.

8 In some states, people who already drive _____ (not/need to) take any exams to get a new license.

9 However, in other states, people who already drive _____ (have to) take an exam to get a new license.

10 You _____ (not/must) forget to bring the right documents to the DMV. This can save you a lot of time and frustration.

*Note: Not all states and provinces call this the Department of Motor Vehicles. However, everyone in the United States and Canada understands the term DMV.

B Unscramble the words to make questions with *have to* and *need to*.

1 have to have / drivers / a driver's license?

   Do drivers have to have a driver's license?

2 a driver / how old / have to be?

3 have to / what / bring / drivers / to the DMV?

4 need to say? / what / an acceptable document

5 have to / be citizens? / drivers

6 need to take / new drivers / a class?

7 pass an exam? / have to / new drivers

8 need to go / drivers / to get their license? / where

C Pair Work Ask and answer the questions in B with a partner. Use the information in A to find the answers.

Getting What You Want **401**

Exercise 2.2 Pronunciation Focus: *Have To* and *Has To*

Have to is usually pronounced "hafta."	I "**hafta**" win the game. You "**hafta**" see my new game!
Has to is usually pronounced "hasta."	She "**hasta**" try harder to win. He "**hasta**" think quickly when he plays this game!

A Listen and repeat the sentences in the chart above.

B Listen. Complete the sentences with *have to* or *has to*.

Welcome to the STACK'EM game website!

Here are some tips on how to win the game!

1. You don't __have to__ know many rules to win the game.

2. A player _____ move around different shapes to make lines.

3. Players _____ turn the pieces to make them fit.

4. The pieces _____ fit together with no spaces to make the line disappear.

5. As players get better, the pieces come more quickly. The player _____ think very quickly.

6. You don't _____ play against someone. You can play by yourself.

7. Players _____ have one of the top five scores for their name to be added to the "champion" list.

8. Stack'em is fantastic! You _____ play a lot to become good, but it's fun!

C Pair Work Write three sentences about the rules of a game you know how to play. Then share them with a partner.

In "Go Fish," players have to ask each other for cards.

1. _____
2. _____
3. _____

Necessity and Conclusions

Exercise 2.3 Necessity and Conclusions

A Complete the sentences with the correct verb combination. Use a verb of necessity or conclusion with the words in parentheses. Then label *N* for necessity and *C* for conclusion. Sometimes more than one answer is possible.

1 Sarah has a lot of work to do in the office, then she goes to school at night. She ___must work___ (work) hard. __N__

2 She always has a lot of homework. She _____ (be) exhausted after a long week of work and school. ____

3 He says that when Sarah _____ (take) a quick break, she can. ____

4 Sarah wants to have a week off.¹ She _____ (talk) to her boss to schedule her time off. ____

5 Her boss _____ (look) at the schedule. ____

6 Her boss _____ (make) sure he has enough workers during the time when Sarah is off. ____

7 She _____ (not/do) any work when she is away on vacation. Her boss will not let her. ____

8 Sarah says her office is a great place to work. She _____ (like) her boss and the people she works with. ____

¹**a week off:** a week without work

B Pair Work Write four sentences about some of the things you have to do to get ahead in your life. Share your sentences with a partner. Make conclusions about what they do with *must*.

A *I have to work all day and go to school at night.*
B *You must be exhausted!*

1 _____
2 _____
3 _____
4 _____

3 Avoid Common Mistakes

1 **Make sure *have to* and *need to* agree with the subject.**

had
She ~~have~~ to be very skilled.

2 **Use the base form of the verb after *have to*, *need to*, or *must*.**

have
He needs to ~~has~~ his passport.

3 **Do not use *to* after *must*.**

I must ~~to~~ follow the rules.

4 **Use the base form of *have to* and *need to* in negative statements and in questions.**

need
He doesn't ~~needs~~ to register.

have
Does she ~~has~~ to write an essay?

5 **Use *have to* or *must* to express conclusions. Do not use *need to* for conclusions.**

has to / must
Today is Tuesday. Tomorrow ~~needs to~~ be Wednesday.

Editing Task

Find and correct 10 more mistakes in this conversation about someone trying to break a record.

Pete   Does Jack ~~needs~~ *need* to have a lot of skill to play the game?

Jim   No, he has to has a lot of luck.

Pete   How many times does he has to win to break the record?

Jim   He have to win three more times.

5   Pete   He won eight times, so the record must to be 10.

Jim   Yes, the world record needs to be 10.

Pete   Does he need to has a certain time to win?

Jim   No, he must to have a certain number of points.

Pete   Jack also has to wins five games in a row.[1] He must to really like this

10   computer game!

Jim   Yeah, he loves it. He doesn't needs to play it every day, but he enjoys it.

[1] **in a row:** without interruption

4 Academic Writing

Opinion Paragraph

Brainstorm > Organize > Write > **Edit**

In Unit 29, you learned ways to introduce and support your opinion and then wrote a paragraph to answer the prompt below. In this unit (30), you will review, revise, and edit your paragraph.

> *The Internet wastes our time. It does not help us do more work. Do you agree or disagree?*

Connecting Ideas

Use the coordinating conjunction *and* or the adverbs *also* and *too* to add information.

My sister uses her computer **and** her smartphone a lot.

My sister uses her computer a lot. She uses her smartphone a lot, **too**.

My sister uses her computer a lot. She **also** uses her smartphone a lot.

Your paragraph about the Internet should include examples to support your opinion. Connecting these examples will make your writing better and easier to understand.

Exercise 4.1 Applying the Skill

Read the paragraph. Rewrite it using *and*, *too*, or *also* to connect ideas.

   I agree that smartphones are extremely useful. First, students can use them to do their homework online. They can read class assignments online. Next, many business people use their smartphones on the subway. For example, they check their email on the way to work. They read reports on the way to work. Finally, smartphones are very helpful to tourists. Tourists use maps to find their way. They use apps to buy tickets to shows and museums. It is difficult to imagine life without smartphones.

My Writing

Exercise 4.2 Revising Your Ideas

1. Work with a partner. Use the questions below to give feedback about the ideas in your partner's paragraph.
   - Which details in your partner's paragraph are the strongest?
   - Which details in your partner's paragraph are unnecessary?
   - What types of details does your partner need to add to make the paragraph stronger?
2. Use the feedback from your partner to revise your paragraph.

Exercise 4.3 Editing Your Writing

Use the checklist to review and edit your paragraph.

Did you analyze the prompt and answer it completely?	
Did you write a clear topic sentence with your opinion?	
Did you include advantages or disadvantages in your paragraph?	
Did you give examples, facts, and reasons to support your opinion?	
Did you use opinion expressions correctly?	
Did you connect ideas correctly with *and*, *also*, and *too*?	
Did you include a concluding sentence?	

Exercise 4.4 Writing Your Final Draft

Apply the feedback and edits from Exercises 4.2 and 4.3 to write the final draft of your paragraph.

UNIT 31

Adjectives and Adverbs

Making a Good Impression

1 Grammar in the Real World

ACADEMIC WRITING

Description and opinion

A Do you know how to give a presentation? What do you do to prepare? Read the article. How many of your ideas are in the web article?

B Comprehension Check Does the article answer these questions? Write *Yes* or *No*. Then answer the questions.

1 What can give you confidence as a presenter?
   _____

2 What are some ways that can help you organize your ideas?
   _____

3 What should you do when you practice?
   _____

4 What should you do after your presentation? Why?
   _____

C Notice Look at the word in bold in each sentence. Circle the word that it describes. How are the words you circled in item 1 different from the words you circled in item 2?

1. a A **confident** presenter always makes a good impression.
   b Think **positive** thoughts.

2. a Smile **confidently**.
   b Before you start, breathe **deeply**.

Next, complete the sentence below. How do you know which word to use?

3 He walks _____.
   a confident
   b confidently

Adjectives and Adverbs

How to Be a SUCCESSFUL PRESENTER

For many people, giving a presentation can be a **scary** experience. If you feel **nervous** about giving presentations, here are some helpful tips that you can follow.

- Prepare your presentation **carefully. Careful** preparation will give you confidence, and this will impress[1] your audience. A **confident**[2] presenter always makes a **good** impression.[3]

- Organize your ideas. Think about what you want to say. Then list your three or four main points on note cards.

- Practice giving your presentation aloud[4] by yourself and with friends, too. Tell your friends to give you **honest** feedback,[5] but make sure they tell you first what you did **well**.

- On the day of the presentation, arrive at the room **early**. Think **positive** thoughts and remember that you can do this.

- Before you start, breathe **deeply** and smile **confidently** at your audience. Speak **slowly** and **clearly**. Make eye contact with people in **different** parts of the room. Look at your notes **quickly** when you need to. Your audience wants you to do **well**. Then relax and do your best.

After your presentation, ask people for feedback and advice. Use the ideas in your next presentation. With practice, you will learn to give **good** presentations, and you may even enjoy giving them.

[1]**impress:** cause people to admire and respect you
[2]**confident:** not having a doubt about yourself or your abilities
[3]**impression:** an idea or opinion of what someone is like
[4]**aloud:** in a voice loud enough that people can hear it
[5]**feedback:** response after seeing an activity or performance

Making a Good Impression

2 Adjectives and Adverbs of Manner

Grammar Presentation

2.1 Adjectives and Adverbs of Manner

A Adjectives give information about nouns. They often come before a noun or after *be*.

ADJECTIVE   NOUN
I want your **honest** feedback.

BE   ADJECTIVE
The slides were **clear**.

B Adverbs give information about verbs.

VERB   ADVERB
The presenter spoke **clearly**.

VERB   ADVERB
She prepared her presentation **carefully**.

C Adverbs of manner usually come after a verb or a verb + object.

VERB   ADVERB
Dress **nicely**.

VERB   OBJ.   ADVERB
She looked at the audience **quickly**.

D Don't put an adverb between a verb and an object. Place it after the object.

VERB   OBJECT   ADVERB
Prepare your presentation **carefully**.

NOT *Prepare carefully your presentation.*

2.2 Basic Forms of Adverbs

	ADJECTIVE	ADVERB
A For most adverbs of manner, add *-ly* to the adjective form.	bad careful clear fluent loud nervous quick	bad**ly** careful**ly** clear**ly** fluent**ly** loud**ly** nervous**ly** quick**ly**
B With adjectives ending in *-y*, change *y* to *i* and add *-ly*.	easy happy	eas**ily** happ**ily**
C With adjectives ending in *-ic*, add *-ally*.	automatic academic	automatic**ally** academic**ally**
D With adjectives ending in a consonant + *-le*, drop *e* and add *-y*.	gentle terrible	gent**ly** terri**bly**

Adjectives and Adverbs

2.2 Basic Forms of Adverbs (continued)

		ADJECTIVE	ADVERB
E	The adverb and adjective form of the following words are the same: *early, fast, hard, late*.	He is **early**. It sounds **fast**. It's a **hard** test. They're **late**.	He went home **early**. He talks **fast**. He studied **hard**. They arrived **late**.
F	*Well* is the adverb form of the adjective *good*.	He's **good** at English.	He speaks English **well**.
	Well can also be an adjective. It means "healthy."	He isn't **well**.	
G	Some adjectives that end in *-ly* do <u>not</u> have an adverb form. Do <u>not</u> use them as adverbs.	elderly, friendly, lively, lonely, lovely, ugly	

▶▶ Adverbs with *-ly*: See page A24.

🌐 DATA FROM THE REAL WORLD

These are the most common adverbs of manner:

well	late	easily	carefully	seriously	automatically
hard	fast	clearly	strongly	differently	properly
early	quickly	slowly	closely	badly	

Grammar Application

Exercise 2.1 Adjectives and Adverbs

A Circle the adjectives and draw an arrow to the nouns they describe. Underline the adverbs and draw a line to the verbs they describe.

I'm a (professional) hairstylist, and I'm very good at my job. I'm friendly and polite to my clients, so I make a good impression. But I don't schedule clients early in the day because I'm not in a good mood until noon.

Of course, I don't get an early start to my day. I wake up late and start my day slowly. I can't think clearly without three cups of strong coffee. After breakfast, I take a shower, get dressed, and check my e-mail. I don't talk to anyone in the morning, except for my elderly neighbor when I leave home. He likes to sit on the front porch. I think he's lonely.

I drive to work, but my commute isn't bad. When I get to work, I check my schedule closely and make a few quick phone calls. At 11:55 a.m., I finish my last cup of coffee and smile warmly at my first client at 12:00 noon.

Making a Good Impression

B Over to You What is your morning routine? Write four sentences using adjectives and adverbs. Then tell a partner.

A *I get up early. I'm awake by 6:00 a.m.*
B *I sleep late. On the weekends, I sleep until 11:00 a.m.*

Exercise 2.2 More Adjectives and Adverbs

A Complete each sentence pair with the adverb or adjective form of the underlined word in the first sentence. The sentences will have a similar meaning. (Remember: Some adjectives do not change form when they are adverbs.)

1 Cindy makes a good impression when she presents in front of a group.
   a She is <u>careful</u> when she researches her topic. She researches her topic _carefully_ .
   b Her voice is <u>clear</u> and easy to understand. She speaks _____.
   c When she starts to speak, her smile is <u>automatic</u>. When she starts to speak, she _____ smiles.
   d She <u>strongly</u> argues her points. She makes _____ arguments for her points.

2 Robert made a good impression at the job interview.
   a He was <u>polite</u>. He talked _politely_ to the interviewer.
   b He was <u>early</u>. He arrived at the company _____.
   c He thought about the questions, and he answered the questions <u>carefully</u>. He was _____ in his answers.
   d He was <u>good</u> at answering the questions. He answered the questions _____.
   e He didn't speak <u>badly</u> about his former employer. He didn't say _____ things about his former employer.

B Pair Work Take turns reading the sentences. Identify the adjective and adverb form of the words.

Exercise 2.3 Adverbs of Manner

A Complete the questions about making a good impression at school and at work. Use the adverb forms of the words in parentheses.

QUESTIONNAIRE

1. Do you get to work or school _early_ (early), or do you arrive _late_ (late)?
2. Do you take your job or your studies _____ (serious)?
3. Do you work _____ (hard), or are you lazy?
4. Do you check your assignments _____ (careful)?
5. Do you try to do every job _____ (proper), or do you do everything _____ (quick)?
6. Do you always dress _____ (appropriate) for work or school?
7. Do you always speak _____ (polite) to your boss or teacher?
8. Do you plan your time _____ (good) and complete your work on time?
9. Do you organize your desk _____ (neat)?
10. Can you give instructions _____ (clear)?
11. Do you like to work _____ (close) with co-workers or classmates?

B Pair Work   Ask and answer the questions in A. Give more information in your answers.

  A *Do you get to work early?*
  B *No, I don't. I usually arrive just in time.*

C What do you think are the six most important qualities of a good employee? What about a good student? Complete the sentences using ideas from A and your own ideas.

A good employee . . .	A good student . . .
1 _works hard_	1 _studies hard_
2 _____	2 _____
3 _____	3 _____
4 _____	4 _____
5 _____	5 _____
6 _____	6 _____

Making a Good Impression

3 Adjectives with Linking Verbs; Adjectives and Adverbs with *Very* and *Too*

Grammar Presentation

3.1 Adjectives with Linking Verbs

A Use an adjective, not an adverb, after these linking verbs: *be, get, seem, look, feel, sound, smell, taste*

I **get confused** [ADJ.] when someone asks difficult questions.

The presentation **looked interesting** [ADJ.].

You may **feel nervous** [ADJ.], but try to **sound confident** [ADJ.].

That coffee **smells good** [ADJ.].

B When *feel* means "have an opinion," use the adverb *strongly*.

FEEL + ADV. (OPINION)
I **feel strongly** that people should speak clearly.

BUT I felt weak when I had the flu, but I feel **strong** now.

3.2 *Very* and *Too* + Adjective or Adverb

A You can use *very* and *too* before adjectives or adverbs to make their meaning stronger. *Very* and *too* do not have the same meaning.

VERY + ADJ.   VERY + ADV.
She is **very serious**. She works **very hard**.

TOO + ADJ.   TOO + ADV.
The talk was **too long**. He spoke **too fast**.

B *Very* makes an adjective or an adverb stronger.

Her ideas were **very helpful**.

He spoke **very fast**. I understood him, but it was difficult.

C *Too* means "more than necessary." It usually has a negative meaning and means there's a problem.

He spoke **too fast**. I couldn't understand anything that he said.

The school is **too expensive**. I can't afford it.

D You can also use *very* (but not *too*) before an adjective + a noun.

ADJ. + NOUN
It's a **very expensive program**.

NOT It's a too expensive program.

Adjectives and Adverbs

3.2 Very and Too + Adjective or Adverb (continued)

E	You can use an infinitive after *too* + an adjective or adverb.	*She's **too tired to study**.* (= She can't study because she's too tired.) *She spoke **too fast to understand**.* (= I did not understand her because she spoke too fast.) *The words on the slides were **too small to read**.* (= No one could read the words because they were too small.)

 ## Grammar Application

Exercise 3.1 Adjectives with Linking Verbs

A Complete the sentences about how people react in new social situations. Choose the correct adjective or adverb in parentheses. When you finish, check (✓) the statements that are true for you.

1 I often get **nervous**/**shyly** in new social situations. _____
2 I am **confident**/**easily** around new people. _____
3 I often feel **excited**/**nervously** before a party. _____
4 I feel **uncomfortable**/**fast** when I'm nervous. _____
5 I hope other people think I look **attractive**/**confidently**. _____
6 I try to be a **nicely**/**friendly** person. _____
7 I like to tell jokes and make people laugh. I tell jokes **bad**/**well**. _____
8 I get **excited**/**well** when I listen to music and sing along to the songs. _____
9 It's never a problem for me to remember people's names. I do that **easily**/**automatic**. _____
10 I give my opinion when I feel **strong**/**strongly** about something. _____

Making a Good Impression

B Pair Work Compare sentences from A. Do you act the same way in new situations?

A *I often get nervous in new social situations. How about you?*
B *I don't get nervous. I'm always excited about meeting new people.*

Exercise 3.2 Adjectives with *Very* and *Too*

A Complete the sentences about a party. Use *very* or *too*.

1. The party lasted for six hours. The party was ___very___ long, so we went home early.
2. The party lasted for an hour. Everyone wanted to stay longer. The party was _____ short.
3. There were 75 people at the party. The living room holds 50. The room was _____ small.
4. There were five people at the table. The table seats 12. The table was _____ big.
5. The party was noisy, and I couldn't hear conversations. The party was _____ noisy.
6. The party was noisy, but I had a great time. The party was _____ noisy.
7. Some people spoke quickly, but I understood most of it. Some people spoke _____ quickly.
8. One man spoke quickly, and I didn't understand a word of it. He spoke _____ quickly.
9. It was 25°F (-4°C) outside on the porch. We had to leave. It was _____ cold.
10. It was 43°F (6°C) outside on the porch. I wore my coat. It was _____ cold.

B Now listen and check your answers.

Adjectives and Adverbs

Exercise 3.3 Adjectives with *Too* + Adjective + Infinitive

A Pair Work Complete the conversations. Use the word given with *too* + adjective + infinitive (*to* + verb). Then practice with a partner.

1 **A** You passed your exams with straight As.
   B That can't <u>be true</u>.

   (good) It's <u>too good to be true</u>.

2 **A** Do you like your new job?
   B I can't <u>say</u>. I only started today.

   (early) It's _____.

3 **A** Mom! Dad! We want <u>to get married</u>.
   B You're only 16!

   (young) You're _____.

4 **A** I want <u>to change programs</u> in school.
   B Well, there's still time.

   (not late) It's _____.

5 **A** Let's <u>go camping</u> this weekend.
   B Camping? It's 10 below outside!

   (cold) It's _____.

6 **A** Is your brother <u>going to work</u> today?
   B Well, I think he has the flu.

   (sick) He's _____.

7 **A** Why don't you <u>ask</u> your boss for help?
   B I can't, I'm afraid of him.

   (scared) I'm _____.

8 **A** You look really stressed today.
   B Do I? You know, I can't <u>think</u>.

   (busy) I'm _____.

Making a Good Impression

B **Group Work** Discuss these questions in a group. Which ideas do you share?

1 Do you ever get too tired to think?
2 Are you ever too scared to ask questions?
3 Do you ever feel too embarrassed to apologize for something?
4 Were you ever too sick to go to work or school this year?
5 What is something you feel is too difficult to do?
6 Are 17-year-olds too young to get married?

 DATA FROM THE REAL WORLD

People often use *not very* + adjective or adverb to make negative statements "softer," less critical, or less direct.

The speaker was**n't very** good. He did**n't** speak **very** well.

NOT ~~The speaker was bad. He spoke badly.~~

Exercise 3.4 *Not very . . .*

Read the notes that an interviewer wrote about a job candidate. Make them less critical, or less direct, and write statements using *not very* and the words in parentheses.

1 unfriendly <u>He wasn't very friendly.</u> (friendly)
2 spoke nervously <u>He didn't speak very confidently.</u> (confidently)
3 wore a dirty shirt _____ (clean)
4 bad at problem solving _____ (good at)
5 answered questions badly _____ (well)
6 looked dishonest _____ (honest)
7 seemed inexperienced _____ (experienced)
8 acted bored _____ (interested)

4 Avoid Common Mistakes

1 Use an adverb when you give information about most verbs. Some adverbs are irregular and do not end in *-ly*.

I work ~~efficient~~ *efficiently*.   I work very ~~hardly~~ *hard*.

2 Use an adjective after the linking verbs *be*, *feel*, *get*, *look*, *seem*, *smell*, *sound*, and *taste*.

He seemed ~~strangely~~ *strange*.

3 Be especially careful with *good* and *well*. People often use *good* instead of *well*, especially when they speak, but do not write this.

I try to do things ~~good~~ *well*.

4 Do not use an adverb between a verb and its object.

I always prepare ~~carefully~~ my answers *carefully*.

5 Do not use *too* when you mean *very*.

My teacher is ~~too~~ *very* good. I'm learning a lot.

Editing Task

Find and correct the mistakes in this article about job interviews.

PREPARING for an INTERVIEW

An interview can be a difficult experience. Prepare ~~carefully~~ your responses *carefully*, and you will make a good impression.

Before the interview, research thoroughly the company. Find out about its products and services. You should always be truthfully about the things you do good. When you talk about
5 something you do bad, choose a weakness that is not serious. Say that you are too aware of the weakness and that you are working hardly to improve yourself. Say you want a new challenge and that you want to progress in your career. Always sound positively and don't complain about your current job.

On the day of the interview, dress nice. Shake firmly hands when you meet the interviewer.
10 Try to sound sincerely and look too confident. Follow these steps and you'll do good.

5 Academic Writing

Description and Opinion

Brainstorm > Organize > Write > Edit

In this writing cycle (Units 31-33), you are going to answer the prompt below. In this unit (31), you will read an article about homestay vacations and then brainstorm ideas for your writing.

> *Describe the place where you live now or where you are from. Write about its positives and negatives. Include your opinions.*

Exercise 5.1 Preparing to Write

Work with a partner. Ask and answer the questions.

1. Think about where you live or where you are from. What kind of place is it? A big city? A small town? Something else?
2. What are the people like in this place? Are they friendly? What do they like to do?
3. Imagine that another student from your class visits this place. What two or three things would he or she probably notice?
4. Would you like to live in this place for your whole life? Why or why not?

Exercise 5.2 Focusing on Vocabulary

Read the definitions. Then complete the sentences with the correct form of the words in bold.

area (n) a region or part of a larger place, like a country or city
cheap (adj) not expensive, or costs less than usual
downtown (adj) the main or central part of a city
expensive (adj) costs a lot of money; not cheap
local (adj) relating to a particular area, city, or town
noisy (adj) loud; makes a lot of noise
quiet (adj) makes little or no noise

1. My hotel is _____ and calm. It is outside of the busy city center, so it isn't loud at night.
2. Central Park is a nice _____ to relax in New York City.
3. When people visit new cities, it's a good idea to ask _____ people for the best restaurants. They know the most about their city.
4. Since the airline was new, they offered _____ flights from New York City to Boston. A lot of new customers bought tickets at low prices.
5. We took the bus to _____ Chicago because that is where the main tourist sites in the city are located.

Adjectives and Adverbs

6 It's getting more _____ to live in a big city, so people who can't pay the high prices are moving away.

7 There was a lot of traffic on my street last night. There were so many _____ cars that I couldn't sleep.

Homestay Vacations

1 These days, homestays are becoming common, and people around the world are offering their homes as hotels. Homestays offer **cheaper** places to stay than normal hotels. They also offer more chances for guests to see the **area** like **local** people. They are popular with students who want to stay in another country and learn a language. We asked three families who run homestays to tell us about where they live.

A Mountain Village – The Atal family

2 Our family home is in the north of Nepal, in the Himalayan Mountains, in the village of Manang. Our mountains are the highest in the world. The village is small and very **quiet**. People here are friendlier than in larger towns. The mountains are extremely beautiful. You can go for long walks and swim in the rivers. You have to plan carefully when shopping because there are no stores or cafés.

A House near the Forest – Kate and Julian Foxton

3 Our two-bedroom house is in the U.S. Pacific Northwest in Washington State. It is a 20-minute drive to Seattle, the nearest city. There are many lakes, rivers, and forests. The surroundings are very quiet. We spend a lot of time reading books, watching movies, and going for walks in the forest, where we see a lot of flowers and small animals. Our area is definitely great for hiking, kayaking, and mountain biking. However, houses here are more **expensive** than in most places, which can be a problem for local people. There are not many buses or trains here, so getting around without a car is difficult.

The Big City – Chafic and Aline Halwany

4 Our home is near the historic **downtown** area of Beirut, Lebanon, one of the largest cities in the Middle East. There are lots of cafés and restaurants, which are open late at night. We love it here because people are so friendly and you can always find what you need. Many people come here to learn Arabic and French. There are also a lot of jobs and businesses here. However, it can be **noisy** at night, and there is a lot of traffic during the day. The best thing about Beirut is the weather. It is nice all year round; it rains in the winter, but there is no snow.

Exercise 5.3 Comprehension Check

Read the text on page 421. Look at the summaries of paragraphs 2–4. Cross out the incorrect words in bold and write the correct words. The first one is an example.

Paragraph 2: The Atal family lives in a **city** *village*. It is a **busy** place. The mountains are very **cold**.

Paragraph 3: Kate and Julian Foxton live in the **Northeast** of the United States. The area is great for **theaters**. The houses are really **cheap**.

Paragraph 4: Chafic and Aline Halwany live in a **small** city. People learn **English** and French in the downtown area. There is a lot of traffic **at night**.

Exercise 5.4 Noticing the Grammar

Work with a partner. Complete the tasks.

1. Find an adjective with a linking verb in paragraph 1. _____

2. Find two examples of an adverb + adjective in paragraph 2. _____
_____

3. Underline the adverb in the last sentence of paragraph 2. What is its adjective form?
_____

4. Read paragraph 3. Write down three adjectives to describe the place where the Foxtons live.
_____ _____

Using a T-chart to Brainstorm

You can use a **T-chart** to brainstorm the positives (+) and negatives (−) of a topic, in this case a place. Write about the positives in one column and the negatives in the other column.

Exercise 5.5 Applying the Skill

Review the text. Choose one of the three places in the article. Use the T-chart to list the positives and negatives about the place you chose.

positive (+)	negative (−)

Unit 31 Adjectives and Adverbs

My Writing

Exercise 5.6 Brainstorming

Think about the place you live now or where you are from. Write down as many words as you can to answer the questions. You do not need to write complete sentences.

1 What kind of place is it? _____

2 What interesting things can you see there? _____

3 What interesting things can you do there? _____

4 What are the people like? _____

5 How do you feel about the place? _____

UNIT 32

Comparative Adjectives and Adverbs

Progress

1 Grammar in the Real World

ACADEMIC WRITING

Description and opinion

A How has modern life changed in the last 15 years? Read the question forum from a website. What changes does the forum discuss?

B Comprehension Check Complete the sentences. Use the text in the forum answer to help you.

1. Highways became _____ and _____.

2. Computers became _____ and _____ but _____ to use.

3. The Internet gave us _____ communication and a _____ world.

C Notice Complete each word or phrase. Use the text to help you.

1. small_____
2. big_____
3. large_____
4. _____ efficient
5. _____ powerful
6. _____ congested

What are the two different ways to change the adjectives?

Comparative Adjectives and Adverbs

Question Forum[1]

Ask your question here

Dear Question Forum

Lorraine San Diego, CA
My grandmother says that everything got **bigger**, **faster**, and **better** in the twentieth century. Is that true? Did some things
5 get **smaller**, **slower**, or **worse** than in the years before?

Rosa San Diego, CA
It's a matter of opinion, but what your grandmother says is generally true. In the twentieth century, buildings became **taller**. Bridges became **longer** than they were in
10 the nineteenth century, and highways became **wider** and **faster** than the old roads. Cities became larger and more **crowded** than they had been before. New airplanes were suddenly **larger** and **heavier** than old airplanes. Large companies joined together to make even **bigger**
15 global corporations.[2] Technology in the home got **better**. Home electrical appliances like refrigerators and washing machines became **better**, **cheaper**, and **more efficient**. Computers became **more powerful** and **more complicated** but easier to use. The Internet gave us
20 **faster** communication and a **smaller** world – what we now call the global village.
Did everything get **larger** and **better**? Not everything. A lot of things did not get **bigger**, and some things got **worse**, like some environmental problems. Some things
25 became **smaller** but **better**. For example, phones became **thinner**, cameras got **lighter**, and modern video cameras became much **smaller** than **older** video cameras. Unfortunately, the ice sheets[3] in the Arctic and Antarctic became **smaller**, too, as the world became
30 **hotter**. Generally, things did not become **slower** – except perhaps traffic in cities, which became **more congested**.[4] The big question is: Are people **happier** now?

[1]**forum:** a place to talk about something of public interest
[2]**corporation:** a large company
[3]**ice sheet:** layer of ice
[4]**congested:** too blocked or crowded

Progress **425**

2 Comparative Adjectives

Grammar Presentation

| You can use comparative adjectives to describe how two people or things are different from one another. | New airplanes were **larger** and **heavier than** old airplanes. |

2.1 Comparisons with *Be* + Adjective

	Be	Comparative Adjective	*Than*	
I	am	older		my brother.
		more serious		my parents.
You We They	are	happier	than	Elisa.
		more successful		our co-workers.
He She It	is	taller		me.
		more excited		the teachers.

2.2 Comparative Adjective + Noun

	Comparative Adjective	Noun
The Internet gave us	faster	communication.
Large companies joined together to make	bigger	corporations.
We now have	more powerful	computers.

2.3 Comparative of Short Adjectives (One Syllable)

	Adjective	Comparative
A For one-syllable adjectives, add *-er*.	low	low**er**
	fast	fast**er**
B For one-syllable adjectives ending in *-e*, add *-r*.	safe	saf**er**
	large	larg**er**

426　Unit 32 Comparative Adjectives and Adverbs

2.3 Comparative of Short Adjectives (One Syllable) *(continued)*

	Adjective	Comparative
C If the adjective ends with one vowel + one consonant, double the last letter and add -er.	hot	ho**tt**er
	big	big**g**er
D If the adjective has two syllables and ends in -y, change the y to i and add -er.	heavy	heav**i**er
	easy	eas**i**er

2.4 Comparative of Long Adjectives (Two or More Syllables)

Adjective	Comparative
crowded	**more** crowded
powerful	**more** powerful
economical	**more** economical
efficient	**more** efficient

2.5 Two-Syllable Adjectives That Take *-er*

Adjective	Comparative
narrow	narrow**er**
quiet	quiet**er**
simple	simpl**er**

2.6 Irregular Adjectives

Adjective	Comparative
good	**better**
bad	**worse**
far	**further (farther)**

🌐 *Further* is over 10 times more frequent than *farther*.

▶▶ Adjectives and Adverbs: Comparative and Superlative Forms: See page A22.

2.7 Using Comparative Adjectives

A	Use comparative adjectives to show a difference between two people, places, things, or ideas.	The Burj Khalifa in Dubai is **taller than** the Sears Tower in Chicago.
B	Use *than* after a comparative and before the second person or thing that you are comparing. Don't use *that* or *then*.	Jessica is older **than** Denise. NOT older ~~that~~ Denise / older ~~then~~ Denise
C	You can use a comparative adjective without *than* when the second part of the comparison is obvious.	I need a **bigger** apartment. (= a bigger apartment than the apartment I have now)
D	*Less* is the opposite of *more*. Do not use *less* with one-syllable adjectives.	The traffic here is **less congested** than in the city. Pennsylvania is **smaller** than California. NOT ~~less big~~
E	You can use a pronoun after *than* instead of a noun.	Mike's sister is taller **than he is**. (= than Mike is) Sue sings better **than I do**.
	In speaking, you can use an object pronoun. In academic writing, always use a subject pronoun.	My brother is older **than me**. My brother is older **than I am**.

🌐 DATA FROM THE REAL WORLD

The 15 most common comparative adjectives ending in *-er* in writing and speaking are:

better	easier	higher	lower	stronger
bigger	further	larger	older	worse
earlier	greater	later	smaller	younger

The 10 most common comparative adjectives with *more* are:

comfortable	efficient	important	powerful	serious
difficult	expensive	interesting	recent	successful

Comparative Adjectives and Adverbs

Grammar Application

Exercise 2.1 Comparisons with *Be*

A How do things today compare with 20 years ago? Write the correct forms of the comparative adjectives in parentheses.

1. Home appliances are _cheaper_ (cheap).
2. Laptop computers are _____ (light).
3. Desktop computers are _____ (quiet).
4. Music is _____ (easy) to share.
5. Bicycles are _____ (fast).
6. Cars are _____ (energy-efficient)
7. Cell phones are _____ (small).
8. Homes are _____ (big).

B Compare cell phones from many years ago and now. Use comparative forms of the adjectives in the box.

Early cellular phone   Smartphone

cheap	fast	powerful	smart
expensive	~~heavy~~	slow	thin

1. _Old cell phones were heavier._
2. _____
3. _____
4. _____
5. _____
6. _____
7. _____
8. _____

Progress **429**

Exercise 2.2 Comparative Adjectives and Nouns

A Read about a city's problems. How can it become a better place to live? Complete the sentences and make solutions. Use comparative forms of the adjectives in the box and nouns. Use each adjective once.

attractive	clean	energy-efficient	new	~~wide~~
cheap	clear	frequent	safe	

Problem	Solution
1 The main highway through the city is narrow.	We should build a _wider highway_.
2 The bridge over the river is old and dangerous.	We should build a _____.
3 The downtown parking is very expensive.	We should have _____.
4 The city parks are not clean.	We should have _____.
5 The city's buses are not energy-efficient.	We should buy _____.
6 The street signs are confusing.	We should install _____.
7 The bus service is infrequent.	We should have _____.
8 The city's website is unattractive.	The city should create a _____.

B Pair Work What changes should happen to improve your town or city? Discuss with a partner.

A *Our city needs a more frequent subway service.*
B *We need nicer department stores downtown. We should have . . .*

C Group Work Compare cities and towns that you know. Work in groups. Then tell the class about them. Use the adjectives in parentheses.

1 (modern) _Houston is more modern than San Antonio._
2 (big) _New York has bigger parks than Miami._
3 (traditional) _____
4 (cheap) _____
5 (good/job market) _____
6 (clean) _____
7 (historic) _____
8 (fancy/stores) _____
9 (crowded) _____

3 Comparative Adverbs

Grammar Presentation

| You can use comparative adverbs to describe how two actions or events are different from each other. | *Ashley drives **more slowly** than her brother.* |

3.1 Comparisons with Adverbs

	Verb	Comparative Adjective	Than	
Joanna	runs	faster		her brother.
The new printer	works	better	than	the old printer.
The population of Italy	is growing	more slowly		the population of Canada.
A diesel car	runs	more efficiently		a gasoline car.

3.2 Comparative of Short Adverbs (One Syllable)

	Adverb	Comparative
For one syllable adverbs, add *-er* or *-r*.	fast	fast**er**
	high	high**er**
	late	late**r**
	long	long**er**
	hard	hard**er**

3.3 Comparative of Longer Adverbs (Two or More Syllables)

	Adverb	Comparative
A For adverbs of two or more syllables, use *more* (or *less*).	often	*more* / *less* often
	carefully	*more* / *less* carefully
	quickly	*more* / *less* quickly
	easily	*more* / *less* easily
B We say *earlier*, not *more early*.	*This flight arrives **earlier than** the other flight.*	

3.4 Irregular Adverbs

Irregular Adverb	Comparative
well	better
badly	worse
far	further or farther

▶▶ Adjectives and Adverbs: Comparative and Superlative Forms: See page A22.

3.5 Using Comparative Adverbs

A	You can use comparative adverbs to compare the way two people do the same action.	Hilda studies **harder than** the other students. My brother drives **more carefully** than my sister.
B	You can use comparative adverbs to compare the way two actions or events happen.	Cairo is growing **more rapidly than** London.
C	You can use comparative adverbs to compare the way an action happened in two different time periods.	Larissa works **harder** now **than** she did last year.
D	Use *than* after a comparative adverb and before the second action or event that you are comparing. Don't use *that* or *then*.	He drives **faster than** his brother. NOT faster ~~that~~ his brother / faster ~~then~~ his brother
E	You can use a comparative adverb without *than*.	I can run fast, but Lorna can run **faster**.
F	*Less* is the opposite of *more*.	The old car runs **less efficiently** than the new car.
	Do not use *less* with one-syllable adverbs.	Meryl arrived **earlier than** Patrick. NOT ~~less late~~

Unit 32 Comparative Adjectives and Adverbs

Comparative Adjectives and Adverbs

 # Grammar Application

Exercise 3.1 Making Comparisons with Adverbs

Listen to the conversation. Complete the chart with comparative adverbs.

New York, New York	Grant, Florida
1 People walk _more quickly_.	4 You drive _____ to get to a mall.
2 People work _____.	5 Joe and Bill go out _____.
3 Restaurants stay open _____.	6 You spend money _____.

Exercise 3.2 More Making Comparisons with Adverbs

A Write the comparative form of the adverb. Then write verbs that go with it from the list. Some verbs can go with more than one adverb.

drive	go to bed	play football	sleep	study
get up	go to the gym	play the guitar	speak English	walk
go out	go to the movies	sing	spend money	work

Adverb, Comparative Adverb	Verb(s)
1 fast _faster_	_run, drive_
2 well	
3 carefully	
4 hard	
5 slowly	
6 early	
7 far	
8 frequently	
9 badly	
10 late	

Progress   **433**

B Over to You How is your lifestyle different from five years ago? In what ways do you do things differently? Use ideas from A.

I speak English better now than I did five years ago.

1 _____
2 _____
3 _____
4 _____
5 _____
6 _____
7 _____

Exercise 3.3 Adverbs and Personal Pronouns

DATA FROM THE REAL WORLD

Research shows that when people use a personal pronoun after *than*, they use the object forms *me, him, her, us, them*. They do not normally use the subject forms *I, he, she, we, they*.

You drive better than me / him.
NOT better than ~~I / he~~

than + object pronoun	▆▆▆▆▆▆▆
than + subject pronoun	▏

People use the subject form of the pronoun with an auxiliary verb (*be, do,* or *have*) or a modal verb (*will, can,* etc.), especially in writing.

He drives faster than I do. (= faster than I drive)
She can speak English better than he can. (= better than he can speak English)

A Over to You Complete the sentences with the names of people you know. Use a subject pronoun and an auxiliary or modal verb after *than*.

1 _____ gets up earlier than I _*do*_ .
2 _____ can run faster than I _*can*_ .
3 _____ eats more slowly than I _____ .
4 _____ exercises more often than I _____ .
5 _____ commutes further than I _____ .
6 _____ studied harder for yesterday's test than I _____ .
7 _____ can speak more fluently than I _____ .
8 _____ did better on the quiz than I _____ .

B Pair Work Tell a partner about each person in A. Use object pronouns (*me, him, them,* etc.).

My friend Charlie gets up earlier than me. He starts work at 7:00 a.m. I get up later than him.

4 Avoid Common Mistakes

1 **Do not use *more* with the *-er* comparative forms of adjectives and adverbs.**
She drives ~~more~~ faster than her brother.
This store is ~~more~~ cheaper than the other one.

2 **Do not use *more* with one-syllable adjectives and adverbs.**
My brother is ~~more tall~~ *taller* than I am.   She speaks ~~more fast~~ *faster* than I do.

3 **Do not use the *-er* ending with most adjectives of two or more syllables.**
His second movie was ~~excitinger~~ *more exciting* than his first movie.

4 **Do not use *more* with *better* or *worse*.**
My English is getting ~~more~~ better this year.

5 **Use *than* after a comparative, not *that* or *then*.**
She works harder ~~then~~ *than* I do.

Editing Task

Progress is change that results in a general improvement in life. Read the ideas about progress. Find and correct eight more mistakes in this blog.

What Is Progress?

It is not easy to answer this question. Here is a list of ideas.

Lisa   Medicines are now more effective and ~~more cheap~~ *cheaper*, so people's health is more better. People expect to live longer then they did 100 years ago.

5 Dan   There is a more shorter work week for everyone. There are powerfuler machines and computers, so people can be free from manual work.

Sanjay   Children reach a more higher level of education.

Cristina   People have more big houses and a comfortabler life that their parents.

5 Academic Writing

Description and Opinion

Brainstorm > **Organize** > Write > Edit

In Unit 31, you read an article and then brainstormed ideas for the prompt below. In this unit (32) you will use a T-chart to organize your ideas and details.

> Describe the place where you live now or where you are from. Write about its positives and negatives. Include your opinions.

Exercise 5.1 Noticing the Grammar

Look at three paragraphs from "Homestay Vacations" on page 421. Circle the comparative adjectives.

These days, homestays are becoming popular, and people around the world are offering their homes as hotels. Homestays offer cheaper places to stay than normal hotels. They also offer more chances for guests to see the area like local people. They are popular with students who want to stay in another country and learn a language. We asked three families
5   who run homestays to tell us about where they live.

A Mountain Village – The Atal family

Our family home is in the north of Nepal, in the Himalayan Mountains, in the village of Manang. Our mountains are the highest in the world. The village is small and very quiet. People here are friendlier than in larger towns. The mountains are extremely beautiful.
10 You can go for long walks and swim in the rivers. You have to plan carefully when shopping because there are no stores or cafés.

A House near the Forest – Kate and Julian Foxton

Our two-bedroom house is in the U.S. Pacific Northwest in Washington State. It is a 20-minute drive to Seattle, the nearest city. There are many lakes, rivers, and forests. The surroundings
15 are very quiet. We spend a lot of time reading books, watching movies, and going for walks in the forest, where we see a lot of flowers and small animals. Our area is definitely great for hiking, kayaking, and mountain biking. However, houses here are more expensive than in most places, which can be a problem for local people. There are not many buses or trains here, so getting around without a car is difficult.

Using Comparative Adjectives to Describe a Place

When writers describe and give their opinion about a place, they often compare the place with another place that they or their readers know to show how the places are different. When they do, they usually use comparative adjectives.

Mexico City is **larger** than New York City.

Seoul is **more modern** than Rome.

Exercise 5.2 Applying the Skill

Complete each sentence with a verb and a comparative adjective. Add a noun if necessary. The first one is an example.

1. Big cities _have better transportation_ than small towns.
2. Living near a forest _____ than living in a city.
3. People in a city can _____ than people in a small town.
4. Places in the north _____ than places in the south.
5. Big cities in Asia _____ than big cities in Europe.
6. People who live on farms _____ than people who live in towns.

Capital Letters and Punctuation

It is important to follow the rules of English capitalization and punctuation when you are writing sentences and paragraphs.

Use a capital letter at the beginning of a sentence. Use a period (.) at the end of a sentence.

He lives in Abu Dhabi**.**

Use commas (,) to separate three or more items in a list.

In her free time**,** she likes to read**,** exercise**,** and play video games.

Use a capital letter with a proper noun (the name of a specific person, place, or thing).

France   **I**stanbul   **J**uly   **S**aturday

Always use a capital letter for the pronoun *I*.

I live in London.

Exercise 5.3 Applying the Skill

Work with a partner. Correct the punctuation and capital letters in the paragraph. The first one is an example.

> I
> i live in montreal it is a city in canada it is a beautiful city there are many Stores and Restaurants the people are friendly there is an Art festival in june people in montreal speak both french and english it is very crowded with tourists in the Summer in the Winter, people like to ice skate and cross-country ski

My Writing

Using a T-chart to Take Notes and Organize Ideas

In Unit 31, you used a T-chart to brainstorm words and ideas for your writing. T-charts are also useful for taking notes and for analyzing and organizing ideas. Writers often review and edit their T-chart notes in later stages of the writing process.

Comparative Adjectives and Adverbs

Exercise 5.4 Applying the Skill

Use the T-chart to make notes and organize ideas for your paragraph.

1 Look at your brainstorming notes on page 423. Organize your notes in the positive and negative columns of the T-chart.

positive (+)	negative (−)

2 Use the list of topics to think of more positives and negatives about the place you will write about. Add these positives and negatives to the T-chart.
- jobs
- types of houses
- people
- things to do
- transportation

3 Highlight the three most important advantages and the three most important disadvantages.

4 Show your T-chart to a partner. Ask and answer questions to give each other feedback.

Exercise 5.5 Planning Your Paragraph

Use the information in your T-chart to plan your paragraph. Make notes in the outline below.

Topic sentence: _____
Advantage/Disadvantage 1: _____
Advantage/Disadvantage 2: _____
Advantage/Disadvantage 3: _____
Disadvantage/Advantage 1: _____
Disadvantage/Advantage 2: _____
Concluding sentence: _____

UNIT 33

Superlative Adjectives and Adverbs

Facts and Opinions

1 Grammar in the Real World

ACADEMIC WRITING

Description and opinion

A What do you know about Vietnam? Read the travel website article. What is the most interesting fact?

B Comprehension Check Answer the questions.
1 Where is Vietnam located?
2 What is the climate like?
3 Why is Hue famous?
4 What is Vietnam's most important export?

C Notice Find the forms of these common adjectives in the text. Write them in the spaces below.

1 big _____
2 hot _____
3 wet _____
4 narrow _____

5 popular _____
6 historic _____
7 important _____
8 beautiful _____

Superlative Adjectives and Adverbs

Vietnam

Vietnam, in Southeast Asia, shares borders with China, Laos, and Cambodia. It is a long country, and at its **narrowest** point it is only about 50 km (31 miles) wide.

Vietnam's population is about 90 million. The capital is Hanoi. The **biggest** city is Ho Chi Minh City, formerly called Saigon.

Vietnam's **most historic** city is Hue. It was the home of the Nguyen kings, and it has many palaces and monuments.

The **most popular** beach is located near the city Nha Trang in the central coast area.

The **most beautiful** area is Ha Long Bay. There are hundreds of small islands and unusual rock formations.[1]

Vietnam has a hot and humid climate, with the **hottest** temperatures in April. The **wettest** month is September.

The **most important** export[2] is crude oil,[3] and the **most important** crop[4] is rice. The industry that is growing the **most rapidly** is tourism.

[1] **rock formation:** a large area of rock that has characteristics different from the land around it

[2] **export:** an item someone sends to another country for sale or use

[3] **crude oil:** oil from underground that nobody has made into different products yet

[4] **crop:** a plant like a grain, vegetable, or fruit that people grow in large amounts on a farm

Facts and Opinions

2 Superlative Adjectives

Grammar Presentation

You can use superlative adjectives to describe how a person or thing is different from all others.	The **most historic** city in Vietnam is Hue.

2.1 Statements

Noun	Be	The	Superlative Adjective	Noun		
Ha Long Bay	is		**most beautiful**	area		Vietnam.
November	isn't	the	**wettest**	month	in	the country.
Ho Chi Minh City	is		**biggest**	city		the area.

2.2 Information Questions

Noun	Be	The	Superlative Adjective	Noun		
Which city	is	the	**most beautiful**	city	in	Vietnam?
What	is		**most important**	export		the country?

2.3 Superlative of Short Adjectives (One Syllable)

		Adjective	Superlative
A	For one-syllable adjectives, add -est.	long	long**est**
		slow	slow**est**
B	For one-syllable adjectives ending in -e, add -st.	large	larg**est**
		wide	wid**est**
C	For adjectives that end in one vowel + one consonant, double the final consonant and add -est.	big	bi**ggest**
		hot	ho**ttest**
D	For two-syllable adjectives ending in -y, change y to i and add -est.	heavy	heav**iest**
		tiny	tin**iest**

Superlative Adjectives and Adverbs

2.4 Superlative of Longer Adjectives (Two or More Syllables)

Adjective	Superlative
beautiful	most beautiful
historic	most historic
important	most important
popular	most popular

2.5 Two-syllable Adjectives That Take -est

Adjective	Superlative
narrow	narrowest
quiet	quietest
simple	simplest

2.6 Irregular Adjectives

Adjective	Superlative
good	best
bad	worst
far	farthest or furthest (farthest is more common)

▸▸ Adjectives and Adverbs: Comparative and Superlative Forms: See page A22.

2.7 Using Superlative Adjectives

A	Use *the* before a superlative adjective followed by a noun.	Ha Long Bay is **the** most beautiful area in Vietnam. NOT ~~is most beautiful area~~
B	Use superlative adjectives to show how one person or thing in a group is different in some way from all the others.	Orla is **the most intelligent** student in the class. The Nile is **the longest** river in Africa.
C	You can use a superlative adjective without a noun.	They have three daughters. Tran is **the youngest**.
D	You can use a possessive item (*my, your, Patrick's, the world's*, etc.) instead of *the* before a superlative adjective.	That book is **my most helpful** guide book. Cheetahs are **the world's fastest** animals.

Facts and Opinions

2.7 Using Superlative Adjectives (continued)

E Use *in* + noun after superlative adjectives when you want to talk about a specific group, for example, *in the world*, *in the class*, etc. Do not use *of*.	The Nile is the longest river **in** the world. NOT ~~the longest river of the world~~
F *Least* is the opposite of *most*. Do not use *least* with one-syllable adjectives.	The Royal is the **least expensive** hotel in town. Rhode Island is the **smallest** U.S. state. NOT ~~the least big~~

DATA FROM THE REAL WORLD

The most common superlative adjectives ending in *-est* in writing and speaking are:

biggest	fastest	largest	lowest	strongest
closest	greatest	latest	oldest	youngest
earliest	highest	longest	smallest	

The most common superlative adjectives with *most* in writing and speaking are:

beautiful	difficult	famous	popular	serious
common	effective	important	powerful	significant[1]
dangerous	expensive	interesting	recent	successful

[1]**significant**: a more formal word for *important*

Grammar Application

Exercise 2.1 Superlative Adjectives

A Pair Work How good is your geography? Complete the sentences with a partner. Use superlative adjectives. Then check the answers at the bottom of the exercise.

444 Unit 33 Superlative Adjectives and Adverbs

Superlative Adjectives and Adverbs

World Geography Quiz

1. The world's _smallest_ (small) continent is _Australia_.
2. The world's _____ (large) continent is _____.
3. The continent with the _____ (more) countries is _____.
4. The _____ (deep) ocean is the _____.
5. The _____ (big) country is _____.
6. The _____ (cold) place in the world is _____.
7. The _____ (high) mountain is _____.
8. The _____ (dry) place on Earth is the _____.
9. The _____ (large) city in the United States is _____.
10. The _____ (long) river in the world is _____.
11. The _____ (populated) country in the world is _____.

B Complete the questions with *the* and superlative adjectives. Note that ↑ shows an affirmative two-syllable superlative (with *most*), and ↓ shows a negative two-syllable superlative (with *least*). Then compare your answers with your classmates. You can find the answers at the bottom of the page.

FACTS ABOUT THE UNITED STATES

What Do You Know About the United States? **Answers**

1. What is _the biggest_ (big) waterfall? — _Niagara Falls_
2. What is _____ (long) river? — _____
3. What is _____ (dry) state? — _____
4. What is _____ (wet) state? — _____
5. What is _____ (popular) national park? ↑ — _____
6. What is _____ (big) city? — _____
7. What is _____ (wasteful) city? ↓ — _____
8. What is _____ (expensive) city to live in? ↑ — _____
9. What large city has _____ (bad) air pollution? — _____
10. What is _____ (famous) bridge? ↑ — _____
11. What is _____ (busy) airport? — _____
12. What is _____ (populated) state? ↑ — _____
13. What is _____ (populated) state? ↓ — _____

2. Mississippi 3. Nevada 4. Hawaii 5. Great Smoky Mountains National Park in Tennessee and North Carolina 6. New York
7. San Francisco 8. New York 9. Los Angeles 10. The Golden Gate Bridge, California 11. Atlanta's Hartsfield-Jackson
12. California 13. Wyoming

C Over to You Think about your city or town. Complete the sentences. Then compare your answers with your classmates. Take a survey. What are the results?

Best (and Worst) of the Town

1 The _nicest_ (nice) neighborhood is _____ .
2 The _____ (delicious) pizza is _____ .
3 The _____ (crowded) area is _____ .
4 The area with the _____ (bad) traffic is _____ .
5 The _____ (dangerous) intersection is _____ .
6 The _____ (unusual) restaurant is _____ .

Exercise 2.2 Superlative Adjectives to Describe People

A Complete the superlative constructions in this conversation. Use *the* when necessary.

Claire So, who are _the most important_ (1) (important) people in your life?

Monika Well, I guess my family and my _____ (2) (good) friends.

Claire OK. Tell me about your family.

Monika Well, let's see. My _____ (3) (close) family members all live near me, so I see them often. I have three brothers: Tim, Liam, and Anthony. Anthony is _____ (4) (young). He's just 13. My grandmother is 75. She's my _____ (5) (old) relative. My friends are mostly from my college days. One really special person is Tina.

Claire Tina? Is she your _____ (6) (good) friend?

Monika Yeah. She's _____ (7) (unusual) person I know, and _____ (8) (interesting). She has a pilot's license and a degree in biology! Of all my friends, she definitely has _____ (9) (exciting) job. She works for a tour company that takes people to some of _____ (10) (exotic[1]) places in the world. When we were in college, she always got _____ (11) (high) grades. She's probably _____ (12) (intelligent) person I know, and _____ (13) (successful).

Claire Amazing!

[1]**exotic:** unusual or interesting because of being from a different culture or country

B Listen to the conversation and check your answers.

C Over to You Answer the questions, and describe your friends or people in your family. Use superlative adjectives. Then share your answers with a partner.

1 Who are the most important people in your life?
2 Who is your best friend?
3 Who is the most successful person you know?
4 Who is the most intelligent? The funniest?

3 Superlative Adverbs

Grammar Presentation

You can use superlative adverbs to describe how a person's actions or the way something happens is different from all others.

*All the students work hard, but Rosa works **hardest**.*

3.1 Statements

	Verb	(The)	Superlative Adjective	
Daniel	ran	(the)	**fastest**	in the men's 100 meters.
This printer	works	(the)	**best**	of all the printers in the office.
Nina	drives	(the)	**most carefully**	of the three women.

3.2 Questions

	Verb	(The)	Superlative Adjective	
Who	arrives	(the)	**earliest**	at school every day?
Which industry	is growing	(the)	**most rapidly**	in Vietnam?
What method	works	(the)	**most effectively**	to learn vocabulary?

3.3 Superlative of Short Adverbs (One Syllable)

	Adjective	Superlative
A For adverbs with one syllable, add -est.	fast	fast**est**
	high	high**est**
	long	long**est**
	hard	hard**est**
B For adverbs with one syllable ending in -e, add -st.	late	lat**est**

3.4 Superlative of Longer Adverbs (Two or More Syllables)

Adjective	Superlative
often	**most** often
recently	**most** recently
quickly	**most** quickly
slowly	**most** slowly

We say *earliest*, not *most early*.
Which flight arrives the **earliest**?

3.5 Irregular Adverbs

Irregular Adverb	Superlative
well	**best**
badly	**worst**
far	**farthest** or **furthest** (*farthest* is more common)

Adjectives and Adverbs: Comparative and Superlative Forms: See page A22.

3.6 Using Superlative Adverbs

A You can use superlative adverbs to describe how one action or event is different from all others.	Hilda studies **the hardest** of all the students in her class. I drive **most carefully** in bad weather or when it's dark.
B You can use a phrase with *of* after a superlative adverb.	The cheetah runs **the fastest of** all the animals.
C *Least* is the opposite of *most*.	Of the three cars, the gasoline car operates **the least efficiently**.

Superlative Adjectives and Adverbs

DATA FROM THE REAL WORLD

People often use superlative adverbs without *the*, especially in spoken language.

You should wear the colors that suit you **best**.
Who do you text **most often**, your family, your classmates, or your friends?
Which of the three movies came out **most recently**?

In academic writing, use *the*.

This method works **the most effectively**.

DATA FROM THE REAL WORLD

Superlative adverbs are much less common than superlative adjectives.

The most common superlative adverbs ending in -est in writing and speaking are:	fastest closest longest	hardest nearest lowest	latest earliest highest
The six most common superlative adverbs used with *most* in writing and speaking are:	easily effectively	economically often	recently frequently

Grammar Application

Exercise 3.1 Superlative Adjectives

A Complete the sentences from a student essay. Use the superlative form of the adverbs in parentheses with *the*.

I live in an apartment with three other students: Shinya, Tomas, and Alex. I arrived ___the most recently___ (1) (recently) – in September this year. Shinya has lived here _____ (2) (long). He moved into the apartment two years ago. Because we are students, we try to spend as little money as possible. Right now, I think that I live _____ (3) (economical) because I almost never go out to eat. Tomas eats out _____ (4) (frequent). Alex probably studies _____ (5) (hard). He always goes to sleep _____ (6) (late). I get up _____ (7) (early) because I travel _____ (8) (far) to school.

Facts and Opinions 449

B Pair Work Complete the sentences with your own ideas. You can use the verbs and adverbs in the boxes to help you. Then share your sentences with a partner.

call	reply	study	work
~~drive~~	speak	text	write

clearly	fast	frequently	hard
early	fluently	good	often

1 Of all my friends, _Hannah drives the fastest_____.
2 Of all my classmates, _____.
3 Of all the people I know, _____.
4 In this class, _____.
5 Of all my family members, _____.
6 Of all my co-workers (or friends), _____.
7 Of all the people I text, _____.
8 Of all the people I send e-mails to, _____.

4 Avoid Common Mistakes ⚠️

1 **Do not use a comparative form instead of a superlative when comparing more than two things.**

Of all the places we visited, Vietnam in April was ~~hotter~~ *the hottest*.

2 **Do not use *most* and *-est* together.**

My ~~most~~ smallest pet was a goldfish.

3 **Do not use *most* with adjectives and adverbs that take *-est*.**

The Hollywood Plaza is the ~~most cheap~~ *cheapest* hotel in town.

4 **Do not use *of* instead of *in*.**

It's the tallest building ~~of~~ *in* the world.

5 **Learn the spelling rules for comparative and superlative adjectives and adverbs.**

Who arrives at school ~~earlyst~~ *earliest* every day, Joanna or Peter?

June 20 was the ~~hotest~~ *hottest* day of the year.

Editing Task

Find and correct 10 more mistakes in the magazine article.

Fascinating Facts About Animals

One of the ~~more~~ *most* amazing things of the natural world is the great variety of animal sizes and behaviors. At 200 tons (180 metric tons) and 108 feet (33 meters), the blue whale is the world's heavyest and bigest animal. However, the world's smaller bird weighs less than one ounce (1.8 grams). Giraffes can be 17 feet (5.2 meters) tall, and they are the tallest animals of the world. The cheetah runs the faster of all animals. It can run up to 75 miles per hour (120 kilometers per hour).

On the other hand, a sloth is perhaps the world's most slowest animal. It often does not move for hours. The loudest land animal is the howler monkey. You can hear its cry about 10 miles (16 kilometers) away. What is the louder marine animal? The blue whale. Blue whales can hear each other up to 1,000 miles (1,600 kilometers) away. What is the animal that lived the most long? It is a clam from the coast of Iceland. Scientists estimate that it is 405 years old. The gastrotrich, a tiny water animal, has the most short life – three days.

5 Academic Writing

Description and Opinion

Brainstorm > Organize > Write > Edit

In Unit 32, you used a T-chart to organize ideas for the prompt below. In this unit (33), you will write, revise, and edit your paragraph.

> *Describe the place where you live now or where you are from. Write about its positives and negatives. Include your opinions.*

Using Contrast Words

When writers describe positives and negatives about a place, they often state the positive points first, then the negative points. A **contrast word** like *however* or *but* can signal the shift from positive to negative within a paragraph.

Exercise 5.1 Applying the Skill

Read the paragraph. Then complete the tasks.

> I am from the only town on an island called Mackinac Island. The island is in Lake Huron in the U.S. state of Michigan, and it is famous for not allowing cars there. Most people get around by riding bicycles or by walking, and we use horses to pull carts full of heavy things. The island is peaceful and quiet without the sound of car engines. Also, the air is cleaner than in most towns. Almost no one gets hurt while traveling because no one travels at high speeds. However, travel is difficult and slow in rainy or snowy weather.

1 Find and underline the contrast word.
2 How did the writer organize the paragraph

   a From positive to negative
   b From negative to positive

My Writing

Exercise 5.2 Writing Your Paragraph

Look at your T-chart and outline on page 439. Write your paragraph on a separate sheet of paper. Include a topic sentence that shows your opinion of the place, its advantages and at least one disadvantage (or its disadvantages with at least one advantage), and a concluding sentence.

Exercise 5.3 Revising Your Ideas

1 Work with a partner. Use the questions below to give feedback on the ideas in your partner's paragraph.

- Which details in your partner's paragraph are the strongest?
- Which details in your partner's paragraph are unnecessary?
- What types of details could your partner add to make the paragraph stronger?

2 Use the feedback from your partner to revise your paragraph.

Using Superlative Adjectives in Your Paragraph

When writers feel strongly about a place, they often use superlative adjectives to express their opinions.

My hometown is **the friendliest** place I know.

In my opinion, San Francisco is **the most beautiful** city in the United States.

Exercise 5.4 Applying the Skill

Add at least one superlative adjective to your paragraph.

Exercise 5.5 Editing Your Writing

Use the checklist to review and edit your paragraph.

Did you answer the prompt completely?	
Did you write a topic sentence?	
Did you include at least three advantages and a disadvantage (or three disadvantages and an advantage)?	
Did you use a contrast word to signal a shift from positive to negative, or from negative to positive?	
Did you include a concluding sentence that summarizes the paragraph or makes your opinion clear?	
Did you use adjectives and adverbs correctly?	
Did you use the correct form of comparative adjectives and adverbs?	
Did you use the correct form of superlative adjectives and adverbs?	

Exercise 5.6 Writing Your Final Draft

Apply the feedback and edits from Exercises 5.3 to 5.5 to write the final draft of your paragraph.

Appendices

1 Capitalization and Punctuation Rules

Capitalize	Examples
1 The first letter of the first word of a sentence	*T*oday is a great day.
2 The pronoun *I*	Yesterday *I* went to hear a new rock band.
3 Names of people	*S*imón *B*olívar, *J*oseph *C*hung
4 Names of buildings, streets, geographic locations, and organizations	*T*aj *M*ajal, *B*roadway, *M*t. *E*verest, *U*nited *N*ations
5 Titles of people	*D*r., *M*r., *M*rs., *M*s.
6 Days, months, and holidays	*T*uesday, *A*pril, *V*alentine's *D*ay
7 Names of courses or classes	*B*iology 101, *E*nglish *C*omposition II
8 Titles of books, movies, and plays	*C*rime and *P*unishment, *A*vatar, *H*amlet
9 States, countries, languages, and nationalities	*C*alifornia, *M*exico, *S*panish, *S*outh *K*orean, *C*anadian
10 Names of religions	*H*induism, *C*atholicism, *I*slam, *J*udaism

Punctuation	Examples
1 Use a period (.) at the end of a sentence.	He is Korean**.**
2 Use a question mark (?) at the end of a question.	Do you want to buy a car**?**
3 Use an exclamation point (!) to show strong emotion (e.g., surprise, anger, shock).	Wait**!** I'm not ready yet. I can't believe it**!**
4 Use an apostrophe (') for possessive nouns.	
Add 's for singular nouns.	That's Sue**'s** umbrella.
Add s' for plural nouns.	Those are the students**'** books. BUT
Add 's for irregular plural nouns.	Bring me the children**'s** shoes.
Use an apostrophe (') for contractions.	I**'ll** be back next week. He can**'t** drive a car.
5 Use a comma (,):	
• between words in a series of three or more items. (Place *and* before the last item.)	I like fish**,** chicken**,** turkey**, and** mashed potatoes.
• before *and, or, but,* and *so* to connect two complete sentences.	You can watch TV**, but** I have to study for a test.

2 Spelling Rules for Noun Plurals

1	Add -s to most singular nouns to form plural nouns.	a camera – two cameras a key – keys	a model – two models a student – students
2	Add -es to nouns that end in -ch, -sh, -ss, and -x.	watch – watches class – classes	dish – dishes tax – taxes
3	With nouns that end in a consonant + -y, change the y to i and add -es.	accessory – accessories	battery – batteries
4	With nouns that end in -ife, change the ending to -ives.	knife – knives wife – wives	life – lives
5	Add -es to nouns that end in -o after a consonant. **Exception:** Add -s only to nouns that end in -o and refer to music.	potato – potatoes piano – pianos	tomato – tomatoes soprano – sopranos
6	Add -s to nouns that end in -o after a vowel.	radio – radios	shampoo – shampoos
7	Some plural nouns have irregular forms. These are the most common irregular plural nouns in academic writing.	man – men child – children foot – feet	woman – women person – people tooth – teeth
8	Some nouns have the same form for singular and plural.	one deer – two deer one fish – two fish	one sheep – two sheep
9	Some nouns are only plural. They do not have a singular form.	clothes glasses headphones jeans	pants scissors sunglasses

3 Verb Forms

Present: *Be*

Affirmative Statements

SINGULAR

Subject	Be	
I	am	
You	are	late.
He / She / It	is	difficult.

PLURAL

Subject	Be	
We / You / They	are	from Seoul.

Negative Statements

SINGULAR

Subject	Be + Not	
I	am not	
You	are not	in class.
He / She / It	is not	

PLURAL

Subject	Be + Not	
We / You / They	are not	students.

Affirmative Contractions

SINGULAR

I am	→	I**'m**
You are	→	You**'re**
He is	→	He**'s**
Jun-Ho is	→	Jun-Ho**'s**
She is	→	She**'s**
His mother is	→	His mother**'s**
It is	→	It**'s**
My name is	→	My name**'s**

PLURAL

We are	→	We**'re**
You are	→	You**'re**
They are	→	They**'re**

Appendices

Negative Contractions

SINGULAR

I am not	→	I**'m not**
You are not	→	You**'re not** / You **aren't**
He is not	→	He**'s not** / He **isn't**
She is not	→	She**'s not** / She **isn't**
It is not	→	It**'s not** / It **isn't**

PLURAL

We are not	→	We**'re not** / We **aren't**
You are not	→	You**'re not** / You **aren't**
They are not	→	They**'re not** / They **aren't**

Singular Yes/No Questions

Be	Subject	
Am	I	
Are	you	in class?
Is	he / she / it	

Singular Short Answers

AFFIRMATIVE

	Subject	Be
Yes,	I	**am**.
	you	**are**.
	he / she / it	**is**.

NEGATIVE

	Subject	Be + Not
No,	I	**am not**.
	you	**are not**.
	he / she / it	**is not**.

Plural Yes/No Questions

Be	Subject	
Are	we / you / they	late?

Plural Short Answers

AFFIRMATIVE

	Subject	Be
Yes,	we / you / they	**are**.

NEGATIVE

	Subject	Be + Not
No,	we / you / they	**are not**.

Negative Short Answer Contractions

SINGULAR

No, I am not.	→	No, I**'m not**.
No, you are not.	→	No, you**'re not**.
		No, you **aren't**.
No, he is not.	→	No, he**'s not**.
		No, he **isn't**.
No, she is not.	→	No, she**'s not**.
		No, she **isn't**.
No, it is not.	→	No, it**'s not**.
		No, it **isn't**.

PLURAL

No, we are not.	→	No, we**'re not**.
		No, we **aren't**.
No, you are not.	→	No, you**'re not**.
		No, you **aren't**.
No, they are not.	→	No, they**'re not**.
		No, they **aren't**.

Information Questions

SINGULAR SUBJECTS

Wh- Word	Be	Subject
Who		your teacher?
What		your major?
When	is	our exam?
Where		the building?
How		your class?

PLURAL SUBJECTS

Wh- Word	Be	Subject
Who		your teachers?
What		your plans?
When	are	your exams?
Where		your books?
How		your classes?

Contractions with Singular Subjects

SINGULAR

Who is	→	**Who's**
What is	→	**What's**
When is	→	**When's**
Where is	→	**Where's**
How is	→	**How's**

There Is / There Are

Affirmative Statements

There	Be	Subject	Place / Time
There	is	a parking lot a free tour	on Alameda Street. at 10:00.
	are	a lot of little shops free tours	in the area. on most days.

Contraction
There is → There's

Negative Statements

There	Be + Not / No	Subject	Place / Time
There	isn't is no	a bank bank	in Union Station.
	isn't is no	a show show	at 8:00.
There	's no	bank	in Union Station.
		show	at 8:00.
There	aren't are no	any cars cars	on Olvera Street.
	aren't are no	any tours tours	in the evening.

Yes / No Questions and Short Answers

Be	There	Subject	Place / Time
Is	there	a visitor's center	on Olvera Street?
		a performance	at 6:00?
Are		any parking lots	in the area?
		any tours	in the evening?

Short Answers
Yes, **there is**.
No, **there isn't**.
Yes, **there are**.
No, **there aren't**.

Appendices A6

Simple Present

Affirmative Statements

SINGULAR

Subject	Verb	
I / You	eat	vegetables every day.
He / She / It	eats	

PLURAL

Subject	Verb	
We / You / They	have	many friends.

Negative Statements

SINGULAR

Subject	Do / Does + Not	Base Form of Verb	
I / You	do not / don't	eat	a lot of meat.
He / She / It	does not / doesn't		

PLURAL

Subject	Do + Not	Base Form of Verb	
We / You / They	do not / don't	exercise	in the morning.

Yes / No Questions

Do / Does	Subject	Base Form of Verb	
Do	I / you / we / they	fall asleep	in 30 minutes?
Does	he / she / it		

Short Answers

AFFIRMATIVE

Yes	Subject	Do / Does
Yes,	I / you / we / they	**do**.
	he / she / it	**does**.

NEGATIVE

No	Subject	Do / Does + Not
No,	I / you / we / they	**do not**. / **don't**.
	he / she / it	**does not**. / **doesn't**.

Information Questions

Wh- word	Do / Does	Subject	Base Form of Verb	
Who	do	I / you / we / they	see	at school?
What			eat	at parties?
When			celebrate	that holiday?
Where	does	he / she / it	study	for school?
Why			live	at home?
How			meet	new people?

Present Progressive

Affirmative Statements

Subject	Be	Verb + -ing
I	am	talking.
You / We / They	are	
He / She / It	is	

Contractions

I am	→	I**'m**
You are	→	You**'re**
We are	→	We**'re**
They are	→	They**'re**
He is	→	He**'s**
She is	→	She**'s**
It is	→	It**'s**

Appendices **A8**

Negative Statements

Subject	Be + Not	Verb + -ing
I	am not	
You / We / They	are not	talking.
He / She / It	is not	

Contractions

I am not →	I'm not	
You are not →	You're not	You aren't
We are not →	We're not	We aren't
They are not →	They're not	They aren't
He is not →	He's not	He isn't
She is not →	She's not	She isn't
It is not →	It's not	It isn't

Yes/No Questions

Be	Subject	Verb + -ing
Am	I	
Are	you / we / they	working?
Is	he / she / it	

Short Answers

AFFIRMATIVE

Yes, I **am**.
Yes, you **are**.
Yes, we **are**.
Yes, they **are**.
Yes, he **is**.
Yes, she **is**.
Yes, it **is**.

NEGATIVE

No, I'm not.	
No, you're not.	No, you aren't.
No, we're not.	No, we aren't.
No, they're not.	No, they aren't.
No, he's not.	No, he isn't.
No, she's not.	No, she isn't.
No, it's not.	No, it isn't.

Information Questions

Wh- Word	Be	Subject	Verb + -ing
Who	am	I	hearing?
What			studying?
When	are	you / we / they	leaving?
Where			going?
Why	is	he / she / it	laughing?
How			feeling?

Wh- Word as Subject	Be	Verb + -ing
Who	is	talking?
What		happening?

Simple Past: Be

Statements

AFFIRMATIVE

Subject	Was / Were	
I / He / She / It	was	in the computer lab.
We / You / They	were	

NEGATIVE

Subject	Was / Were + Not	
I / He / She / It	was not / wasn't	in class.
We / You / They	were not / weren't	

Yes/No Questions and Short Answers

Was / Were	Subject	
Was	I / he / she / it	very smart?
Were	we / you / they	in college?

AFFIRMATIVE

Yes	Subject	Was / Were
Yes,	I / he / she / it	was.
	we / you / they	were.

NEGATIVE

No	Subject	Was / Were + Not
No,	I / he / she / it	was not. / wasn't.
	we / you / they	were not. / weren't.

Information Questions

Wh- Word	Was / Were	Subject	
Who	was	your best friend	as a child?
What	was	your favorite class	last semester?
When	was	her birthday party?	
What time	was	the meeting	on Monday?
Where	were	his partners?	
Why	were	they	successful?
How	were	the concerts	the other night?
How old	were	their cars	in 2011?

Simple Past

Statements

AFFIRMATIVE

Subject	Simple Past Verb	
I You We They He She It	started	in 1962.

NEGATIVE

Subject	Did + Not	Base Form of Verb	
I You We They He She It	did not didn't	sign	a contract.

Yes/No Questions

Did	Subject	Base Form of Verb	
Did	I you we they he she it	finish	the report?

Short Answers

AFFIRMATIVE

Yes	Subject	Did
Yes,	I you we they he she it	did.

NEGATIVE

No	Subject	Did + Not
No,	I you we they he she it	did not. didn't.

Information Questions

Wh- Word	Did	Subject	Base Form of Verb	
Who	did	I you we they he she it	write	about?
What			do	yesterday?
When			finish	our report?
Where			visit	on vacation?
Why			start	a company?
How			save	enough money?

A11 Appendices

Past Progressive

Statements

AFFIRMATIVE

Subject	Past of *Be*	Verb + *-ing*
I / He / She / It	was	working.
You / We / They	were	

NEGATIVE

Subject	Past of *Be* + *Not*	Verb + *-ing*
I / He / She / It	was not / wasn't	working.
You / We / They	were not / weren't	

Yes / No Questions

Past of *Be*	Subject	Verb + *-ing*
Was	I / he / she / it	working?
Were	you / we / they	working?

Short Answers

AFFIRMATIVE

	Subject	Past of *Be*
Yes,	I / he / she / it	was.
	you / we / they	were.

NEGATIVE

	Subject	Past of *Be* + *Not*
No,	I / he / she / it	were not. / weren't.
	you / we / they	were not. / weren't.

Information Questions

Wh- Word	Past of *Be*	Subject	Verb + *-ing*
Who	was	I / he / she / it	studying?
What			doing?
When			researching?
Where	were	you / we / they	working?
Why			experimenting?
How			feeling?

Wh- Word as Subject	Past of *Be*	Verb + *-ing*
Who	was	talking?
What	was	happening?

Future: Be Going To

Statements

AFFIRMATIVE

Subject	Be	Going To	Base Form of Verb	
I	am	going to	get	a job.
You We They	are			
He She It	is			

NEGATIVE

Subject	Be + Not	Going To	Base Form of Verb	
I	am not	going to	get	a job.
You We They	are not			
He She It	is not			

Yes/No Questions

Be	Subject	Going To	Base Form of Verb	
Am	I	going to	get	a job?
Are	you we they			
Is	he she it			

Short Answers

AFFIRMATIVE

	Subject	Be
Yes,	I	am.
	you we they	are.
	he she it	is.

NEGATIVE

	Subject	Be + Not
No,	I	'm not.
	you we they	aren't.
	he she it	isn't.

Information Questions

Wh- Word	Be	Subject	Going To	Base Form of Verb	
Who	Am	I	going to	interview	tomorrow?
What	Are	you we they		do	after graduation?
When				leave	for New York?
Where				work	after college?
Why	Is	he she it		move	to Canada?
How				pay	his loans?

Information Questions

Wh- Word as Subject	Be	Going To	Base Form of Verb	
Who	is	going to	get	a job after college?
What	is	going to	happen	after school?

Future: *Will*

Statements

AFFIRMATIVE

Subject	Will	Base Form of Verb	
I / You / We / They / He / She / It	will / 'll	have	a healthy life.

NEGATIVE

Subject	Will + Not	Base Form of Verb	
I / You / We / They / He / She / It	will not / won't	have	a healthy life.

Yes/No Questions

Will	Subject	Base Form of Verb	
Will	I / you / we / they / he / she / it	have	a healthy life?

Short Answers

AFFIRMATIVE

Yes, I / Yes, you / Yes, we / Yes, they / Yes, he / Yes, she / Yes, it	will.

NEGATIVE

No, I / No, you / No, we / No, they / No, he / No, she / No, it	won't.

Information Questions

Wh- Word	Will	Subject	Base Form of Verb	
Who	will	I / you / we / they / he / she / it	meet	at the interview tomorrow?
What	will	I / you / we / they / he / she / it	do	in your training program?
When	will	I / you / we / they / he / she / it	return	your documents?
Where	will	I / you / we / they / he / she / it	find	information about careers?
Why	will	I / you / we / they / he / she / it	travel	to South America?
How	will	I / you / we / they / he / she / it	build	new apartments?

Appendices **A14**

Imperatives

Statements

AFFIRMATIVE	
Base Form of Verb	
Smile	and be helpful.
Look	at people when you talk to them.

NEGATIVE		
Do + Not	**Base Form of Verb**	
Don't/ Do not	**interrupt**	people who are very busy.
	do	this in the beginning.

4 Common Regular and Irregular Verbs

Regular

Base Form	Past Form
call	called
decide	decided
happen	happened
like	liked
live	lived
look	looked
move	moved
start	started
talk	talked
try	tried
work	worked

Irregular

Base Form	Past Form
come	came
do	did
get	got
go	went
have	had
make	made
put	put
read	read
say	said
see	saw

5 Irregular Verbs

Base Form	Simple Past
be	was / were
become	became
begin	began
bite	bit
blow	blew
break	broke
bring	brought
build	built
buy	bought
catch	caught
choose	chose
come	came
cost	cost
cut	cut
do	did
draw	drew
drink	drank
drive	drove
eat	ate
fall	fell
feed	fed
feel	felt
fight	fought
find	found
fly	flew
forget	forgot
forgive	forgave
get	got
give	gave
go	went
grow	grew
have	had
hear	heard
hide	hid
hit	hit
hold	held
hurt	hurt

Base Form	Simple Past
keep	kept
know	knew
leave	left
lose	lost
make	made
meet	met
pay	paid
put	put
read	read
ride	rode
run	ran
say	said
see	saw
sell	sold
send	sent
set	set
shake	shook
show	showed
shut	shut
sing	sang
sit	sat
sleep	slept
speak	spoke
spend	spent
stand	stood
steal	stole
swim	swam
take	took
teach	taught
tell	told
think	thought
throw	threw
understand	understood
wake	woke
wear	wore
win	won
write	wrote

6 Spelling Rules for Possessive Nouns

1	Add 's to singular nouns to show possession.	The **manager's** name is Mr. Patel. (one manager) The **boss's** ideas are helpful. (one boss)
2	Add an apostrophe (') to plural nouns ending in -s to show possession.	The **managers'** names are hard to remember. (more than one manager) The **bosses'** ideas are very good. (more than one boss)
3	For irregular plural nouns, add 's to show possession.	The **men's** uniforms are heavy. (more than one man) The **children's** room is messy. (more than one child)
4	*My, your, his, her, our,* and *their* can come before a possessive noun.	**My friend's** sister is in Peru. **Our parents'** names are short.

7 Noncount Nouns and Containers

Common Noncount Nouns

Food and Liquids		Materials	School Subjects	Weather	Other
beef	rice	leather	algebra	fog	advice
bread	salt	metal	art	ice	furniture
butter	seafood	oil	biology	rain	garbage
cheese	shrimp	plastic	economics	snow	help
coffee	soup	silk	English	weather	homework
fish	spinach	wood	geography		information
ice cream	sugar		history		jewelry
meat	tea		music		mail
milk	water		physics		money
olive oil			psychology		noise
			science		traffic
					vocabulary
					work

Measurement Words and Containers

a bag of potatoes rice	**a bowl** of soup pasta	**a glass** of water soda	**a piece** of cake meat
a bar of chocolate soap	**a bunch** of grapes bananas	**a head** of lettuce cabbage	**a plate** of eggs chicken
a bottle of oil ketchup	**a can** of beans tuna	**a jar** of mustard pickles	**a pound** of butter cheese
a box of cereal candy	**a carton** of milk juice	**a loaf** of bread	**a slice** of pie pizza

8 Metric Conversion

1 ounce = 28 grams
1 gram = .04 ounce

1 pound = .45 kilogram
1 kilogram = 2.2 pounds

1 liter = .26 gallon
1 gallon = 3.8 liters

1 mile = 1.6 kilometers
1 kilometer = .62 mile

1 foot = .30 meter
1 meter = 3.3 feet

1 inch = 2.54 centimeters
1 centimeter = .39 inch

9 Subject and Object Pronouns

Subject Pronoun	Possessive Adjective	Object Pronoun	
I	my	me	*I* can't find the calculator. *My* desk is so messy. My boss is unhappy with *me*.
you	your	you	*You* are very organized. *Your* desk is so neat. I want to be like *you*.
he	his	him	*He* is a new employee. *His* old job was in Hong Kong. This is very exciting to *him*.
she	her	her	*She* went home. *Her* computer is off. I'll call *her*.
it	its	it	*It's* a new company. *Its* president is Mr. Janesh. He wants *it* to be successful.
we	our	us	*We* are looking for the reports. *Our* boss wants to read them. The reports are important to *us*.
they	their	them	*They* are writing a report. *Their* team members will help *them*.

10 Indefinite and Definite Articles

Indefinite Article

1	Use *a/an* with singular count nouns.	She made **a decision** about her job. **An analyst** examines something in detail.
2	Use *a* when the noun begins with a consonant sound.	She made **a decision** about her job.
3	Use *an* when the noun begins with a vowel sound.	**An analyst** examines something in detail.
4	Use *a* before adjectives or adverbs that begin with a consonant sound.	Tony found **a great** apartment in Chicago.
5	Use *a* before words that begin with *u* when the *u* makes a "you" sound.	James went to **a university** in Boston. The economy is **a universal** concern.
6	Use *a/an* to introduce a person or thing for the first time to a listener. When you mention the person or thing again, use *the*.	Tom bought **a car**. (The listener does not know about this car.) **The car** was not very expensive. (Now the listener knows about this car.)

Definite Article

1	You can use *the* before singular or plural count nouns, and before noncount nouns.	**The job** is a good one. **The choices** were interesting. **The information** is very useful.
2	Use *the* to talk about people or things that both the listener and speaker know about.	**The president** discussed **the plan**. (Everyone knows the president and the plan.) **The moon** and **the stars** were beautiful last night. (Everyone knows the moon and the stars.)
3	Use *the* to talk about a specific noun.	"**The teacher** gave us difficult homework tonight." (The speaker and listener know this teacher.) "**The game** was interesting." "I agree." (The speaker and listener are thinking of the same game.)

11 Spelling Rules for Verbs Ending in *-ing*

1. For most verbs, add *-ing**.
   go → going   say → saying   talk → talking

2. If the verb ends in a silent *-e*, delete *e* and add *-ing*.
   live → living   make → making   write → writing

3. For *be* and *see*, don't drop the *e* because it is not silent.
   be → being   see → seeing

4. If the verb ends in *-ie*, change the *ie* to *y* and add *-ing*.
   die → dying   lie → lying

5. If the verb has one syllable and follows the pattern consonant, vowel, consonant (CVC), double the last letter and add *-ing*.
   get → getting   put → putting   sit → sitting

6. Do not double the consonant if the verb ends in *-w*, *-x*, or *-y*.
   grow → growing   fix → fixing   say → saying

7. If the verb has two syllables, ends in the pattern CVC, and is stressed on the last syllable, double the last letter and add *-ing*.
   beGIN → beginning

8. If the verb has two syllables and is stressed on the first syllable, do not double the last letter.
   LISten → listening   TRAVel → traveling   VISit → visiting

* Verbs that end in *-ing* are also called *gerunds* when they are used as a noun. The same spelling rules above apply to gerunds as well.

12 Spelling and Pronunciation Rules for Simple Present

Spelling of Third-Person Singular Verbs

1. Add *-s* to most verbs.
   Add *-s* to verbs ending in a vowel* + *-y*.
   drinks, rides, runs, sees, sleeps   buys, pays, says

2. Add *-es* to verbs ending in *-ch*, *-sh*, *-ss*, *-x*.
   Add *-es* to verbs ending in a consonant** + *-o*.
   teaches, pushes, misses, fixes   does, goes

3. For verbs that end in a consonant + *-y*, change the *y* to *i* and add *-es*.
   cry → cries   study → studies

4. Some verbs are irregular.
   be → am / are / is   have → has

* **Vowels:** the letters *a, e, i, o, u*
** **Consonants:** the letters *b, c, d, f, g, h, j, k, l, m, n, p, q, r, s, t, v, w, x, y, z*

Pronunciation of Third-Person Singular Verbs
1 Say /s/ after /f/, /k/, /p/, and /t/ sounds. laugh**s**, drink**s**, walk**s**, sleep**s**, write**s**, get**s**
2 Say /z/ after /b/, /d/, /g/, /v/, /m/, /n/, /l/, and /r/ sounds and all vowel sounds. grab**s**, ride**s**, hug**s**, live**s**, come**s**, run**s**, smile**s**, hear**s**, see**s**, play**s**, buy**s**, goe**s**, studie**s**
3 Say /əz/ after /tʃ/, /ʃ/, /s/, /ks/, /z/, and /dʒ/ sounds. teach**es**, push**es**, kiss**es**, fix**es**, us**es**, chang**es**
4 Pronounce the vowel sound in *does* and *says* differently from *do* and *say*. do /duː/ → does /dʌz/   say /seɪ/ → says /sez/

13 Spelling and Pronunciation Rules for Regular Verbs in Simple Past

Spelling of Regular Verbs	
1 For most verbs, add *-ed*.	work → worked
2 For verbs ending in *-e*, add *-d*.	live → lived
3 For verbs ending in consonant + *-y*, change the *y* to *i* and add *-ed*.	study → studied
4 For verbs ending in vowel + *-y*, add *-ed*.	play → played
5 For one-syllable verbs ending in consonant-vowel-consonant (CVC), double the consonant.	plan → planned
6 Do not double the consonant if the verb ends in *-x* or *-w*.	show → showed
7 For two-syllable verbs ending in CVC and stressed on the first syllable, do not double the consonant.	TRAvel → TRAveled
8 For two-syllable verbs ending in CVC and stressed on the second syllable, double the consonant.	conTROL → conTROLLED

Pronunciation of Regular Verbs		
1 When the verb ends in /t/ or /d/, say *-ed* as /ɪd/ or /əd/.	wait → waited	deci**d**e → decided
2 When the verb ends in /f/, /k/, /p/, /s/, /ʃ/, and /tʃ/, say *-ed* as /t/.	laugh → laughed look → looked stop → stopped	miss → missed finish → finished watch → watched
3 For verbs that end in other consonant and vowel sounds, say *-ed* as /d/.	agree → agreed borrow → borrowed change → changed	listen → listened live → lived play → played

14 Adjectives and Adverbs: Comparative and Superlative Forms

	Adjective	Comparative	Superlative
1 One-Syllable Adjectives a Add -*er* and -*est* to one-syllable adjectives.	cheap new old small strong tall young	cheaper newer older smaller stronger taller younger	the cheapest the newest the oldest the smallest the strongest the tallest the youngest
b If the adjective ends with one vowel + one consonant, double the last letter and add -*er* or -*est*. Do not double the consonant *w*.	big hot sad thin	bigger hotter sadder thinner	the biggest the hottest the saddest the thinnest
2 Two-Syllable Adjectives a Add *more* or *the most* to most two-syllable adjectives.	boring famous handsome patient	more boring more famous more handsome more patient	the most boring the most famous the most handsome the most patient
b Some two-syllable adjectives have two forms.	narrow simple	narrower / more narrow simpler / more simple	the narrowest / the most narrow the simplest / the most simple
c If the adjective has two syllables and ends in -*y*, change the *y* to *i* and add -*er* or -*est*.	angry easy friendly happy lucky pretty silly	angrier easier friendlier happier luckier prettier sillier	the angriest the easiest the friendliest the happiest the luckiest the prettiest the silliest

	Adjective	Comparative	Superlative
3 Three-or-More-Syllable Adjectives Add *more* or *the most* to adjectives with three or more syllables.	beautiful difficult enjoyable expensive important serious	more beautiful more difficult more enjoyable more expensive more important more serious	the most beautiful the most difficult the most enjoyable the most expensive the most important the most serious
4 Irregular Adjectives Some adjectives have irregular forms.	bad far good	worse farther/further better	the worst the farthest/the furthest the best

	Adjective	Comparative	Superlative
1 -*ly* Adverbs Most adverbs end in -*ly*.	patiently quickly quietly slowly	more patiently more quickly more quietly more slowly	(the) most patiently (the) most quickly (the) most quietly (the) most slowly
2 One-Syllable Adverbs A few adverbs do not end in -*ly*. Add -*er* and -*est* to these adverbs.	fast hard	faster harder	(the) fastest (the) hardest
3 Irregular Adverbs Some adverbs have irregular forms.	badly far well	worse farther / further better	(the) worst (the) farthest / furthest (the) best

People usually only use *the* with superlative adverbs in formal writing and speaking.

15 Adverbs with -ly

Adjective	Adverb	Adjective	Adverb
bad	badly	loud	loudly
beautiful	beautifully	nervous	nervously
careful	carefully	nice	nicely
clear	clearly	patient	patiently
close	closely	polite	politely
confident	confidently	proper	properly
deep	deeply	quick	quickly
fluent	fluently	quiet	quietly
honest	honestly	slow	slowly
interesting	interestingly	strong	strongly
late	lately		

Spelling Rules for Adverbs

		Adjectives	Adverbs
1	After most adjectives, add -ly.	accidental interesting nice peaceful	accidentally interestingly nicely peacefully
2	After -y, delete y and add -ily.	easy happy	easily happily
3	After -ic, add -ally.	automatic terrific	automatically terrifically
4	After a consonant + -le, drop the e and add -y.	gentle terrible	gently terribly

16 Modal Verbs and Modal-like Expressions

Modals are helper verbs. Most modals have multiple meanings.

Function	Modal Verb	Time	Example
Ability	can	present	I **can** speak three languages.
	could	past	She **couldn't** attend class yesterday.
	be able to	present, past	I'm **not able** to help you tomorrow.
	know how to	present, past	I **know how to** speak two languages.
Possibility	can	present	I **can** meet you at 3:00 for coffee.
	could	past	People **could** read the newspaper online many years ago.
Requests less formal	can	present, future	**Can** you stop that noise now?
more formal	could would	present, future	**Could** you turn off your cell phone, please? **Would** you please come to my party?
Permission less formal	can could	present, future	You **can** give me your answer next week. Yes, you **could** watch TV now.
more formal	may	present, future	You **may** leave now.
Advice	should ought to might want to	present, future	What **should** you do if you live in a noisy place? You really **ought to** save your money. You **might want to** wait until next month.
Suggestions	Why don't Let's	present, future	**Why don't** we study together? **Let's** read the chapter together.
Necessity	have to need to must	past, present, future	We **had to** cancel our date at the last minute. She **needs to** make a schedule. All students **must** send their applications out on time.
Conclusion	must	present, future	Today is Monday, so tomorrow **must** be Tuesday.

17 Stative (Non-Action) Verbs

1 Stative verbs describe states, not actions. These are stative verbs: *love, know, want, need, seem, mean,* and *agree*. Use the simple present with stative verbs, not the present progressive.	I **don't like** rude people. NOT ~~I'm not liking~~ rude people. What **do** you **know** about this? NOT What ~~are you knowing~~? They **seem** upset. NOT They ~~are seeming~~ upset. Experts **don't agree** on the meaning of some gestures. NOT Experts ~~are not agreeing~~ on the meaning of some gestures.
2 Some verbs have a stative meaning and an action meaning.	STATIVE I **think** grammar is fun. (= an opinion) ACTION I'**m thinking** about my homework. (= using my mind) STATIVE The book **looks** interesting. (= appears) ACTION We'**re looking** at the book right now. (= using our eyes) STATIVE Do you **have** a dog? (= own) ACTION Are you **having** a good time? (= experiencing)
3 You can use *feel* with the same meaning in the simple present and the present progressive.	I **feel** tired today. OR I'**m feeling** tired today. How **do** you **feel**? OR How **are** you **feeling**?

18 Verbs + Gerunds and Infinitives

Verbs Followed by a Gerund Only

admit	keep (= continue)
avoid	mind (= object to)
consider	miss
delay	postpone
deny	practice
discuss	quit
enjoy	recall (= remember)
finish	risk
imagine	suggest
involve	understand

Verbs Followed by an Infinitive Only

afford	help	pretend
agree	hope	promise
arrange	intend	refuse
attempt	learn	seem
decide	manage	tend (= be likely)
deserve	need	threaten
expect	offer	volunteer
fail	plan	want
forget	prepare	

Verbs Followed by a Gerund or an Infinitive

begin	like	start
continue	love	
hate	prefer	

Index

a, 28, 30, 33, 37, 56
   before adjectives, 63
   as an indefinite article, 228, 230–231, 239, A19
   pronunciation of, 232
   with singular count nouns, 196, 230
ability, 270, 272, 273, 277–278, 281, A25
about, 78
above, 78
absolutely, 390
adjectives, 54, 56, 408, 410, 411
   a / *an* before, 56, 63
   answers with, 59–60
   after *be*, 63
   comparative, 424, 426–428, 435, A22–A23
      irregular, 427
      with *than*, 428, 435
   how +, 59–60
   after linking verbs, 414, 419
   not very +, 418
   before nouns, 56, 63
   possessive, A18
   superlative, 442–444, A22–A23
      in + noun after, 444
      irregular, 443
      possessive items before, 443
      the before, 443
   with *too* and infinitive, 415
   very and *too* +, 414
adverbs, 408, 410, 411, 419

comparative, 424, 431–432, 434, 435, A24
   irregular, 432
   with *than*, 432, 434, 435
   forms of, 410, A24
   of frequency, 106–107, 308
   of manner, 410–411
   maybe, 375, 381
   not very +, 342
   superlative, 447–449, 450, A24
      irregular, 448
      phrases with *of* after, 448
      with *the*, 449
   with *too* and infinitive, 415
   very and *too* +, 414
   with *will*, 374–375
advice, 386, 387, 389–390, 393, A25
a few, 219, 220
after, 184, 186, 187
   to introduce an event, 187
   as a preposition, 187
   spelling of, 190
ago, 152
a little, 212, 219, 220
a lot of, 212, 219, 220, 223, 224
always, 106, 107, 264
an, 28, 30, 33, 37, 56
   before adjectives, 63
   as an indefinite article, 228, 230–231, 239, A19
   pronunciation of, 232
   with singular count nouns, 196, 230
and, 37, 134, 136–137, 142

any, 212, 214, 215, 224
   any + *-one* / *-body* / *-thing*, 249, 250, 253
   are there any, 91, 215
   there aren't any, 87, 91
are, 37
   aren't, 304
around, 78
articles, 235
   definite, 230, 231, A19
   indefinite, 230–231, A19
   no article, 235
at, 71
   + address, 80
   at night, 101
   with locations, 74
   + specific time, 77, 80, 101
at the moment, 301, 303, 306, 308
be, 4, 16–17, 20, 21, 33
   with *a* / *an* + noun, 33
   + adjective, 5, 63
      comparisons with, 426
   adjectives after, 410
   be able to, 277–278, A25
   contractions of, 4–5, 17, 20, 23, A3
   with demonstratives, 43
   full forms of, 4, 5, 8
   information questions with, 14, 20–21, 23, A5
   to link ideas, 4, 5, 11
   negative contractions of, 8, 17, A5
   + *not*, 8, 11, 16, 17, 174
   + noun, 5

+ number, 5
+ preposition, 5
short answers with, 16–17, 23, A4, A5
simple past of, 172, 174, 176–178, A10
statements with present of, 2, 4–5, 8, A3
what +, 20–21
yes / *no* questions with, 16–19, 23, 177–178, A4, A10
because, 134, 139–140, 142
before, 184, 186–187
to introduce an event, 187
as a preposition, 187
spelling of, 190
be going to, 356, 358–359, 360, 364
answers to questions with, 374
for possible plans and intentions, 367
statements, 367
behind, 70
best, 448
better, 432
between, 71, 77
body
some + / *any* + / *every* + / *no* + *-body*, 249, 250, 252
but, 134, 136–137, 142
can, 281
for ability or possibility, 272, 273, 278, A25
cannot, 273, 287
can't, 287
+ *not*, 272, 273
for permission, 290, A25
pronunciation of *can* / *can't*, 275
for requests, 286–287, 295, A25
capitalization, A1
certainly, 287, 291, 375
certainty, levels of, 375
clauses
main, 186, 190, 323, 324
with past progressive, 323, 324

with simple past, 323, 324
time, 184, 186–187, 190, 324
with past progressive, 323, 324
with simple past, 323, 324
comparatives, 424, 426–428, 431–432, 434, 435, A22–23
conclusions, 396, 398, 399, 404, A25
conjunctions, 134, 136–137
consonants, 56, A21
consonant sounds, 30, 56, 232, 239, A19, A22
contractions, 300, 301, A3, A4, A5, A8
negative, 319
there's, 86, A6
of *will* after a *Wh*- word, 366
could, 281
for ability or possibility, 272, 281, A25
could not, 272
+ *not*, 272
for permission, 290, A25
for requests, 286–287, 295, A25
definitely, 375, 390
demonstratives, 40, 42–44
did, 167–169
did not / *didn't*, 154, 156, 164
do, 295
do / *does*, 109, 116, 117, 119
does not / *doesn't*, 100, 109, 116
do not / *don't*, 100, 109, 116, 258, 265
earlier, 431
earliest, 447
every
every day, 101
every + day, 101
every + *-one* / *-body* / *-thing*, 249, 250
every week, 308
feel, 308, A26
feel strongly, 414

frequency expressions, 130
from . . . to . . ., 101
future
with *be going to*, 356, 358, 360, A13
may / *might* for possibility in the, 374, 381
with present progressive, 356, 358, 359, 367
with *will*, 356, 363–364, 372, 374, 381, A14
gerunds, 342, A20
forming, 347, 352
go +, 351
verb + contrasted with present progressive, 348
following verbs, 347–348, 352, A26
go
go ahead, 291
go + gerund, 351
good, 411, 419
has, 37
has to, 402
have, 28, 35
with *did not* / *didn't*, 156
with *do* / *does*, 119
do not have to, 398, 399
have to, 398–400, 402, 404, A25
+ noun, 35
how, 20, 21, 124, 125, 130, 167–168, 178
how + adjective, 59–60
how many, 21, 202, 203, 207
how much, 21, 44, 202, 203, 207
how often, 130
how old, 21, 178
imperatives, 256, 258–259, 265, A15
with *always* and *never*, 264
in, 70
in front of, 71
in the morning / *afternoon* / *evening*, 77, 101
with locations, 74
+ month, 77, 80

Index **12**

+ noun after superlative adjectives, 444, 450
+ parts of the day/ season, 77, 101
infinitives, 342
   forming, 344, 352
   after *too* + an adjective or adverb, 415
   following verbs, 344–345, 352, A26
   with *would like*, 352
   would you like +, 352
isn't, 304
it, 244
   it is, 87, 91, 94
   its, 51
   it's, 51, 87
I think, 387
know how to, 277, 278, A25
last, 152
least, 444, 448
less, 428, 431, 432
let's, 386, 387, A25
like
   I'd / she'd / they'd like, 345
   I'd like to, 345
   I'd like to contrasted with *I like to*, 345, 352
   would like, 345
   would you like + infinitive, 345
likely, 375
many, 212, 219, 220, 223, 224
may, 295, 374–375
   to answer questions with *be going to* or *will*, 374
   for future possibility, 372, 374, 375, 381
   may be contrasted with *maybe*, 375, 381
   may not, 374
   for permission, 290, A25
maybe, 375, 381, 387, 390, 393
might, 374–375, 393
   to answer questions with *be going to* or *will*, 374

   for future possibility, 372, 374, 375, 381
   might not, 374
   might want to, 386–387, A25
more, 427–428, 431–432, 435
most, 443–444, 447–448, 450
much, 212, 219, 220, 223, 224
must, 398, 399, 400, 404, A25
   must not, 399
   mustn't, 399
near, 71
necessity, 396, 398–399, A25
need to, 398–400, 404, A25
   do not need to, 398
never, 106, 107, 264, 308
next to, 70–71
no, 16, 17, 20, 287, 291, 390
   no + *-one* / *-body* / *-thing*, 249, 250
   no problem, 287, 291
not
   's not /re not, 304
nouns, 30, 196
   adjectives describing, 56, 63
   count, 30–31, 194, 196–197, 202, 203, 207, A19
   articles with, 230, 235
   noncount, 194, 196–197, 202, 203, 205, 207, 224, A17, A19
   articles with, 230, 235, 239
   plural, 30, 31, 33, 37, 42, 47, 48, 51, A2
   possessive, 47, 51, A17
   proper, 31
   singular, 31, 32, 42, 47, 48, 51
now, 301, 303, 306
   right now, 301, 303, 306, 308
objects, 332–333
   questions and answers about, 335–336
obligation, 398, 399
of, 444, 450
   of course, 287, 291

offers, 379–380
   with *I'll*, 379
   with *will*, 379
often, 106, 107, 308
OK, 287
on, 70
   + day/ date, 77, 80
   with locations, 74
   on top of, 70
   + street name, 80
   + *the* + ordinal number + *floor*, 75, 80
one
   some + / *any* + / *every* + / *no* + *-one*, 249, 250, 252, 253
   there is one, 91
or, 134, 136–137, 142
ordinal numbers
   with floors, 74, 80
   with streets, 74
ought to, 386–387, 393, A25
   ought not to, 387
past progressive, 316, 318–319
   forming the, 327
   information questions in, 319, 327
   main clauses with, 324
   with the simple past statements, 318, A12
   time clauses with, 323, 324
   use of, 319, 320
permission, 284, 290–291, A25
please, 258, 286, 290
possessives, 40, 42, 47, 48, 51
possibility, 270, 272, 273, A25
   in the future, 372, 374, 375, 381
predictions, 363–365, 381
prepositions
   common expressions with, 75
   in past time expressions, 152
   of place, 68, 70–71, 74–75
   of time, 77, 78
present progressive, 298, 300–301
   for the future, 356, 358, 360

for plans and arrangements
  already made, 367
with present time expressions,
  303, 306, 308
questions, 305–306, 359
contrasted with simple present,
  307–308
spelling -ing forms, 301
statements, 359, A8
contrasted with verb + gerund,
  348

probably, 375, 387, 390, 393

promises, 380, 381

pronouns, 332, 333, 338
  gender in, 338
  indefinite, 242, 249–250, 253
  object, 330, 332–333, 338, 428,
    435, A18
  possessive, 242, 244–245, 253
  in second clause, 324
  subject, 330, 332–333, 338, 428,
    435, A18
  after *than*, 428, 435

punctuation, A1

quantifiers, 212, 219–220, A17

questions
  with days, dates, and times, 78
  with demonstratives, 44
  with *how* + adjective, 60
  information
    with *be*, 16, 20–21, 23, 177,
      178, A5, A10
    with *be going to*, 358, A13
    with *can / could*, 273
    about necessity, 399
    past progressive, 319, 327,
      A12
    present progressive, 305, 359,
      A9
    simple past, 167–168, 169, A11
    simple present, 122, 124–125,
      A8
    for suggestions / advice,
      389–390
    with superlative adjectives,
      442

with superlative adverbs, 447
with *will*, 365, 367, A14
to get information
  with *might* about possibility,
    374
  about objects, 335–336
  about subjects, 335–336
  Wh- questions, 336
  with *what . . . like?*, 60
  word order in, 327, 367, 393
Yes / No
  with *be*, 16–17, 23, 177–178,
    A4, A10
  with *be able to*, 277
  with *be going to*, 358, A13
  with *can / could*, 273
  about necessity, 399
  with *no* +, 251
  past progressive, 318, A12
  present progressive, 305, 359,
    A9
  simple past, 164, A11
  simple present, 114, 116–117,
    A7
  with *some* and *any*, 214
  with *some* + / *any* + / *every*
    +, 250
  for suggestions / advice,
    389–390
  with *there is / there are*, 91, A6
  with *will*, 364, A14
  with *why don't you / we*, 387

rarely, 106

requests, 284, 286–287, 291, A25
  word order for, 295

short answers, 21
  with *a lot, a few*, and *not many*,
    219
  with *a lot, a little*, and *not much*,
    219
  with *be*, 16–18, 23, A4, A5, A10
  with *be going to*, A13
  about necessity, 399
  to past progressive questions,
    318, A12
  to present progressive
    questions, 306, A9

to requests, 287
to simple past questions, 164,
  177, A11
to simple present questions,
  114, 116–117, A7
with *there are / aren't*, 91, A6
with *there is / isn't*, 91, A6

should, 386–387, 389–390, 393,
  A26
  should not, 386, 393
  what should I / we, 391
  where should we, 391

simple past, 148, 162, 316
  of *be*, 172, 174, 176–178, A10
  information questions, 167–168,
    169
  irregular verbs, 153–154
  statements, 148, 153–154, A11
  time clauses with, 323, 324
  and time expressions, 152
  regular verbs, 148–149, 151, A22
  Yes / No questions, 164, A11

simple present, 100, 102–103, A7
  with adverbs of frequency, 308
  information questions, 122, 124,
    A8
  contrasted with present
    progressive, 307–308
  spelling rules for verbs, 101, A21
  with stative verbs, 308, A27
  and time expressions, 102–103
  Yes / No questions, 114, 116, A7

some, 212, 214, 215, 224
  some + *-one* / *-body* / *-thing*,
    249, 250
  there are some, 87, 91

sometimes, 106, 107

sorry, 287, 291
  I'm sorry, 287, 291

stative verbs, 308, A26
  stative meaning, 308, A26

subjects, 332
  questions and answers about,
    335
  for suggestions and advice, 387

suggestions, 384, 386, 387, 389–390, A25
superlatives, 440, 442–444, 447–449, A23–24
sure, 287, 291
   I'm not sure, 390
surely, 375
than, 428, 431–432, 435
that, 43–44, 51
   that's, 43
the, 228, 230–231, 235, 239, A19
   before a superlative adjective, 443
   before a superlative adverb, 447
theirs, 244, 248
there is / are, 84, 86–87, 94, A6
   with nouns, 94
   there are some, 86, 87
   there is / are no, 86, 87
   there isn't / aren't, 86, 87
   there's, 86, 87, 93
   there's no, 86
   Yes / No questions and answers with, 91, A6
these, 43–44, 51
   these days, 301, 306
they, 44
   they are, 87, 91, 94
thing
   some + / any + / every + / no + -thing, 249–250
this, 43–44, 51
   this morning / afternoon / evening, 303
   this semester / year, 303
   this week / month, 301, 303, 306
those, 43–44, 51
time clauses, 184, 186–187, 190
time expressions, 100–101
   for the past, 152, 164, 174, 177
   present with present progressive, 301, 303, 306, 308

to, 346, 404
today, 303, 308
tonight, 303
too, 414, 415, 419
units of measure, 202–203, 207, A18
usually, 106, 107
verbs
   adverbs to give information about, 409, 419
   followed by gerunds, 347–348, 352, A25
   followed by infinitives, 345–346, 348, 352, A26
   -ing, A20
   irregular simple past, 153–154, 156, A15–A16
   linking, 414, 419
   regular simple past, 148–149, 151, 156, A15, A22
very, 56, 414, 419
   not very + adjective or adverb, 418
vowels, 56, A21
   vowel sounds, 56, 63, 101, 196, 230, 239, A19, A21, A22, A26
want, 281
   might want to, 386–387
   want to, 346, 352
was / were, 174, 180
   + *born*, 174, 180
   in past progressive, 327
   wasn't / weren't, 174, 177
well, 411, 418, 432
   well, . . ., 117
Wh- words, 20, 21, 124, 125
   contractions of *will* after, 366
   with *might* to ask questions about possibility, 374
   in past progressive information questions, 327
   in present progressive information questions, 306
   with simple past of *be*, 177–178

   in simple past information questions, 167–168
   as subjects, 359, 360, A9
what, 20, 21, 124, 125, 168, 178
   Wh- questions with, 335
   what day is, 78
   what is, 44
   what . . . like, 59
   what should I / we, 391
   what time, 124, 125, 168
   what time is, 78
when, 20, 21, 23, 124, 125, 168, 178
   to introduce an event, 187
   spelling of, 190
   time clauses with, 184, 186, 187, 323, 324
   when is / are, 78
where, 20, 21, 124, 125, 168, 178
   where should we, 391
while, 323–324
who, 20, 21, 124, 125, 168, 178
   Wh- questions with, 335
   who is, 44
whom, 336
whose, 48, 245
why, 124, 125, 168, 178
   why don't, 387, 390, A25
will
   adverbs with, 378
   answers to questions with, 374
   contraction of after *Wh-* word, 366
   for the future, 356, 364–365, A14
   for future certainty, 381
   for future possibility, 372, 374
   with *I think / I suppose / I guess*, 365
   with *I'll / we'll*, 365
   for offers, 381
   for offers and promises, 372, 374
   for predictions, 367
worse, 432
worst, 448

would
   for requests, 286–287, 295, A25

writing
   academic
      forms of *be* in, 5
      forms of *be going to* in, 360
      forms of *there is / are* in, 86, 94
      irregular plural nouns in, 31
      subject pronoun after *than* in, 428, 435
      the before a superlative adverb, 448
      will in, 365

informal
   contractions of *be* in, 5
   contractions of *be going to* in, 360
   contractions of *will* in, 365
may in, 375
about the past, 174

yes, 16, 17, 20, 23, 287, 291, 390

Yes / No questions
   with *be*, 16–17, 23, 177–178, A4, A10
   with *be able to*, 277
   with *be going to*, 358, A13
   with *can / could*, 273
   about necessity, 399
   past progressive, 318, A12
   present progressive, 305, 359, A9
   simple past, 164, A11
   simple present, 114, 116–117, A7
   with *some* and *any*, 214
   with *some +* / *any +* / *every +* / *no +*, 250
   for suggestions / advice, 389–390
   with *there is* / *there are*, 91–92, A6
   with *will*, 364, A14

yesterday, 152

Art Credits

Acknowledgements

The authors and publishers acknowledge the following sources of copyright material and are grateful for the permissions granted. While every effort has been made, it has not always been possible to identify the sources of all the material used, or to trace all copyright holders. If any omissions are brought to our notice, we will be happy to include the appropriate acknowledgements on reprinting and in the next update to the digital edition, as applicable.

Key: U = Unit

Photography

All the photos are sourced from Getty Images.

U16: Jasmina007/iStock/Getty Images Plus; DMEPhotography/iStock/Getty Images Plus; Poike/iStock/Getty Images Plus; Electravk/Moment; Fridholm, Jakob/Johner Images; Harneshkp/iStock/Getty Images Plus; Jamesmcq24/iStock/Getty Images Plus; Gary Sergraves/Dorling Kindersley; Michael Barrow Photography/Moment; Dave King/Dorling Kindersley; WesAbrams/iStock/Getty Images Plus; Anuchit kamsongmueang/Moment; Stanislav Sablin/iStock/Getty Images Plus; jswax/iStock/Getty Images Plus; Tachjang/iStock/Getty Images Plus; Antonio Ciufo/Moment Open; edo73/iStock; Bridget Davey/Moment Mobile; Julia_Sudnitskaya/iStock; Kelvin Kam/EyeEm; Jennifer Levy/StockFood Creative; MarenWischnewski/iStock; **U17**: Milkos/iStock/Getty Images Plus; Tetra images; StockPhotosArt/iStock/Getty Images Plus; Lauren Burke/Photodisc; Robert Daly/OJO Images; lunanaranja/iStock/Getty Images Plus; **U18**: PeopleImages/E+; Kennan Harvey/Aurora Open; Milanvirijevic/E+; Image Source; Alistair Berg/DigitalVision; Oversnap/E+; Globe Turner, LLC/GeoNova Maps; Maciej Nicgorski/EyeEm; **U19**: caziopeia/iStock/Getty Images Plus; Twomeows/Moment; Oxygen/Moment; Bpperry/iStock/Getty Images Plus; Ana Guisado Photography/Moment; Pakin Songmor/Moment; Arctic-Images/The Image Bank; Erin Donalson/iStock/Getty Images Plus; Yagi Studio/DigitalVision; Jacobs Stock Photography Ltd/DigitalVision; Caziopeia/iStock/Getty Images Plus; Ann Cutting/Photolibrary; **U20**: Tashi-Delek/E+; Ariel Skelley/DigitalVision; Werner Büchel/Moment; Yuri de Mesquita Bar/iStock/Getty Images Plus; Tim Mosenfelder/Getty Images Entertainment; PAUL ELLIS/AFP; Christian Kober/AWL Images; **U21**: Santypan/iStock/Getty Images Plus; Andresr/E+; Jose Luis Pelaez/Photodisc; **U22**: Hill Street Studios/DigitalVision; Westend61; Leland Bobbe/DigitalVision; Dave & Les Jacobs/DigitalVision; Jhorrocks/E+; Jacqueline Veissid; Kupicoo/E+; Ariel Skelley/DigitalVision; **U23**: Siphotography/iStock/Getty Images Plus; FatCamera/E+; Hero Images; Mike Hewitt; **U24**: David Arky; Jose Luis Pelaez Inc/DigitalVision; Grassetto/iStock/Getty Images Plus; SherSor/iStock/Getty Images Plus; Pioneer111/iStock/Getty Images Plus; **U25**: Andy Roberts/OJO Images; Dima_sidelnikov/iStock/Getty Images Plus; Justin Sullivan; Johnnieshin/iStock/Getty Images Plus; Em-m/iStock/Getty Images Plus; HasseChr/iStock Editorial; technotr/E+; **U26**: Bruce Glikas/FilmMagic; Andresr/E+; Steve Hix/Corbis; Reggie Casagrande/Stockbyte; GlobalStock/E+; **U27**: Sam Edwards/OJO Images; Martin-dm/E+; Kali9/E+; John Lund/Marc Romanelli/Blend Images; Michele Falzone/AWL Images; DEA/W. BUSS/De Agostini; Spaces Images/Blend Images; Moodboard/Cultura; T2 Images/Cultura; **U28**: Westend61; Rafal Rodzoch/Caiaimage; Ariel Skelley/DigitalVision; Ismagilov/iStock/Getty Images Plus; BJI/Blue Jean Images; **U29**: Digital Vision/Photodisc; Dougal Waters/DigitalVision; Ariel Skelley/DigitalVision; Eva-Katalin/E+; Sam Edwards/Caiaimage; **U30**: Henrik Weis/DigitalVision; PeopleImages/E+; Kali9/E+; Neustockimages/E+; Joshblake/E+; JGI/Tom Grill; **U31**: Hero Images; Nancy Honey/Cultura; Radius Images; XiXinXing/iStock/Getty Images Plus; Fancy/

Veer/Corbis; mangostock/iStock/Getty Images Plus; **U32**: Christopher Kimmel/Aurora Photos; LockieCurrie/E+; T3 Magazine/Future; Fuse/Corbis; Pgiam/iStock; **U33**: Fototrav/E+; Alex Stoen/Moment; Godong/Universal Images Group; Klaus Vedfelt/Taxi; Martin Harvey/Corbis NX; Buddy Mays/Corbis NX; Juan Carlos Munoz/Nature Picture Library; VW Pics/Universal Images Group; Borut Furlan/WaterFrame; Guy Edwardes/The Image Bank; Nnehring/E+; Dennis Macdonald/PhotoLibrary.

Illustrations

Ben hasler; Ed Fotheringham; Maria Rabinky; Michael Mantel; Monika Roe; Pat Byrnes; Richard Williams; Rob Schuster.

Audio

Audio production by John Marshall Media.

Typeset

Q2A Media Services Pvt. Ltd.